WERTZ
WIRT
WUERTZ
Etc.
Families
of
Pennsylvania

1400s-1990

Carolyn Cell Choppin

HERITAGE BOOKS
2008

HERITAGE BOOKS
AN IMPRINT OF HERITAGE BOOKS, INC.

Books, CDs, and more—Worldwide

For our listing of thousands of titles see our website
at
www.HeritageBooks.com

Published 2008 by
HERITAGE BOOKS, INC.
Publishing Division
100 Railroad Ave. #104
Westminster, Maryland 21157

International Standard Book Numbers
Paperbound: 978-1-55613-352-7
Clothbound: 978-0-7884-7259-6

WERTZ-WUERTZ-WURTZ FAMILY HISTORY
Table of Contents

PREFACE

The initial intention of this work was to preserve the family history of the ancestors and descendants of our Franklin County, Penn. Wertz families. However, as our research and correspondence progressed it seemed clear that additional chapters should be added noting the several other Pennsylvania Wertz-Wirt-Wurtz families and the few others who settled in other states. These records are by no means complete, but they are included here to assist others and prevent needless duplication of efforts. Hopefully future generations will begin where we left off, as we have begun where those before us concluded.

A genealogy is always an ongoing compilation of never ending records and generations yet unborn, and thus never complete or finished. But there also comes a time when the volume of records collected, and the number of generations recorded needs to be presented in a published work for the benefit of present and future generations. Many in our Wertz clan have felt this need for some years now and encouraged the writing of this book. To them I am grateful for their influence and support, and I sincerely hope they are not disappointed with the result.

Carolyn Cell Choppin
Jacksonville, Florida
1988

INTRODUCTION

Primarily this family history proceeds from the earliest known families forward to the present generations. Because this author has a dislike for numbering systems, which take up space and are at best confusing, and prefers a narrative style, families are outlined under headings, with numbers given to the children in each outlined family corresponding to their order of birth as best that could be determined. Page references are then given to the location within this book where preceding and descendent generations are recorded. Occasionally summary information reviewing preceding records moves backwards in time, but the wording of such passages should make them clear. For the most part family groups have been maintained by chapter and subchapter headings, except in Chapters 1, 7, 10, and 11, where misc. records for several perhaps unrelated Wertz families are included.

Some common abbreviations have occasionally been used, such as: b.=born, m.=married, d.= died, and a.=about or approximately. The standard abbreviations for states, months, etc. have also been utilized, but for the most part complete words, and always complete dates, are presented throughout this book to minimize any possible misinterpretations. The use of a letter in parentheses, such as (A), denotes references or footnotes, which are given at the conclusion of the text of the book, just preceding the two indexes. In cases where a source or reference is used only once or twice, those notations may be included in the text.

Every effort has been made to make this book readable and informative for the family member seeking to learn of their Wertz heritage, and at the same time useful to the family researcher who perhaps seeks only specific pieces of data or clues to missing links.

ACKNOWLEDGMENTS

The record keeping efforts of many, in generations past as well as present, have contributed to the total collection of data here assembled. Some records are of course from public documents or books in courthouses and libraries. But the bulk of this work began with the efforts of Estelle Ryan Snyder of Chicago, Illinois, who in 1912 to 1915 compiled a record of the descendants of Unstatt Wurtz, born about 1605 in Bretten, Karlsruhe, Baden, Germany.

Mrs. Snyder recorded this family tree on a large "butcher paper" in map style. A sample piece of that chart is reprinted at the end of Chapter 1. Many years ago that chart was filmed to preserve it and to produce copies for other family members and libraries, and in this filming process the size of the writing was so reduced that reading is difficult now, and even magnification does not much help to clarify the blurred ink or unclear writing.

So that over the years many interpretations of the original work have led to errors. Thus throughout this work, where other records could not be found to verify questionable dates, question marks appear to call the readers attention to the possible errors of interpretation or transcription.

Nevertheless, we owe a great debt to Estelle Ryan Snyder and those of her generation who recorded this family tree.

Among the more recent generations, we extend appreciation to the following contributors:

William H. Brindle, of Erie, Penn.

Christian Heckman Cell, now deceased.

Clark Wesley Cell, now deceased.

Lottie Catherine Cell, now deceased.

Samuel Wesley Cell, now deceased.

Robert Franklin Cell, of Edinburg, Texas.

Mrs. Shirley Jo Cunningham, of Fort Wayne, Indiana.

John M. Fisher, of Chambersburg, Penn.

Mrs. Naomi Haughham, of Franklin, Indiana.

Ila Hoskins, of Indianapolis, Indiana.

Kathryn Shockey Huber, of Newtown, Penn.

Kathy Knepper, of Kensington, Maryland.

Mrs. Esther McAllester, of Elk Grove, Calif.

Mrs. Bonnie G. Moats, of Waynesboro, Penn.

Miss Janet Myers, of Washington D.C.

Mrs. Wanda C. Smith, of Auburn, Indiana

Mrs. Robert (Thelma Shafer) Ungerer, of Wooster, Ohio.

Mrs. Annette L. (Rock) Webb, of Marsing, Idaho.

Leslie H. Weber, of Saugus, California.

Gerald W. Wertz, of McHenry, Illinois.

Kathy Wertz Zerbe, of Santa Rosa, California.

Chapter 1

ANCESTORS IN BRETTEN, KARLSRUHE, BADEN, GERMANY

Oral tradition, handed down among the Wertz families in Franklin County, Pennsylvania for several generations and finally written down about 1910, was that "the Wertz family is descended from two brothers who were knighted in Germany at the time of Charlemane (742-814). The name was then spelled: Von Wirz. One of these two brothers settled in Switzerland; records are available there for this branch of the family. (see Chapter 8) The other brother settled in Germany and from him comes our branch of the family, using the spelling Wurtz and Wuertz in Germany, and Wertz in America."

There is of course no proof that this tradition is correct. But we have learned nothing to disprove it either over the many years of research done by numerous members of this family. There is also no proof that any of the Wirtz-Wurtz crests (see next page) belong to our direct ancestors.

The earliest proven records that we do have, date to 1585 in Bretten, a town about 20 miles East of Karlsruhe, in Baden, Germany. Most birth, marriage and death records of that area were destroyed during the French invasion. But in 1912, Mrs. Estelle Ryan Snyder of Chicago, Illinois was able, by correspondence with the Pastor, Karl Renz, of the Reformed Lutheran Church of Bretten, to locate church records dating from 1600. A few earlier records now appear in the IGI. (E)

WERTZ

Wertsch Nördlingen | Werttorf Prov. ...

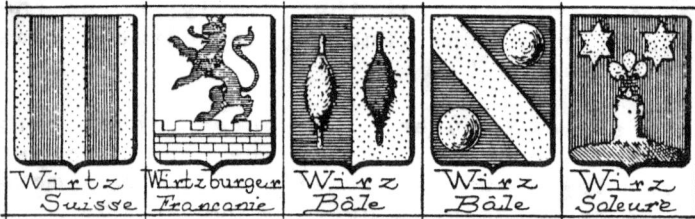

Wirtz Suisse | Wirtzburger Franconie | Wirz Bâle | Wirz Bâle | Wirz Soleure

Würtz Strasbourg | Würtz Suisse | Würtz und Burg Silésie | Wurtzel Aut. | Würz (and Wirz) Aut.

IGI Records, BRETTEN,KARLSRUHE,BADEN, GERMANY

1585,October 5th, Alexander Wurtz married to
       Barbara Fleiner.
1600,December 14th, Anstet Wurtz christened,
       parents = Alexander Wurtz & Barbara
       Fleiner.
1659,December 10th, Unstatt Wurtz married to
       Margarita Zeigler
1665, November 28th, Hans Conrad Wurtz born to
       Unstatt Wurtz and Margarita.
1681, June 26th, Unstatt Wurtz born to Unstatt
       Wurtz and Margarita

The last three records, 1659 and 1681, were
submitted by this author in 1968 from the
records obtained by Estelle Ryan Snyder.
However, the first two records are of unknown
origin.   They would seem to pertain to this
family, and if so may add another generation
to the pedigree established by Mrs. Snyder.
They are included here as questionable, but
possible.

The Reformed Lutheran Church Records of
Bretten, obtained in 1912 by Estelle Ryan
Snyder and charted by her in 1915, shows the
following outline:

Unstatt Wurtz, born about 1605, Bretten...
       two sons indicated:

I. Hans Bunkardt Wurtz, born about 1630,
Bretten; married 11 June 1653 to Maria
Duscheur; eight children all recorded in the
Bretten Church records:

1. Catarina Wurtz, born 18 Feb. 1657.
2. Susannah Wurtz, born 17 Oct. 1658.
3. Anna Maria Wurtz, born 13 Sept. 1660.
4. Justina Wurtz, born 15 Sept. 1662.
5. Anna Barbara Wurtz, born 26 March 1664.
6. Anna Margaretha Wurtz, born 10 Oct. 1665.
7. Anna Elizabeth Wurtz, born 29 Sept. 1669.
8. Hans Bunkardt Wurtz II, born 2 April 1674.

Birth Record of Hans Conrad Wurtz
born 28 November 1665
parents: Unstatt Wurtz and
Margaret Ziegler

From the Reformed Luthern Church Record
Book, in Bretten; page 128.

II. Unstatt Wurtz II, born about 1635, Bretten; Bootmaker; married 10 December 1659 to Margarita Zeigler; ten children, all born in Bretten:

1. Anna Catherina Wurtz, born 27 --?-- 1660.
2. Anna Barbara Wurtz, born 1 August 1662.
   (this child probably died before 1672.*)
3. Margarita Wurtz, born 10 March 1664.

4. Hans Conrad Wurtz, born 28 Nov. 1665;
   married by 1699 to Anna Maria Ursula;
Bootmaker; ten children; all born in Bretten:
   (1) Margarita Elizabeth Wurtz, b.7 Oct. 1699
   (2) Bernhard Englehard Wurtz, b.25 Nov. 1701
   (3) Johann Jacob Wurtz,born 29 Oct.1702.
       (this child probably died by 1711.*)
   (4) Hans Jacob Wurtz, born 20 June 1705.
       emigrated to America 21 September 1731;
       m. 29 Dec. 1734 to Anna Barbara Hoff;
       will dated 10 March1775, Quincy,Franklin
       Co.,Penn., five children; see Chapter Two.
   (5) Franz Wurtz, born 21 Sept. 1706.
   (6) Anna Elizabeth Wurtz, born 8 March 1709.
   (7) Johann Jacob Wurtz, born 28 May 1711.
   (8) Alexander Wurtz, born 25 March 1714.
   (9) Anna Maria Wurtz, born 13 Oct. 1716.
   (10) Johanna Maria Wurtz, born 26 Nov. 1721.

5. Josysh or Joseph Wurtz, born 8 Feb. 1668.
6. Anna Maria Wurtz, born 19 Nov. 1670.
   (probably died by 1677. *)
7. Anna Barbara Wurtz, born 7 Nov. 1672.
8. Anna Maria Wurtz, born 10 Feb. 1677.
9. Anna Elizabeth Wurtz, born 6 March 1679.
10. Unstatt Wurtz III, born 26 June 1681.

* Where two children in a family were given the same name, usually the first had died young. This was probably the case in our Wurtz families, but we have no proof of their deaths. It is also possible that the birthdates quoted above are in reality christening dates.

Birth Record of Hans Jacob Wurtz
born 20 June 1705
parents: Hans Conrad Wurtz and
Anna Maria Ursula

From the Reformed Luthern Church Record
Book, in Bretten; page 64.

Additional IGI records show another Wurtz family in Bretten at the same time period. Their connection to our family is unknown, and thus their records are included here for information only. No statement of relationship is indicated or intended.

Hans Wurtz and Elizabeth Winter... parents of:
1. Hans Wurtz, christened 18 January 1567.
2. Agnes Wurtz, christened 19 Dec. 1568.
3. Anna Wurtz, christened 27 Nov. 1569.
4. George Wurtz, christened 6 May 1571.
5. Margaretha Wurtz, christened 1 Dec. 1572.
6. Martinus Wurtz, christened 10 March 1575.
        (see below)
7. Jacob Wurtz, christened 15 June 1576.
8. Christoph Wurtz, christened 6 Feb. 1579.
9. Veit Wurtz, christened 6 Feb. 1579.
10. Hans Jorg Wurtz, christened 6 March 1581.

Children numbers 8 and 9 may have been twins, or just christened on the same date. These records do not give any clue to their age or birthdates.

Martinus Wurtz married 12 Oct. 1597, Bretten to Barbara Wesinger; parents of:
    1. Catharina Wurtz,chr.21 July 1598, Bretten Perhaps the first wife, Barbara, died in childbirth or soon after, because the records show Martinus Wurtz and a Maria Salomea Creutz as parents of the following children... all christened at Bretten:
    1. Margaretha Wurtz, chr. 14 Feb. 1603. *
    2. Margaretha Wurtz, chr. 14 Feb. 1613. *
    3. Hans Martin Wurtz, chr. 14 Feb. 1616.
    4. Anna Maria Wurtz, chr. 6 Dec. 1620.
    5. Hans Michael Wurtz, chr. 18 May 1623.
    6. Magdalena Wurtz, chr. 3 April 1626.
    7. Johann Melchiro Wurtz, chr. 8 June 1627.
    8. Peter Wurtz, chr. 13 October 1629.

* A Margaretha Wurtz married Oct. 1632 to Hans Michael Strauss. It is not known if this is one of the above Margaretha's or not, or if there were two Margaretha's in this family.

15

Perhaps, since the day and month are the same, an entry error in the year has resulted in a duplicate entry.

There are many other Wurtz families listed in the Baden IGI files, but these were living in or near Bretten during the same time period as our Unstatt Wurtz families, thus adding probability to some kinship, through none is known at this time.

OTHER KARLSRUHE MARRIAGES

Anna Maria Wurtz, m. 14 June 1768, to Philipp Jacob Deuchler.

Anna Rosina Wurtz, m. 7 June 1783, to Philipp Jacob Herrmann.

Catharina Barbara Wurtz, m. 14 Aug. 1801, to Johann Philipp Bittmann.

Catharina Philippina Wurtz, m. 18 April 1809, to Johann Wilhelm Eberle.

Christina Auguste Wuertz, m. 10 July 1770, to Johannes Bohnenberger.

Christoph Wuerz, m. 28 May 1720, to Elizabeth Trautwein.

Christoph Wilhelm Wuertz, m. 2 August 1825, to Margaretha Mueller.

Eleonore Magdalene Wuerz, m. 17 May 1791, to Johann Jakob Ewinger.

Elisabeth Wilmelmina Wurtz, m. 26 July 1803, to Johann Sigmund Seis.

Eva Margaretha Wuertz, m. 3 Jan. 1747, to Johann Melchior Kuntz.

Franz Jacob Wuertz, m. 15 April 1806, to Jacobina Juliana Kyri.

Franziscus Wurtz, m. 22 Sept. 1722, to Susanna Juliana Kustner.

Friedrich Jacob Wurtz, m. 11 Feb. 1744, to Elizabeth Catharina Schmidt.

Friedrich Karl Wurtz, m. 30 May 1837, to Sophie Dobelin.

Friedrich Juliana Wuertz, m. 16 Feb. 1832, to Christoph Heinrich Sprang.

Heinrich Jacob Wurtz, m. 27 Nov. 1759, to Anna Catharina Hoffmann.

Heinrich Jacob Wurtz, m. 9 Feb. 1768, to
    Juliana Clara Schmidt.
Heinrich Jacob Wurtz, m. 20 Nov. 1796, to
    Maria Dorothea Langenbach.
Heinrich Jacob Wuertz, m. 18 Feb. 1841, to
    Rosina Karolina Wuertz.
Jacob Casimir Wuertz, m. 15 Dec. 1808, to
    Maria Elisabeth Schwarz.
Jacob Friedrich Wuertz or Wurts, m. 13 Jan.
    1811, to Maria Susanna Rothengatter.
Johann Friedrich Wurtz, m. 16 Nov. 1773, to
    Anna Maria Zeltmann.
Johann Georg Wurtz, m.5 Nov. 1748, to Juliana
    Hermann.
Johann Jacob Wurtz, m. 4 Nov. 1704, to
    Catharina Fuegen.
Johann Jacob Wurtz, m. 20 Nov. 1725, to Anna
    Barbara May.
Johann Jacob Wurtz, m. 5 Feb. 1731, to Maria
    Barbara Kossmann.
Johann Jacob Wurtz, m. 1 August 1752, to
    Johanna Bischoff.
Johann Jacob Wurtz, m. 22 Nov. 1757, to Rosina
    Wendel.
Johann Jacob Wurtz, m. 17 Feb. 1799, to Ursula
    Huegie.
Johann Karl Christian Jacob Wurtz, m. 11 Feb.
    1838, to Anna Maria Bittmann.
Johann Martin Wurtz, m. 23 Nov. 1779, to
    Susanna Christina Fung.
Johann Philipp Wurtz, m. 18 Nov. 1687, to
    Johanna Christina Druechler.
Johann Philipp Wurtz, m. 1 May 1714, to Maria
    Catharina Vetter.
Johann Philipp Wurtz, m. 4 Feb. 1738, to Maria
    Salome Umbgelter.
Johann Philipp Wurtz, m. 10 June 1766, to Anna
    Margaretha Wurster.
Johannes Wurtz, m. 10 August 1688, to Anna
    Christina Rottengatter.
Johannes Wurtz, m. 13 March 1691, to Maria
    Juliana Rollwagen.
Johannes Wurtz, m. 27 June 1713, to Rosina
    Schmid.
Johannes Wurtz, m. 2 June 1722, to Dorothea
    Catharina Mutz.

Johannes Wurtz, m. 26 April 1746, to Maria
    Elisabeth Lenzinger.
Johannes Wurtz, m. 16 Nov. 1756, to Anna
    Rosina Frey.
Johannes Wuertz, m. 6 July 1790, to Maria
    Elisabetha Rothengatter.
Margaretha Juliana Wuertz, m. 6 Oct. 1827,
    to Friedrich Hetzel.
Maria Elisabeth Wurtz, m. 5 Dec. 1786, to
    Johann Georg Belz.
Maria Friedrike Jacobina Wuertz, m. 26 Nov.
    1771, to Jerg Martin Dieterle.
Philipp Friedrich Wurtz, m. 22 Nov. 1709, to
    Elisabeth Catharine Hoffmann.
Philipp Friedrich Wurtz, m. 11 Feb. 1744, to
    Maria Catharina Frey.
Philipp Jacob Wurtz, m. 29 Jan. 1782, to
    Maria Elisabeth Langfahr.
Philipp Jacob Wurtz, m. 2 April 1792, to
    Rosina Catharina Beitemann.
Rosina Karolina Wuertz, m. 18 Feb. 1841, to
    Heinrich Jacob Wuertz.
Rosina Sophia Wurtz, m. 31 Oct. 1797, to
    Philipp Jacob Hetzel.

BIRTHS or CHRISTENINGS in KARLSRUHE

Christoph Wuerz, born 1698, Oberoewisheim,
Karlsruhe, son of Franz Stephen Wuerz and
Agnes Maria.

Eva Margaretha Wuerz, born 14 Sept. 1724,
Oberoewisheim, Karlsruhe, daughter of
Christoph Wuerz and Elizabetha.

Michael Wuerz, born 6 Sept. 1721,
Oberoewisheim, Karlsruhe, son of Christoph
Wuerz and Elizabetha.

SUMMARY of our BRETTEN ANCESTORS

Our immigrant ancestor, Hans Jacob Wurtz, was born 20 June 1705 in Bretten, Karlsruhe, Baden, Germany, the fourth child, and third son of Hans Conrad Wurtz and Anna Maria Ursula. Records in both Germany and America substantiate this. Records of his immigration, marriage, and family will be outlined in Chapter 2.

Hans Conrad Wurtz, was born 28 Nov. 1665, in Bretten, the fourth child and eldest son of Unstatt Wurtz and Margaretha Zeigler. The church records in Bretten also indicate that Hans Conrad was a bootmaker.

Unstatt Wurtz and Margaretha Zeigler were married 10 December 1659, probably in Bretten or nearby Karlsruhe. (Karlsruhe is both a town and a "county" in this part of Germany.) This Unstatt Wurtz was probably born about 1635, probably the second son of Unstatt/Anstet Wurtz and --?--. (Name of this women is as yet unknown. It is possible that the senior Unstatt Wurtz is the same person as the Anstet Wurtz, christened 14 December 1600 in Bretten, son of Alexander Wurtz and Barbara Fleiner.

Alexander Wurtz and Barbara Fleiner were married 5 October 1585 in Bretten, so Anstet would have probably been one of their younger children. Since the Bretten records prior to 1585 were destroyed, we have no way to ascertain Alexander's birth or parentage.

Chapter 2

OUR EMIGRANT ANCESTOR, HANS JACOB WURTZ

When Queen Anne was on the throne of England the rulers decided too many Englishman were being sent to the colonies and they began looking for others to settle the new world lands. In the section of Germany known as the Palatinate the people were oppressed by war and poverty and religious persecution. So they listened eagerly to the glowing tales of America, and in just two years some thirty thousand Germans moved first to England, where they were sheltered mostly in tents, and then transported, a few to Ireland, but most of them to Pennsylvania, New York and the Carolinas. Thus began the great German emigration to America.

In 1731 Hans Jacob Wertz, now 26 years old, having learned his father's trade of bootmaking, joined a band of pilgrims who left the Palatinate, passing through Holland and then boarded a ship probably at Rotterdam. There were one hundred and six Palatines, with their families, making two hundred and sixty nine persons who sailed on the Ship Britannia of London, with Master Michael Franklin at the helm. The list of passengers, made upon their arrival at Philadelphia 21 September 1731 includes Jacob Wirtz or Wurts, age 26. He signed by mark, indicating that he probably could not write. Jacob is also the only Wurtz listed in the entire company, so it is assumed that he came alone, leaving all of his family behind in Germany.

The original ships log is now in the custody of the state of Pennsylvania, and can be seen at the capitol building in Harrisburg.

21

These lists have been published in several books, available in many libraries. (A)(B)

No proof has yet been found to indicate exactly where Jacob lived from 1731 to 1733. However, on March 3rd 1734 he purchased a pre-empted claim of 118 acres in Coventry township, in the county of Chester. This farm was known as "Pleasant Dale".

The autobiography of David Wertz, written in 1896 (DD), states that "Jacob Wertz was born in Mineheim, in the village of Muastad, Germany, July 17, 1705, and he married Barbara Hoff, of the same place... She was the daughter of Jonas Hoff. Barbara Hoff was born Dec. 29, 1707, in Germany, and died in America Feb. 11, 1788." (DD)

Some family researchers have theorized that perhaps Jacob left a sweetheart behind in Germany and during these first few years in Pennsylvania worked to earn enough to send for her. This is of course possible, but makes a better legend then fact, as the records give no indication as to how or where he met Anna Barbara Hoff whom he married on the 29th of December 1734 at Coventry. The marriage was performed by the Rev. Johann Caspar Stoever, one of the early traveling ministers, and is recorded in his records, which are now on file at Harrisburg. Note that Jacob's surname is spelled Wuertz in this record.

Anna Barbara Hoff

Several family researchers have cited the emigration records of the Ship "Samuel" that arrived in Philadelphia 17 August 1733 and list the names of a Hans Jacob Hoff, age 33; Anna Barbara Hoff, age 33; and Christina Hoff, age 2. It has been claimed that this Anna Barbara Hoff was the sweetheart of our Jacob Wurtz, and the woman he married in December of 1734. However this author has found no proof of this claim, and suspects that haste in locating a similar name of the right age and time of emigration may have clouded reality. The assumption that Hans Jacob Hoff was Anna Barbara's twin brother, ignores the two year old child, and if this was a family of three upon arrival, unless the father and daughter died soon after, and the widow married our Jacob Wurtz, one would expect to find mention of Christina in the Wurtz family records, as a child this young would no doubt have been adopted by a step father.

Also, in Yoder's compilation of Pennsylvania German Church Records (I), his record of the marriage of Jacob Wertz on 3 Dec. 1734, gives Anna Barbara's maiden surname as "Hofin(?)" and in Knepper records Anna Barbara's maiden surname is recorded as "Huff". (AA) Thus it is with great reservation as to the connections in fact, that this emigration record of Anna Barbara Hoff is mentioned at all. Several Hoff researchers have been contacted, but as yet none have records of an Anna Barbara who might have married our Jacob Wurtz. Early Pennsylvania records do indicate that several Hoff families had arrived in Pennsylvania prior to 1734, and perhaps one of them had a daughter whom Jacob met and married.

The David Wertz autobiography of 1896 (DD) states that Barbara Hoff Wertz was a daughter of Jones Hoff. But he also implies that they were married in Germany, which the Coventry records clearly disproves. And David Wertz also gives a date and place of birth for Jacob which is disproved by the Bretten Church records. Thus we can hardly conclude that he is correct about Barbara's date and place of birth or her father's name, though we have not been able to prove or disprove any of these.

Family of JACOB & BARBARA WURTZ

The will of Jacob Wurtz, dated 14 March 1775, probated 25 Sept. 1775 names three sons and two daughters. The baptismal records of the

23

eldest son and two daughters were recorded at Coventry, and are now on file at Harrisburg. The descendants of the youngest son have a birth certificate that indicates he was born in York County. The family lived in Coventry for ten or twelve years, and it is not know exactly when they moved to York County. So the other son could have been born in Coventry or in York County. But the existence of five surviving children is certain.

The eldest son, John Cunradt Wertz, was born 15 Oct. 1735 and baptized 25 October 1735 at Coventry, Chester Co., Penn. He was know all of his life as Conrad Wertz. He was married twice, but all of his eight children were by this first wife, Mary. Twelve generations of his descendants are outlined in Chapter three.

The second child, daughter Maria Catherina Wertz, was born 8 August 1738, baptized 10 January 1739 at Coventry. She married Abraham Knepper, and they had five children. This family is outlined in Chapter four.

The third child, Anna Margaretha Wertz, was born 14 June 1740, baptized 22 Sept. 1740, at Coventry. Her fathers will says she married a Mr. Flood or Hood, but no record of such a family has been found. She may have married Henry Hoover. (CC)

The fourth child, John Wertz, was probably born about 1742 or 1743. He died in Franklin County, Penn. and his will, proved there in 1815, names only two sons. Their families are outlined in Chapter five.

The youngest son, Johann George Wertz, was born 31 January 1745 in York County, Penn. He inherited his father's farm in Quincy twp. of Franklin County, and with his wife, Catherina Stoner and their eight children lived there until his death 27 November 1798. Many of his descendants are still living in Franklin Co. This family is outlined in Chapter six.

24

The historical records of Franklin county (C) indicate that Quincy township was first settled by "a mixed population of Germans and Scotch-Irish. Frederick Fisher located in 1737; George Wertz came from York county in 1745; Adam Small settled about the same time. John Snowberger, a Swiss, settled in 1750; John M'Cleary, of Scotland, in 1768, and his descendants occupied the same tract of land for one hundred and two years. Christopher Dull, Abraham Knepper, Adam Small, George Royer, John and George Cook, Samuel Toms, John Heefner and others were early settlers."

The deeds indicate that it was Jacob Wertz who first purchased four adjoining tracts of land, by 1747, in what was then Cumberland County. Part of the property is described as "100 acres of land adjoining the widow Snowberger, Lodwick Stull, and Frederick Foreman, on a branch of Little Antetum Creek, in Antrim township in the said county of Cumberland."

This land is now in Quincy township, Franklin County, near the little town of Quincy. Onto this tract of land, Jacob and Barbara Wertz moved with their five children. It is believed that they first built a house on this land in 1756, which was rebuilt in 1826, and was still standing and in the possession of their descendants over 150 years later.(D) Hans Jacob Wurtz signed his will the 14th day of March in 1775. He wrote his own name, spelling it "Jacob Werts". This will is on file at Carlisle, Pennsylvania, in Will Book B, page 198. It reads as follows:

"In the name of God Amen. I, Jacob Wertz, of Antrim Township, Cumberland County and Province of Pennsylvania, yeoman, imperfect health of body, but of perfect mind and memory, thanks be given unto God, calling unto mind the mortality of my body, do make and ordain this my last Will and Testament in manner following: I recommend my soul into the hand of Almighty God that gave it, and my

25

body I recommend to the earth to be buried in decent Christian burial at the discretion of my Executors and as touching such worldly Estate wherewith it has pleased God to bless me with in this life, I give, devise and dispose of the same in the following manner and form: First I give and bequeath to Barbarey, my dearly beloved wife, out of my estate, as long as she lives, to be given yearly to her from my three sons Conrad, George and John Wertz, 10 bushels of wheat a year, and likewise 10 bushels of rye a year from each of my three sons, Conrad, George, and John Wertz. Likewise 2 cows, 2 sheep, and my sons to find feed for the cows and sheep, for her lifetime, every year 1/4 acre of hemp for her lifetime, each of my sons Conrad, George, and John Wertz shall give her 20 shillings apiece yearly for her lifetime, and a good dwelling house to live in for her during her life.

"I give to my well beloved sons Conrad, George and John Wertz my estate of land as it is parted and surveyed already. Likewise all my moveable estate such as horses, cows, and goods the three sons Conrad, George and John Wertz is to have and no other. Likewise the land in the Mountain, my three sons is to have every one to have share of it alike.

"My beloved wife Barbarey is to have a share with my three sons in the moveable goods, likewise I give to my daughter Catherine Knipper one English shilling. Likewise I give to Abraham and Catherine Knipper's children, 50 pounds Pennsylvania currency out of my estate to be paid 10 pounds a year. Likewise I give to my daughter Margrat Flood 50 pounds Pennsylvania currency to be paid her at 10 pounds a year. The said 50 pounds to Abraham Knipper's children and Margrat Flood to commence payable one year from or after my decease. This is to certify that if any of my sons Conrad, George or John Wertz should sell any of their land or places, they shall, must and will give good freeholders, two at least, for security for my wife's maintenance during her life. If any of my sons should want to sell their place they should give the first offer to their other brother or brothers, and if they will not give as much as another person they are at liberty to sell it to whom they please. Likewise my wife is to have the bed and bed clothes and stone household goods both in room and kitchen and her firewood to be cut and hauled home free from all costs and charge. Likewise a horse, the use of it, when she is in want of one. Likewise my wife is to raise the young cattle that she has from the two cows till they are three years old. My sons is to find feed for them, and she is to put one away, once every three years.

"Likewise the servant girl is to have, when she is free, her choice of the cows, and to have one cow given her, a spinning wheel, a feather bed, good freedom clothes.

"I likewise constitute, make, and ordain Conrad, George and John Wertz, and Barbarey, my wife, the sole executors of this my last Will and Testament, and I do hereby utterly disallow and revoke all former Testaments and Wills and executors ratifying and confirming this and no other to be my last Will and Testament. In witness whereof I have here unto set my hand and seal this 14th day of March in the year of our Lord 1775."

    (Signed) Jacob Werts

Witnesses: James Murray, Lodowick Stull, Richard Heckom, George Adam Cook.

The various spellings of the Wertz surname are of interest, but seem to have no particular significance. In the Bretten Church records the name was most often spelled Wurtz. The ship's log of the "Brittania" shows the name spelled Wirtz twice and Wurts once, each list written by someone other than Jacob himself, since he signed by mark. Rev. Johann Casper Stover's records show the name spelled Wuertz. Jacob signed his will "Jacob Werts", but whoever transcribed the will used the Wertz spelling. Jacob's descendants have continued to use the Wertz spelling.

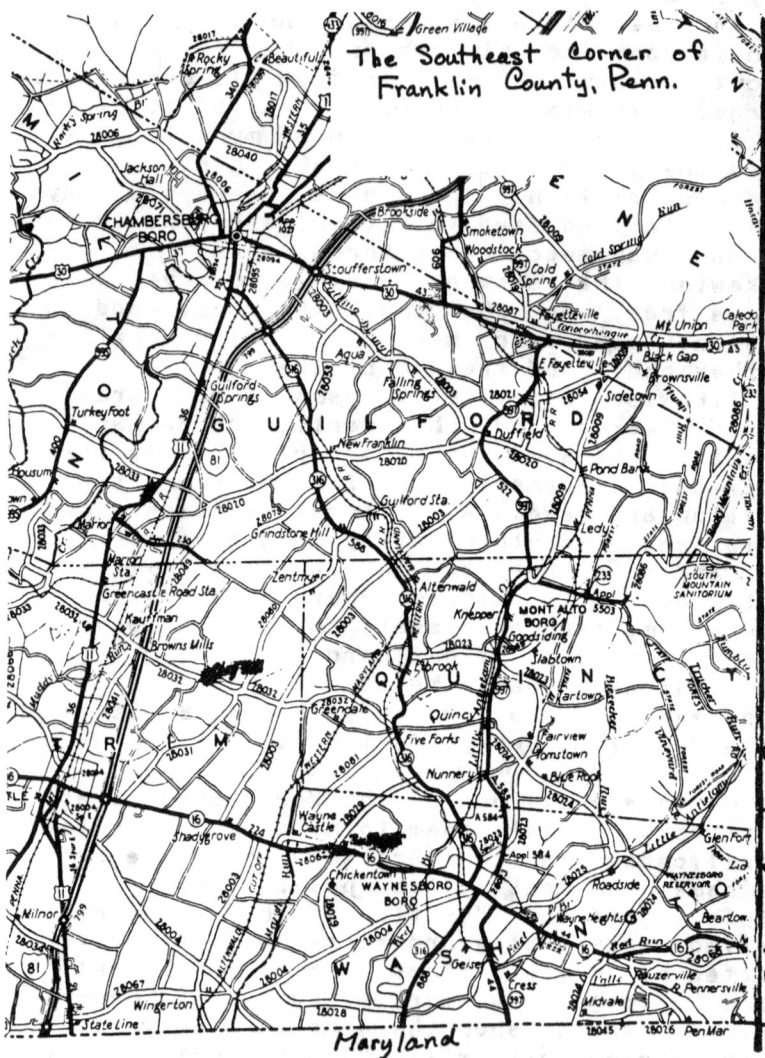

The Southeast Corner of
Franklin County, Penn.

Chapter 3

JOHN CUNRADT WERTZ, 1735 - 1793

John Conrad **Wertz** was born 15 October 1735 at Coventry, Chester County, Pennsylvania, the eldest son of Hans Jacob Wurtz and Anna Barbara Hoff. He spent his early boyhood in Chester County and moved with his family when he was 6 to 10 years old, first to York County and soon after to what is now Quincy township in Franklin County. Here he remained for the rest of his life. He was known throughout his life as Conrad Wertz, though many records spell his name in various ways. (The IGI lists him as Conrad Worts!)

Sometime about 1758, probably in Quincy township, Conrad married. His first wife's name was Mary, but we do not yet know her maiden surname. She was the mother of all of his eight children. Mary died sometime between 1781 and 1792, and soon after her death, Conrad remarried. His second wife was Catherine, and to date we do not know her maiden surname either. She lived until sometime after 1810, and is named in Conrad's will. Catherine Wertz is listed as head of the household in the 1810 Census for Washington township, Franklin County, Penn.

Conrad Wertz died in 1793, and his will, dated 27 January 1792 is found in Will Book Volume A, page 237 at the Franklin County Courthouse in Chambersburg. The will reads as follows:

WILL of CONRAD WERTZ

"In the name of God, Amen, are the following articles by me and a last will and testament of Conrad Wertz being of good understanding hath ordained and set forth in the presence of Samuel Royer, Daniel Royer, Christian Miller, and William Brown.
"1st I recommend my soul unto the Almighty God, my body to the earth to be buried in a

Christian like manner. Unto my beloved wife Catherine I give and bequeath what she is entitled to by law besides one good bed. Next I bequeath unto my eldest son, John, one shilling sterling for his prerogative right. Next all my estate real and personal shall be sold by public vendue on these conditions all my real estate to be sold at any opportunity. Next all my surviving children, namely, John, Jacob, Peter, Conrad, Christian, Andrew, Daniel, and my daughter Mary shall all have an equal and alike portion. Next it is my will that my son Jacob shall have possession of the mill or the benefit thereof until the first of May 1793 for the expense he has been on the same.

"Next it is my will for the whole estate and all my property herein mentioned I do hereby declare, nominate and appoint Daniel Royer and Christian Miller to be Executors to act agreeable to equity and conscience whereby and at any times the said Executors, Daniel Royer and Christian Miller shall have full power and authority to collect all my just outstanding debts and also to pay and discharge all my just debts and to give title and deed of all the property to be sold as if the same had been done in my lifetime. Next I desire and is my will that my chosen and appointed executors, Daniel Royer and Christian Miller, shall at the same time have the same power and authority fully in my name and after all cases laid to give good title in my name for the plantation of George and John Wertz, my brothers, as they think fit, wherein shall be no dispute and all demands of any heirs against my estate shall have full power in my name to settle and justify the same and this my last will and testament by me pronounced, declared, signed, sealed in the presence of the present witnesses this 27th day of January Anno Domini 1792."

(signed) Conrad Wertz

Witnesses present: Frederick Foreman, William Brown, and Samuel Royer.

FAMILY of CONRAD and MARY WERTZ

1. **John Wertz**, born Sept. 1758 or 1759, in Quincy township, Franklin County, Penn. Died in 1833 or 1834, probably in Somerset County. He married by 1796 to Catherine Starr. They had eleven children, most of whom were born in Somerset County, Penn. See page 32 for an outline and records of his family.

2. **Jacob Wertz**, born the 5th or 8th of June, 1763, in Quincy township. He probably died between 1830 and 1840 in Franklin County. On 4 April 1784 he married Hannah Emmons or Emerson, who was born 4 Feb. 1765. They had eight children, all of them probably born in Franklin County. See page 37 for outline and records of this family.

3. **Mary or Maria Wertz**, probably born about 1765 in Quincy township. She married Peter Coffman, and they had several children, but no records of this family have been obtained to date. It is believed that this family moved from Pennsylvania perhaps soon after their marriage.

4. **Peter Wertz**, born about 1768, Quincy township; died in 1807. No record has yet been found to indicate the name of his wife, but they are known to have had three children. See page 40 for records of this family.

5. **Conrad Wertz**, born the 5th or 6th of August 1770, Quincy township, Franklin County; He lived in Quincy township, at least until 1819, as all eleven of his children were born there. He married by 1793 to Anna Maria Cook, born 3 March 1775; died 29 April 1867. See page 43 for an outline and records of this family.

6. **Christian Wertz**, born 12 January 1772, in Quincy township, Franklin County; died 24 February 1851 in Harrison township, Bedford County, Penn. In 1795 he married Elizabeth Fisher, who was born 24 May 1776, and died 17

31

December 1845. They had twelve children, probably all born in Bedford County. See page 57 for an outline and records of this family.

7. Andrew Wertz, born the 2nd or 7th of May, 1774, Quincy township. He married by 1801 to Magdalena Berkey, born 1 January 1779. They had twelve children. See page 65 for outline and records of this family.

8. Daniel Wertz, born 20 December 1781, in Quincy township, Franklin County, Penn. Died 28 September 1873 or 1878 in Montgomery County, Ohio. By 1803 he married Sarah Weimer, daughter of Frederick Weimer Jr. Sarah was born 23 November 1787 in Somerset County, Penn. and died the 10th or 20th of March 1854 or 1859 in Montgomery County, Ohio. Both Daniel and Sarah are buried at the Ellerton Cemetery, Ellerton, Montgomery County, Ohio. They had fourteen children, the first two born in Franklin County, Penn. and the rest born in Ohio. Outline and records of this family begin on page 74.

The reader will note that some dates are not certain due to the poor writing on the charts made in 1914 by Estelle Ryan Snyder. Others are disputed by several records or different descendants. Where dates are in question, all possibilities are indicated. If a "best" or primary source exists, only that date has been given.

JOHN WERTZ and CATHERINE STARR

John Wertz was born September 1758 or 1759 in Quincy township, Franklin County, and died in 1833 or 1834, probably in Somerset County. He is listed as John Werty in the 1810 Somerset County Census.
John Wertz married by 1796 to Catherine Starr, and they had eleven children. It is not yet know just when they moved to Somerset County, but at least two of their children were

32

christened there in April of 1799. It is possible that the two or three eldest children were born before they arrived in Somerset County, but at least the eight younger children were born there.

1. Elizabeth Wertz, born 1796; christened 14 April 1799, at the German Reformed Church in Stoystown, Somerset County, Penn. (IGI) She married John Fisher, and they had eight children whose names on the chart are not clear, but appear to be: Mary, Catherine, Jonathan, Martin, David, Elizabeth, Susan, and Jacob.

2. Mary Wertz, born 1797; died 1882; married David Kissinger and had ten children: Catherine, Susan, Jacob, Eliza Ann, Stephen, Margaret, Esther (Hettie), John, Lewis, and Andrew.

3. Catherine Wertz, born 3 Dec. 1798; christened 14 April 1799, at the German Reformed Church in Stoystown, Somerset County, Penn. (IGI) She died 22 June 1885. Catherine married Elias Crissman, and they had four children: George Washington, Mary, Lucinda, and Elias.

4. John Wertz, born 23 Nov. 1802; died 25 March 1887; married Susan Berkey, and they had thirteen children. See next page for an outline and records of this family.

5. Susan Wertz, born 1805; died 30 Dec. 1899; married John Hoffman, and had three children: Jacob, Samuel, and Aaron.

6. Rebecca Wertz, born 18 March 1807; died 22 January 1892; married Samuel Kung, and had four children: Sarah Ann, Aaron, Mary, and Lydia.

7. Sarah Wertz, born 1808 or 1809; married Tobias Yoder, and had at least one daughter: Sara Yoder, who married John Keafer.

8. Barbara Wertz, born 13 July 1810, Somerset County (IGI); died 20 April 1903; married Jacob Lint, and had six children: Eliza, Catherine, Susanna, Lydia, Sarah, and John.

9. Andrew Wertz, born 1813; died August 1848; married Esther Brallier, born 17 Sept. 1817; died 3 June 1896. They had four children: David Wertz, Samuel Wertz, Mary Wertz, and Andrew (?) Wertz. The youngest son had at least three children, but names and other records of this family have not been located.

10. Jacob Wertz, born 31 August 1815; died 24 May 1888; married Mary Hoffman, and they had seven children. Outline of this family is on page 36.

11. George Wertz, born 1818; died 12 April 1881; married Sarah Martin, and had nine children, but their names are very blurred on the chart and impossible to read. The eldest two appear to be Elizabeth and Catherine, and the youngest two seem to be Clara and Mary. (This George Wertz might be the George Wertz, age 36 listed in the Franklin County 1850 Census, with wife Hetty, age 30, and six children. – See Chapter 7)

JOHN WERTZ and Susan Berkey

John Wertz was born 23 November 1802 or 1803 and died 25 March 1887; son of John Wertz and Catherine Starr. He married about 1829 to Susan Berkey, born 15 December 1811, died 9 November 1904. They had thirteen children. Records of this family are found in the 1850 Census, Conemaugh twp., Somerset County, Penn. and have been entered into the IGI for most of the children.

1. Rachel Wertz, born June 1830 (age 19 in the 1850 Census, Paint twp., Somerset Co. – see IGI); m. Andrew Berkey; five children: Elizabeth, David, Marinda, Hiram, and Alice.

2. Caroline Wertz, born June 1832 (?); in 1850 Census, Paint twp., Somerset Co. (E); married Jacob Gordon, and had six children: Henry, Andrew, Leon, Noah, Jacob, and Lewis.

3. Hattie Wertz, born 10 March 1833(?); married William Schunk, and had six children: Franklin, Lucy, Mary, Seth (?), John, and William.

4. Elizabeth Wertz, born about 1834 (age 16 in 1850 - see IGI); married Samuel Roddy, and had seven children: Mary Jane, Alice, Elsie, Nelson W., Amanda, Sydney E., and Wilson L.

5. William Wertz, born about 1836 (age 14 in 1850 - see IGI); married Polly Alvine, and they had seven children: (1) Josiah Wertz, who died before 1915; (2) Catherine Wertz, who married twice, to Les R--?--, and to J. Mason; (3) Malinda Wertz, who died before 1915; (4) Lucy Wertz, married Leon --?--; (5) Thomas Wertz, married Carrie Miller and lived at Johnstown, Penn.; (6) Polly Wertz, died before 1915; and (7) Samuel Wertz, died before 1915.

6. David B. Wertz, born about 1838 (age 12 in 1850 - see IGI); married 1st to Susan Coble, and second to Susan --?--; six children: (1) Mary Jane Wertz, married; (2) Amanda Wertz, married; (3) Newman Wertz, born 26 March 1868, died before 1915; (4) Dayton Wertz, born August 1870 or 1871; (5) Ellen Wertz, born 1873, died 1882; and (6) Henry Wertz, born 1875, died before 1915.

7. Susan Wertz, born about 1841 (age 9 in 1850 - see IGI); married. Children, if any, are not listed.

8. Catherine Wertz, born about 1843 (age 7 in 1850 - see IGI); married Jacob Holsopp, and they had seven children: Agustus (?); Emma, born March 1868; Leona (?); Sarah; Marion (?); Lucy; and Jacob.

9. John Wertz, born 16 February 1843; died young, probably before 1850.

10. Jacob Wertz, born about 1846 (age 4 in 1850 - see IGI); married Mary Miller. Lived in Pennsylvania. Children, if any, are not listed.

11. Peter Wertz, born 26 February 1849 (age 1 in 1850 - see IGI); unmarried; lived in Indiana.

12. Lucinda Wertz, born 1852 (?); married Ephraim Seese (?). Children, if any, are not listed.

13. Mary A. Wertz, born 1856 (?); married Albert A. Kinsey. Children, if any, are not listed.

JACOB WERTZ and Mary Hoffman

Jacob Wertz, born 31 August 1815; died 24 May 1888; son of John Wertz and Catherine Starr. Jacob married about 1837/8 to Mary Hoffman, born 18 May 1818; died 23 January 1906. They had seven children:

1. Hannah Wertz, born 2 Dec. 1838; married David Reid, and had two children.

2. Catherine Wertz, born 1840; married 7 Feb. 1869 in Juniata County, Penn. to John Lauber. (see IGI) Children, if any, are not listed.

3. Elizabeth Wertz, born 1844; married Jacob W--?--. Children, if any, are not listed.

4. Susan Wertz, born 25 Dec. 1845; married Samuel Harrison. Children, if any, are not listed.

5. John A. Wertz, born 19 Feb. 1848; married Susan Strayer. Lived Johnstown, Penn. Children, if any, are not listed.

6. George M. Wertz, born 19 July 1856; married Louisa Glitch. Lived Johnstown, Penn. Children, if any, are not listed.

7. Jacob M. Wertz, born 29 Sept. 1859; married Lena Glitch. Lived Johnstown, Penn. Children, if any, are not listed.

JACOB WERTZ and HANNAH EMMONS

Jacob Wertz, born 8 June 1762/3, Quincy twp., Franklin Co., Penn.; son of John Cunradt and Mary Wertz; probably died in Franklin County between 1830 and 1840. He is most likely the Jacob Wertz listed in the 1810, 1820, and 1830 Census of Washington twp., Franklin County. Jacob married 4 April 1784 to Hannah Emmons (or Emersons), who was born 4 February 1765. They had eight children, all born in Franklin County, Pennsylvania:

1. John Wertz, born 13 March 1785. Nothing further is known of him. (Possibly this is the John Wertz who m. 25 Feb. 1808 at the East Conococheague Pres. Church, Greencastle, Franklin Co., to Elizabeth Foulkman.) (6)

2. Elizabeth Wertz, born 5 Sept. 1786. Possibly the Elizabeth Wertz m. 1811 to John McFerren. (see Chapter 4, page 101.)

3. George Wertz, born 2nd or 3rd of August 1788; married Catherine --?--, and they had eleven children. See next page for outline and records of this family.

4. Mary Wertz, born 1 December 1790; married George Smith, and they had seven children: Melinda, Jacob, James, George, Hannah, Thomas, and Margaret.

5. James Wertz, born 1 January 1793. Nothing further is known of him.

6. Priscilla Wertz, born 21 June 1795. Nothing further is known of her.

7. Henry Wertz, born 14 August 1797; married 19 June 1823 to S. Witner, born 26 May 1798. They had seven children. See page 39 for outline of this family.

8. Nancy Wertz, born 16 June 1800; married 22 November 1825 to Spencer Sayers, born 19 Feb. 1804; one son: Hiram Sayers, born 3 August 1826.

GEORGE and Catherine WERTZ

George Wertz, born 2 or 3 August 1788; son of Jacob Wertz and Hannah Emmons; married Catherine --?--, had eleven children:

1. John Andrew Wertz, born 25 Dec. 1823; died before 1915, unmarried, and without issue.

2. Jerome Wertz, born 17 August 1825; died before 1915. No record of any children.

3. Daniel Wertz, born 18 Nov. 1827; married, but no record of any children.

4. Mary Wertz, born 26 August 1829; married a Mr. Larkkins, and had two children; George W., and Addie F. Lived in Ohio.

5. John Wertz, born 20 April 1831; wife's name unknown; seven children: (1) Thomas Wertz; (2) James Wertz, who died before 1915 without issue; (3) Jerome Wertz, who was living in South Bend, Indiana in 1915; (4) Milan Wertz, who was living in South Bend, Indiana in 1915; (5) Harold Wertz, who was living in Niles, Michigan in 1915; (6) William Wertz, who was living in South Bend, Indiana in 1915; and (7) Cora Wertz, who was married and living in South Bend, Indiana in 1915.

6. Harriet Wertz, born 5 January 1833; married a Mr. Stutz. No record of children.

7. Elizabeth Wertz, born 30 July 1835; died before 1915, unmarried, and without issue.

8. Catherine Wertz, born 20 June 1837; died before 1915; married John Christian Warner, born 30 June 1837; died 25 Feb. 1910; eight children: (1) Emma Warner, born 4 Dec. 1863, married Peter Hartman; (2) Cora Warner, born 4 Sept. 1865, married Milton Woodlong (?); (3) George Warner, born 26 April 1867; (4) Amanda Warner, born 14 June 1869, married Daniel Baker; (5) Catherine Warner, born 16 June 1871, married Manley (?) Shaffer; (6) Daniel Warner, born 16 March 1873, married Sara Geintz (?); (7) Ida Warner, born 19 June 1875, married Edmund Davy; (8) Henry Warner, born 28 April 1877, married Annie Schaffer.

9. Margaret Wertz, born 17 Sept. 1839, married a Mr. Fisher. Family if any not known.

10. George Wertz, born 25 April 1841, died 12 January 1854 (?).

11. Amanda Wertz, born 20 Feb. 1845, married a Mr. Davis. Family if any not known.

HENRY WERTZ and S. Witner

Henry Wertz, born 14 August 1797, son of Jacob Wertz and Hannah Emmons; married 19 June 1823 to S. Witner, born 26 May 1798. They had seven children:

1. George Wertz, born 8 July 1824.

2. Joseph Wertz, born 12 August 1826.

3. Mary Wertz, born 28 Feb. 1829.

4. Harriet Wertz, born 17 August 1832.

5. Henry Wertz, born 20 Sept. 1833, married 1872 to Edna Sh--?--; four children. See next page for outline of this family.

6. William Wertz, born 28 Feb. 1836.

7. Jesse Wertz, born 5 April 1839.

39

HENRY WERTZ and Edna

Henry Wertz, born 20 Sept. 1833, son of Henry Wertz and S. Witner; married in 1872 to Edna Sh--f--dy (?), and they had four children:

1. William Wertz, born 14 Sept. 1874; married 12 July 1898 to Nora Park. Three children: (1) Ruth Wertz, born 7 May 1899; (2) Glen Martin Wertz, born 2 June 1906; and (3) Clifford M. Wertz, born 22 Sept. 1908.

2. Gracie G. Wertz, born 16 Sept. 1877.

3. Jennie Wertz, born 16 March 1880.

4. Sofia Wertz, born 22 Nov. 1893.

PETER WERTZ, died 1807

Peter Wertz, born about 1768, third son of John Cunradt and Mary Wertz. It is not known who Peter married, but he died before his third child, Jacob, was born in 1807.

1. John Wertz, probably born about 1805, died in infancy.

2. a daughter, probably born about 1806, also died in infancy.

3. Jacob Wertz, born 14 June 1807, died April 1865; married 16 Sept. 1830, Holmes Co., Ohio (E) to his first cousin, Catherine or Catrina Wertz, daughter of Andrew Wertz and Magdalena Berkey, see page 65. Catherine was born 21 March 1811, and died 18 June 1879. They had eleven children:

Family of JACOB and CATHERINE WERTZ

1. John Wertz, born 23 August 1831; lived at South Haven, Michigan.

2. Jerome Wertz, born 21 May 1833; married Fannie Hummell; seven children. See next page.

40

3. Amanda Wertz, born 4 Sept. 1835; died 9 June 1908(?); married David Profit. Family, if any unknown.

4. Daniel or David Wertz, born 6 Dec. 1837; unmarried; living in Davenport, Iowa in 1915.

5. Catherine Wertz, born 20 Sept. 1840; died 16 August 1864, unmarried.

6. Jacob Wertz, born 19 June 1843; married Rose Miller.

7. Cornelius Wertz, born 28 January 1845; married 1st to Jennie Gray; married 2nd to Miss Dougherty; lived Bedford, Iowa. Three Children; nine grandchildren known. See page 42 for outline of this family.

8. George W. Wertz, born 11 June 1847; lived Marina, Iowa.

9. Henry Wertz, born 26 Oct. 1849; died before 1915; no heirs.

10. Emily Wertz, born 29 July 1851; died January 1901; married David Snyder; one son: Jacob Leroy Snyder, born 2 April 1890; living in Eldridge, Iowa in 1915.

11. Louis Wertz, born 16 March 1855; married Cora B. Johnson; lived at Sterling, Illinois.

JEROME WERTZ and Fannie Hummell

Jerome Wertz, born 21 May 1833, son of Jacob and Catherine Wertz; married Fannie Hummell and they had seven children:

1. Charles Wertz, born May 1857; died Jan. 1860.

2. Frank Wertz, born Feb. 1859; married Elizabeth --?--; lived at Kellogg, Iowa.

3. Eliza Ann Wertz, born March 1861; married James Molloy (?); lived Albion, Iowa.

4. Amanda Wertz, born 1863; married Frank Pierce; lived at Kellogg, Iowa.

5. Mary Wertz, born 186?; married Sam Davis; lived in Iowa.

6. Emily Wertz, born 24 Sept. 186?; married George Schuman (?); lived at Albion, Iowa.

7. George Wertz, born 187?; married Anna Bell; lived at Lauerl (?), Iowa.

CORNELIUS WERTZ and Jennie Gray

Cornelius Wertz, born 28 January 1845, son of Jacob and Catherine Wertz; married 1st to Jennie Gray; married 2nd to Miss. Dougherty; three children. It is not known if all three children were from Cornelius' first marriage.

1. Ora E. Wertz, born 5 Nov. 1875; married Nellie B. Taylor; three children: (1) Wylda C. Wertz, born 14 Sept. 1903, St. Joseph, Michigan; (2) Jerome Wertz, born 19 Oct. 1905, St. Joseph, Michigan; and (3) Hallene Wertz, born 23 June 1910, St. Joseph, Michigan.

2. John J. Wertz, born 1881; married Florence Hamilton (?); lived in Colorado. Three children born by 1915: (1) Melvin Donald Wertz, born 19 Sept. 1905, Colorado; (2) Mable Caroline Wertz, born 16 Sept. 1909, Colorado; and (3) Francis Marie Wertz, born 2 May 1913, Colorado.

3. Ida M. Wertz, married William H. Miller; lived Marathon, Iowa; three children: (1) George Franklin Miller, born 5 June 1898, Iowa; (2) Claude William Miller, born 24 May 1901, Iowa; and (3) Gladys Marie Miller, born 19 June 1908, Iowa.

42

CONRAD WERTZ and ANNA MARIA COOK

Conrad Wertz, born 6 August 1770, Quincy township, Cumberland (now Franklin) County, Pennsylvania; son of John Cunradt and Mary Wertz; married by 1793 to Anna Maria (Mary) Cook, born 3 March 1775; died 29 April 1867, age 92 years, 1 month, and 26 days; buried at the Lutheran Churchyard, St. Thomas; daughter of Johann George Adam Cook, 1751-1842 and Rebecca Ankenny, of Washington Twp. Conrad and Mary had eleven children, all born in Quincy township, of Franklin County, Penn.:

1. George Wertz, born 15 Feb. 1794. He is believed to have married, but nothing further is known of him or his family, if any. (This could be the George Wertz in the 1830 Census, Letterkenny twp., Franklin Co., Penn.)

2. Catherine Wertz, born 23 May 1796; married 1st to a Mr. Williston, and 2nd to a Mr. Anderson. Nothing further is known of them.

3. Anna Maria Wertz, born 30 Oct. 1798; married a Mr. Rafflespanger. Nothing further is known of this family.

4. John Wertz, born 15 March 1801; married Catherine Houk, and had five children and at least thirteen grandchildren. See next page for an outline of this family.

5. Rebecca Wertz, born 7 July 1803; married a Mr. Whistler, according to the 1915 chart. Or maybe this is the Rebecca Wertz m. a. 1825 to George McFerren. (see Chapter 4, page 101.)

6. Elizabeth Wertz, born 12 January 1806; married Godfrey Brecker, and had six children: (1) Jeremiah Brecker, married a Miss Newbery; (2) Anna Brecker, married a Mr. Stouffer; (3) Margaret Brecker, married a Mr. Powell; (4) Martha Brecker; (5) Wesley Brecker; and (6) John Brecker.

7. Nancy Wertz, born 2 July 1809; married 26 March 1829 to Mathias Brindle, son of Marks Brindle of St. Thomas twp., Franklin Co., Penn. Their marriage record is on file at Chambersburg, Franklin County, Penn. and a copy of their marriage certificate is included on page 47. Six children. See page 46 for an outline of this family.

8. Rachel Wertz, born 3 January 1812; married John Coble, and had six children, and at least twelve grandchildren. See page 48 for outline and records of this family.

9. Henrietta Wertz, born 16 July 1814; married Thomas Morgan. Nothing further is known of this family, if any.

10. Magdalena (Martha) Wertz, born 23 October 1816; died 6 January 1903; married 7 April 1836 to John Croft, born 9 August 1815; died 2 Feb. 1892, son of David Croft Jr. John and Martha Wertz Croft had nine children, and 31 grandchildren. Outline of this family is on page 49 of this book, and in the Croft and Cell family histories by this author. John and Martha Wertz Croft were the 2nd great grandparents of this author. Pictures of this couple are found on pages 50 and 51.

11. Conrad Wertz, born 2 October 1819; married Fannie Bush and they had five children and 19 grandchildren. See page 55 for outline of this family.

JOHN WERTZ and Catherine Houk

John Wertz, born 15 March 1801, Quincy twp., Franklin County, Penn.; died in 1869; son of Conrad Wertz and Anna Maria Cook; married Catherine Houk, born 25 Nov. 1806; died 1892; they had five children: This family is on the 1830, 1840, 1850, and 1860 Census of St. Thomas twp., Franklin Co., Penn.

44

1. Elizabeth Wertz, born 6 Oct. 1826; died 4 March 1890; married 19 Sept. 1850 by Rev. Adam Height, near St. Thomas to Frederick Byers. They had ten children: (1) John Byers, born 10 Sept. 1845, married Mary Richardson; (2) Susan Byers, born 28 May 1848, married Peter Honker, and lived in Chambersburg and later Pawnee City, Nebraska; (3) Hiriam Byers, born March 1850, married Anna Bunkhold(?), lived St. Thomas and Chambersburg, Penn.; (4) Annie E. Byers, born 3 January 185?, married David E. Yeager, had twelve children, lived St. Thomas, Penn.; (5) Maggie C. Byers, born 2? March 1856, married Jacob Meredeth, lived St. Thomas, Penn.; (6) Rachael A. Byers, born 28 Oct 1858, married Jacob Dutinler, three children; (7) William M. Byers, born 23 Dec. 1863, married Maggie Slatzer(?), lived Chambersburg, Penn.; (8) Charles C. Byers, born 29 July 1867, married Martha Anderson, lived in Nebraska; (9) Philip W. Byers, born 28 May 1870, married Susan Stoner; (10) Jacob W. Byers, born 27 Sept. 1872, married Anna Baker, lived Chambersburg, Penn.

2. Mary Ann Wertz, born 26 January 1832; died 1903; married William Byers. Family if any, unknown.

3. John Conrad Wertz, born 17 March 1836, married Mary A. Goodale, born 16 August 1837; three children, and at least two grand children, see next page.

4. Catherine Margaret or Margaret Catherine Wertz, born 4 January 1839; married 18 Dec. 1857 by Rev. T.F. Hallowell in Pleasant Hall to Solomon Neff; lived at Upper Strassburg, Franklin County. Their marriage notice was in the Franklin Repository Newspaper on Dec. 16th, 1857. Family, if any, unknown.

5. Rachel F. Wertz, born 14 Dec. 1842, married August Eckhardt, lived Pawnee City, Nebraska. Family, if any, unknown.

JOHN CONRAD WERTZ and Mary A. Goodale

John Conrad Wertz, born 17 March 1836, and Mary A. Goodale, born 16 August 1837, had three children:

1. Arlene Wertz, born 1863, married Alfred William Cavanough(?), born 23 Nov. 1860, lived Pawnee City, Nebraska. Family, if any, unknown.

2. Katie L. Wertz, born 21 November 1865, married Nathaniel C. Morrison, who died before 1915; two children: Etta Morrison, married and living in Tennessee in 1915; and Leo W. Morrison, living in Los Angeles, California in 1915.

3. John Conrad Wertz, born 1870, married Luella Gaston, lived Lincoln, Nebraska. No further record of this family to date.

MATHIAS BRINDLE and Nancy Wertz

Mathias or Matthias Brindle, born 28 August 1803, died 6 August 1844 at Millcreek, Erie County, Penn. He was the fourth of twelve children of Marks or Marcus Brindle and Mary Houck or Houcker of St. Thomas, Franklin Co., Penn. Nancy Wertz, born 2 July 1809, Quincy twp., Franklin Co., Penn., died 22 Jan. 1871 at Millcreek, Erie Co., Penn., daughter of Conrad Wertz and Anna Marie Cook also of St. Thomas. Mathias and Nancy were married 26 March 1829 at Chambersburg, and a copy of their marriage certificate is on the next page. They had six children and at least 17 grandchildren. Information on this family has been obtained from their great grandson, William H. Brindle of Erie, Penn. by correspondence with this author since 1976.

1. George Brindle, born 8 July 1830; died 18 December 1887; married Margaret Boyer or Royer; two children.

46

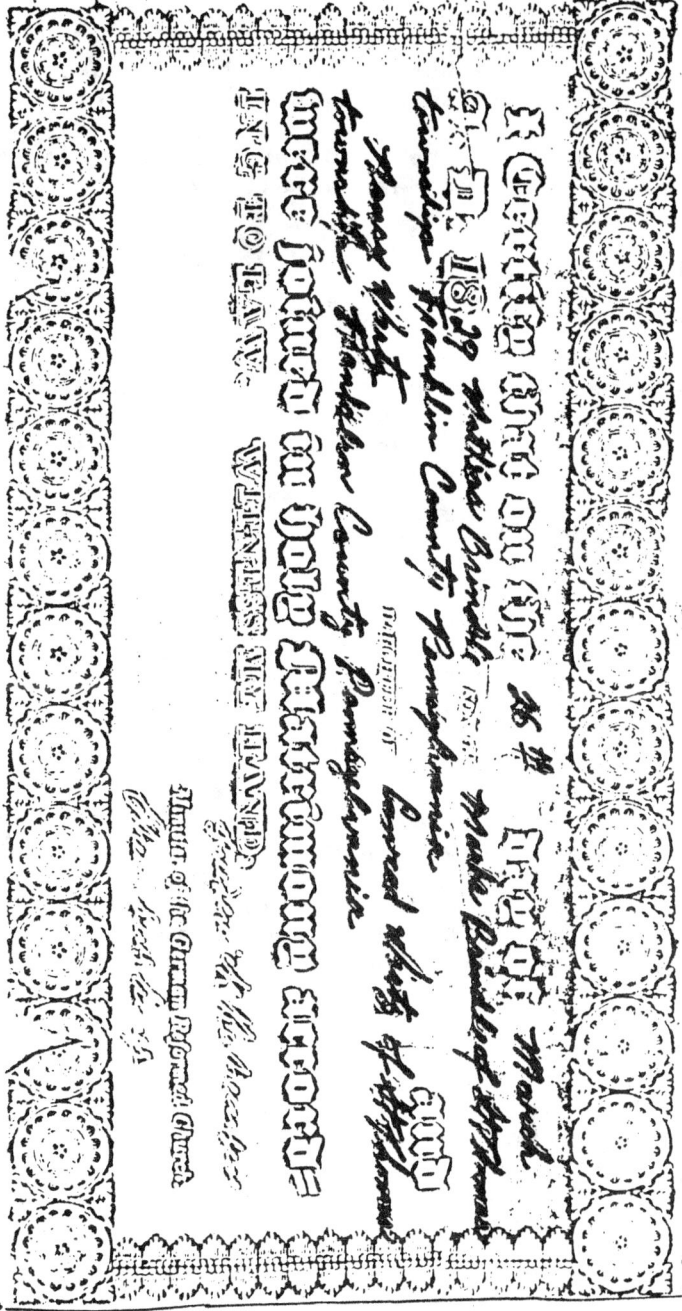

I Certify That on the 26 th day of March

A.D. 1899 Arthur Burns of Markes, and

township Franklin County Pennsylvania Lizzie Huff of

township Franklin County Pennsylvania

were joined in Holy Matrimony according

to law.

WITNESS MY HAND

Minister of the German Reformed Church

2. Mary Brindle, born 25 April 1832; died 6 May 1912; married John Miller, born 1818; died 1891; four children.

3. John Brindle, born 4 June 1834; died 3 May 1915; married Louise Sherwin; two children.

4. Wesley Brindle, born 10 April 1836; died 6 June 1908; married Fannie Waidley, born 1842; five children.

5. Rachel Brindle, born 13 April 1838; married a Mr. Dougherty; no records yet of their family.

6. William Brindle, born 5 May 1841; died 19 January 1916; married Susan E. Ricker; four children, including Edward Brindle, the father of William H. Brindle.

JOHN COBLE and Rachel Wertz

John Coble, born in 1815 or 1818 in St. Thomas twp., Franklin County, Penn.; died 1887; eldest son of Captain John Coble and Susanna Wiland. Further data on this family can also be found in the Coble family history by this author. Rachel Wertz, born 3 January 1812 or 1813, Quincy twp., Franklin County, Penn, daughter of Conrad Wertz and Anna Maria Cook. John and Rachel were married in Franklin County about 1835, and they had eight children, all born at St. Thomas, Franklin County, Penn. Records of this family can be found in the 1850 and 1860 Census of St. Thomas twp., Franklin Co.

1. Jonathan Coble, born 1836; living in St. Thomas, Penn. in 1915.

2. Elmira Margaret Coble, born 1838; nothing further is known of her.

3. Jerome C. Coble, born 1840; lived at Waynesboro, Penn.; four children: Howard; Wertz Coble; Otilla; and William Coble.

4. M. Joanna Coble, born 1842; nothing further is known of her.

5. Lucretia Coble, born 1845; married a Mr. Sackman and they had seven children: Annie; Edward; Katie; Mary; John; Cora; and Jerome Sackman.

6. Samuel Coble, born a. 1848 (age 2 in 1850) and probably died before 1860.

7. Catherine C. Coble, born a. 1850 (age 10 in 1860). No further record of her.

8. Daniel Coble, is not listed in this family in either the 1850 or 1860 Census, but the Coble family records state that he was a son of John W. and Rachel Wertz Coble, and that he married and had one son, Charles Coble.

JOHN CROFT and Martha Wertz

John Croft, born 9 August 1815, Hamilton twp., Franklin Co., Penn.; died 2 February 1892, St. Thomas twp., Franklin Co., Penn.; was the only son of John David Croft Jr. and Mary Magadelene Coble. Further records of this family can be found in the Croft and Coble family histories by this author.
Magdalena (or Martha as she was known throughout her adult life) Wertz, was born 23 October 1816, Quincy twp. and died 6 January 1903 in St. Thomas twp., Franklin Co.; daughter of Conrad Wertz and Anna Maria Cook. John and Martha were married 7 April 1836 in Franklin County, and they had nine children, all born in Franklin County, Penn.:

1. Rev. Samuel Croft M.D., born 16 November 1836; died 15 March 1907; married 24 Dec. 1861 to Anna Mary Embich, born 17 Dec. 1838, daughter of Henry Embich; nine children and at least sixteen grandchildren: (1) Charles Luther Croft, born 17 Dec. 1862, m. Amanda Smucker, one son, Paul Croft; (2) Carrie Lucretia Croft, born 21 Aug. 1865, m. John

Martha Wertz Croft
1816–1903

John Croft
1815–1892

Irvin Croft (son of David & Eleanor, see below), two children, Chester A. & Ruth; (3) Sarah Ellen Croft, born 10 April 1867, died 3 August 1868; (4) George Albert Croft, born 16 August 1869, married Nell Pressman, no children. (George was a photographer at Uniontown, Penn. and produced most of the family photos, including those of his grandparents included here.); (5) Martha Blanche Croft, born 21 Feb. 1871, married Frisby Sherts Brake, seven children; (6) William Henry Croft, born 2 April 1873, married Verna Creary or Cleary, two daughters; (7) John Clarence Croft, born 17 Jan. 1876, married Amy --?--, three daughters; (8) Walter Samuel Croft, born 7 July 1878, married Sarah McGann, one son, Walter H. Croft, living in Hagerstown, Maryland in 1905; (9) Mary Catherine Croft, married Stafford Pyne or Pine. There is an article about Rev. Dr. Samuel Croft in the Biographical Annals of Franklin County Pennsylvania, page 247. (F)

2. David Croft, born 20 January 1840, died 3 August 1892 or 1902; married 27 Nov. 1861 to Eleanor/Ellen/Elnora W. Kinnard, married 2nd to Mrs. Emma Brewer; six children by first marriage: (1) William H. Croft, born 13 July 1864, died 18 Feb. 1898, unmarried; (2) John Irvin Croft, born 11 August 1867, died 8 Jan. 1895, married Carrie Lucretia Croft (daughter of Samuel and Anna Mary Croft, see above), two children, Chester A. and Elva Ruth; (3) Harry C. Croft, born 27 March 1869, married Nettie Hawbecker or Hawbaker, four children, Helen, Elizabeth, Kathryn, and Don K.; (4) Martha Myrtle Croft, born 8 Sept. 1871, married Harry S. Lesher, four children, Donald, Thelma, Owen, and Ethel; (5) Ida Grace Croft, born 31 March 1874, married J. Ambrose Welsh, three children, Harold, Jacob, and Mary Ellen; (6) Clayton Howard Croft, born 17 April 1879, died 6 Dec. 1910, unmarried.

3. John Croft, born 26 June 1842, died 24 Feb. 1912 at Waynesboro, Penn.; married 18 Feb.

1869 to Clara S.Gelwix, no children; married
2nd to Lydia Strock, born 11 May 1841, one
son: Frank Wesley Croft, who married Laura
Statler and had two children, Ella May and
Mary Grace.

4. George Wertz Croft, born 6 August 1844,
died 25 May 1928; m. Sarah Jane Walker and had
three children: (1) Dr. John Walker Croft, m.
Carrie Brendt, two children, Robert and
Sylvia; (2) Clarence Croft, m. Almeda Summer,
one son, George Croft; (3) Martha Elizabeth
Croft, died July 1914, unmarried.

5. a daughter, born 11 Oct. 1846, died 22
December 1846, age two and one half months.

6. Mary Ellen Croft, born 18 Feb. 1848, died 1
Sept. 1924, Hinsdale, Illinois; married 25
Dec. 1867 at the Croft farmhome near St.
Thomas, Penn. to John W Cell, born 2 Dec.
1844, Franklin Co., Penn., died 5 Jan. 1911,
Topeka, Kansas, son of Christian Cell and
Catherine Heckman; twelve children: (1) Martha
Ellen Cell, born 24 Oct. 1870, St. Thomas,
died 29 August 1879, Ness Co., Kansas, age 7
years, 10 months; (2) John Franklin Cell, born
31 May 1873, St. Thomas, died May 1953,
Marionville, Missouri, married in 1905 to Mary
Florence Musson, six children; (3) George
Croft Cell, born 20 Feb. 1875, St. Thomas,
died 18 April 1937, Reading, Mass., married 26
June 1901 to Cornelia Ellen Clark, three
children (George and Ella are the grandparents
of this author); (4) Daniel Edward Cell, born
25 June 1876, St. Thomas, died 23 December
1881, Osage Co., Kansas, age 5 years, 6
months; (5) Charles Wertz Cell, born 23 Feb.
1878, St. Thomas, died 27 Feb. 1944, married
Ada Almeda Burk, one daughter; (6) Lottie
Catherine Cell, born 7 Feb. 1880, Ness Co.,
Kansas, died 7 June 1974, LaJolla, Calif.,
never married; (7) Rachel Cell, born 1 Feb.
1882, Osage Co., Kansas, died 13 Sept. 1882,
Osage Co., Kansas, age 7 months; (8) King
Cell, born prematurely, in 8th month of

The John and Molly Cell Family

(picture probably taken about 1900)

Charles W.,   J. Frank,   George C.

Mary Ann,   M. Luther,   Lottie C.

Samuel W.,   Christian H.

John W. Cell and Mary Ellen Croft Cell

pregnancy, in about 1884, Osage Co., Kansas, "the baby did not live"; (9) Martin Luther Cell, born 15 April 1885, Scranton, Osage Co., Kansas, died 24 Nov. 1942, Calif., married first in 1911 to Helen Mauzey, one daughter, married second in 1914 to Olive Patterson, one son; (10) Mary Ann Cell, born 22 Feb. 1887, Scranton, Kansas, died 13 June 1868, Topeka, Kansas, married in 1911 to Sherman Shoup, eight children; (11) Christian Heckman Cell, born 27 January 1889, Scranton, Kansas, died 24 July 1981, Vista, Calif., married three times, no surviving children; (12) Samuel Wesley Cell, born 6 January 1892, Scranton, Kansas, died 18 June 1968, Amesbury, Mass., married first to Helen Bertha Magnuson, two children, and married second to Clara Matilda Magnuson, two children. Further records of these Cell families are available in the Croft and Cell family histories by this author.

7. Rachel C. Croft, born 22 June 1850, died 24 May 1922, Marion, Penn.; married George W. Myers; five children: (1) Homer Wertz Myers, died unmarried before 1969; (2) Ethel Croft Myers, never married; (3) Janet Myers, never married; (4) John Croft Myers, married Josephine Croswell, no children; (5) Martha Myers, married John W. Miller, two children, Robert and Rachael.

8. Daniel Calvin Croft, born 29 July 1853, died 6 March 1931; married in 1878 to Etta Sellers; no children. An excellent article on Daniel Croft is on pages 247 and 248 of the Biographical Annals of Franklin County Pennsylvania.

9. Charlotte Elizabeth Croft, born 31 August 1855, died 5 November 1948; married William James Clark, born 1855, died 1919; no children.

CONRAD WERTZ and Fannie Bush

Conrad Wertz, born 2 Oct. 1819, youngest child

of Conrad Wertz and Anna Maria Cook; married
Fannie Bush.   They had five children and
nineteen grandchildren:

1. Alonzo/Alanza Wertz; five children: (1) Lee
Wertz; (2) Emma Wertz Cresky, one son, John
Cresky; (3) Nellie Wertz Coyle, one daughter,
Nona Coyle; (4) Grace Wertz Betz, one child;
Dollie Wertz Parce, one son, Thomas Parce.

2. Mary Ellen Wertz, married a Mr. Bates,
seven   children: (1)   Frank   Bates,   three
children; (2) Lee Bates, two children; (3)
Harry Bates, two children; (4) Conrad Bates,
three children; (5) Logan Bates, two children;
(6) Linnie Bates Goodman, five children; (7)
Nettie Bates.

3. Amanda Wertz, married a Mr. Eisenzimmer,
two children: Perry and James.

4. Rose Wertz, married a Mr. Barr, three
children, Harry, Mable (?), and Nellie.

5. Lee Wertz, married Myra --?--, two sons:
Roy O. Wertz; and Clyde H. Wertz.

LUTHERAN CHURCHYARD, ST. THOMAS

Our Mother, Mary Wertz,

d Apr. 29, 1867 aged 92 yrs., 1 mo., 26 days
∴ b. 3 March 1775

(This is with the: "Ellen Elmira Patterson:
  Mary Henry, Mary Hay, lot of markers)
(Elizabeth Wilson and John Fries)

TOMBSTONE INSCRIPTION

CHRISTIAN WERTZ and ELIZABETH FISHER

Christian Wertz, born 3 (Y) or 12 January 1772, Quincy twp., Franklin Co., Penn.; died 24 Feb. 1851, Harrison twp., Bedford Co., Penn.; will dated 11 January 1851, on file in Bedford Co. names twelve children. Christian was the 6th child of John Cunradt and Mary Wertz. Christian married in 1795 to Elizabeth Fisher, born 24 May 1776, died 17 Dec. 1845; daughter of Frederick Fisher, born 27 Dec. 1747; died 27 July 1810 and Susanna, born 15 Dec. 1747, died 9 Nov. 1817; Frederick and Susanna Fisher are both buried at Quincy Cemetery, Franklin County., Penn. (H) Frederick Fisher's will is on file at the Franklin County Courthouse, Book B, page 412. Christian and Elizabeth Wertz are both buried at the Old Union Church Cemetery, at the intersection of New Baltimore Road and Route 31, in Bedford Co., Penn. (Y) Records of all twelve of their children can also be found in the IGI (E); and most of this family is in the 1850 Census, Harrison twp., Bedford County.

1. Ann Maria (Mary) Wertz, born 25 August 1796, living in 1851; The 1850 Census, Harrison twp., Bedford Co. shows Christina Wertz, age 78, living with John Didy, age 55, and his wife, Mary, age 54, and a Betsey Gardner, age 42. Chart says "no heirs".

2. Frederick Wertz, born 8 Oct. 1798, Bedford County, Penn.; chart says "no heirs".

3. Susanna Wertz, born 24 Dec. 1800, Bedford Co.; married John Rock, eight children, and at least 16 grandchildren. See next page.

4. Elizabeth "Polly" Wertz, born 28 April 1803, Bedford Co.; chart says she married John Dedy, but the 1850 Census, Harrison twp. indicates it was her sister, Mary who married John Dedy/Didy; and thus perhaps this is the "Betsey Gardner" living with them. The chart says "no heirs".

5. Catherine Wertz, born 7 July 1803/5; m. a Mr. Willis; "no heirs". A Catherine Willis, born 20 Aug. 1761, died 7 July 1805, is buried in the Old Union Cemetery, Bedford Co. (Y), but this must be an aunt or mother-in-law of our Catherine Wertz Willis.

6. David Wertz, born 7 July 1807; died 10 April 1890; married Cordelia Dorsey; five children. See page 59 for this family.

7. Amos Wertz, born 4 or 19 January 1810; died 10 June 1893; married Mrs. David Rock; six children. See page 61 for this family.

8. Nancy Wertz, born 19 May 1812; died 26 February 1894; married June 1834 to Simon Knepper; eleven children. See page 62 for outline and records of this family.

9. Hester "Hetty" Wertz, born 12 October 1814; died 1 June 1896; married first to a Mr. Sullivan and had six children; married second to William Hart. Outline of these families are on page 63.

10. Christian Wertz, born 5 March 1817, Bedford Co.; no further record of him.

11. Lydia Wertz, born 13 June 1818; married John E. Rider; three children. See page 64 for outline of this family.

12. Sarah Wertz, born 20 June 1822; married David or Dewald Kinzey; four children. See page 64 for outline of this family.

JOHN ROCK and Susanna Wertz

Susanna Wertz, born 24 Dec. 1800 in Bedford County, daughter of Christian Wertz and Elizabeth Fisher; married John Rock, and they had eight children:

1. Josiah Rock, born 30 June 1823; lived in Iowa.

2. Elizabeth Rock, married Lewis Launchbaugh, and they had two children: Keith and Anna. Keith Launchbaugh married Martha Upton, and Anna Launchbaugh married a Mr. Baker.

3. David Rock, married his 1st cousin, Louise Rock, and they had two daughters: Ida and Susan, who were both married by 1915.

4. George A. Rock; lived in Kansas.

5. John Rock, born 28 April 1833, married Harriet Lone; lived in Kansas; nine children: (1) Jesse F. Rock, born Sept. 1856, married Ella Alexander, lived in Oklahoma; (2) Melissa Rock, born June 1858, married Mr. Richer, lived in Oregon; (3) Roxina Rock, born 23 April 1861, lived in Oklahoma; (4) A.F.Rock, born 10 May 1864, lived in Oklahoma; (5) Oneida Belle Rock, born Nov. 186?, lived in Colorado; (6) Alverda Rock, born Feb. 187?, lived in Colorado; (7) Olive Rock, born 12 April 1873, lived in Iowa; (8) Perry Rock, born 15 August 187?, lived in Iowa; and (9) Essie Rock, born Feb. 188?, married 1st to Perry Shaskston, and 2nd to Ford Dale, lived in Iowa.

6. Katherine Rock, died before 1915; no heirs.

7. Anna Marie Rock, married a Mr. Peck. No further data on family, if any.

8. Henry C. Rock, married Maggie Vance, three children; lived at Fairfield, Iowa.

Information on the Rock families was obtained from Mrs. Annette L. Rock Webb, of Marsing, Idaho, a second great granddaughter of John Rock and Susanna Wertz, by correspondence from 1973 to 1977.

DAVID WERTZ and Cordelia Dorsey

David Wertz, born 7 July 1807, died 10 April 1890; son of Christian Wertz and Elizabeth

Fisher; married Cordelia or Coralelia Dorsey, born 13 May 1819, died 17 May 1852. Cordelia Wertz is buried at the Old Union Cemetery, Bedford Co. (Y) They had six children. The David Wertz family can be found in the 1850 Census, Harrison twp., Bedford Co., Penn. and these records have been entered in the IGI, with the surname spelled Wirtz. (E) All of these children were undoubtedly born in Harrison township of Bedford County.

1. Mary C. or E. Wertz, born 24 April 1836 (age 14 in 1850); married G.M. Gelber; lived in Iowa.

2. Charlotte or Sharlott Wertz, born 21 July 1838 (age 12 in 1850); died 27 April 1905; married J. W. Batlorf; five children: (1) William Batlorf, lived in Kansas; (2) Emma Batlorf, married a Mr. Harrison, lived in Kansas; (3) Mary Batlorf, died 1892, married a Mr. Watson, one daughter, Amy Watson, lived in Kansas; (4) David Batlorf, lived in Kansas; and (5) Cora Batlorf, married a Mr. Bennett, lived in Kansas.

3. Lewis H. Wertz, died 13 July 1842, 6 mo., and 14 days old; buried at Old Union Cemetery in Bedford County. (Y) (= born 12 Jan. 1842)

4. Sarah Wertz, born 31 July 1843 (IGI says age 2 in 1850, but that is most likely incorrect); (E) died 1889; married R. K. Ocheltree; they had six children: (1) Charles Ocheltree, lived in Iowa; (2) Elma Ocheltree, lived at Iron River, Michigan; (3) Marion Ocheltree, lived at Hoopertown, Illinois; (4) Ella Ocheltree, born 2 April 1910, married a Mr. Henderson, and had four children by 1915: Florence, Madge, Nellie, and Freida Henderson, all lived at Tipton, Iowa; (5) Bert Ocheltree, died before 1915, lived at Tipton, Iowa; and (6) Walter Ocheltree, lived Iron River, Mich.

5. William Wertz, born 12 Feb. 1846 (age 4 in 1850); m. Ollie Cronch; lived Harrison, Neb.

6. Cyrus or Cyris Wertz, born 5 July 1848 (age 2 in 1850); married Ellie Wireck; lived at Bozeman, Montana.

AMOS WERTZ and Mrs. David Rock

Amos Wertz, born 19 June 1810, died 10 June 1893; married a "Mrs. David Rock", born 24 Feb. 18??. The record does not indicate if Mrs. David Rock was a widow when she married Amos Wertz, or if she had previous children. She and Amos had six children. This family is in the 1850 Census, Harrison twp., Bedford County, Penn. and the first five children are listed in the IGI. In 1850, Amos Wertz' wife is shown as Nancy, age 41. All of their children were probably born in Harrison twp., Bedford Co.

1. John Wertz, born 20 Sept. 1836 (age 14 in 1850), died 9 June 1906; married Rebecca A. Elliott; four children: (1) Nellie Wertz, born 27 Dec. 1868, died 1 May 1880, no heirs; (2) Cora Wertz, born 25 May 1870, married Herman Hungerford, lived Burlington, Iowa; (3) Frank E. Wertz, born 13 March 1872, wife's name was Charlotte, and they lived in Chicago, Ill; and (4) Estelle Wertz, born 25 Jan. 1877, m. Vernon Cooper, lived Minneapolis, Minnesota.

2. Caroline Wertz, born 11 Jan. 1839 (age 11 in 1850), died 31 Jan. 1899; married Bill McCoy; three children: (1) Ella Mae McCoy, born April 1871, married Jay Picksal, lived in Iowa; (2) Frank McCoy, born 19 March 1873, died before 1915; and (3) Ralph McCoy, born 16 July 1877, died 26 Sept. 1896, unmarried.

3. Elizabeth Wertz, born 12 April 1841/2 (age 8 in 1850); married Lowery McMakers; lived at Burlington, Iowa.

4. Mary Wertz, born 20 March 1843/4 (age 7 in 1850), died 27 Dec. 19?? (before 1915); married Herman Hungerford; no heirs.

61

5. Elmira Wertz, born 19 March 1848 (age 2 in 1850), died 22 Dec. 1860; no heirs.

6. Lemuel Wertz, born 26 August 1851; married 1st to Kate Bush, married 2nd Maggie --?--; lived at Novenger, Missouri.

SIMON KNEPPER and Nancy Wertz

Nancy Wertz, born 19 May 1812, died 26 Feb. 1894, daughter of Christian Wertz and Elizabeth Fisher; married June 1834 to Simon Knepper, b. 1809, d. 1857; eleven children:

1. Amanda Knepper, born 20 May 1835, died 2 Jan. 1884; married 1st to Joseph Pritts, three children; married 2nd to Abram Musser.
Children by 1st marriage: (1) Milton J. Pritts, lived Somerset, Penn.; (2) Ella Pritts, married Walter Heffby, lived at Johnstown, Penn.; and (3) Irvin Pritts, died before 1915, no heirs.

2. Oliver Knepper, born June 1837, killed in the battle of New Musket on 28 Jan. 1899; married Mary Pugh, born 10 Oct. 1836; seven children: (1) Laura Knepper, born 5 May 1860, married Peter Baush, lived at Somerset, Penn.; (2) Chester Knepper, born 10 Dec. 1861, married Helen Todhunter; (3) Ada Knepper, born 20 Aug. 1863 (twin), married Hyman H. Anderson; (4) Cora Knepper, born 20 Aug. 1863 (twin), married A.R. Helmas, lived in Oklahoma; (5) Edith May Knepper (E), born 5 May 1867, christened 17 Dec. 1867 at Trinity Luthern Church in Somerset Co., Penn.(E), married Reubon M. Linton, lived in Somerset, Penn.; (6) Orlo Smith Knepper (E), born 16 June 1875 or 7 Oct. 1876 (E) Somerset Co., Penn., married Susan C. Lantz, lived at White Plains, New York; and (7) Florence Knepper, born 10 Jan. 1878, married John H. Benetz, lived Somerset, Penn.

3. Henry Franklin Knepper (E), born 19 April 1839; married 14 February 1860, Somerset Co.,

Penn.(E) to Margaret "Magie" Spangler; lived at Johnstown, Penn.

4. Amos Knepper, born 14 April 1841; married Sabina Smith; lived Somerset, Penn.

5. William Knepper, born 25 July 1843; died 15 May 1864, no heirs.

6. Sarah Ellen Knepper, born 31 Dec. 1845; married William Weigle, born 10 Jan. 1847; lived in Pennsylvania.

7. Emiline "Emma" Knepper (E), born 28 May 1848; married 5 Oct. 1872, Somerset Co.,Penn. (E) to Samuel A. Deetz; lived at Windbar, Penn.

8. David W.Knepper, born 7 Sept. 1850, died 21 July 1870; no heirs.

9. Cyrus Knepper, born 26 August 1852; married Annie Pile; lived Somerset, Penn.

10. Ann Lucinda Knepper, born 6 Oct. 1854; married Edward Rice.

11. Mary Elizabeth Knepper, born 17 April 1857; m. Edward Horner; lived Johnstown, Penn.

Mr. SULLIVAN and Hester Wertz

Hester Wertz, born 12 October 1814; daughter of Christian Wertz and Elizabeth Fisher; m.1st to a Mr. Sullivan and had six children:

1. Susan Sullivan; lived in Pennsylvania.

2. Elizabeth Sullivan, married a Mr. Philips.

3. Mary Sullivan, married George Safton; lived at Denver, Colorado.

4. Ida Sullivan, married; lived in Penn.

5. William Sullivan.

63

6. a child not named, nor sex given.

Hester Wertz Sullivan, married 2nd to William Hart, born 27 June 1815; died 24 May 1890. Hester died 1 June 1896, and both of them are buried at the Old Union Cemetery, Bedford Co. (Y), along with a "dau. Emma, 1859-1886."

JOHN E. RIDER and Lydia Wertz

Lydia Wertz, born 13 June 1818, daughter of Christian Wertz and Elizabeth Fisher; married John E. Rider; three children:

1. Martin M. Rider, born 23 Sept. 18?9; married Mary E. Karr; one daughter: Grace B. Rider, married William Files, lived at Iowa City, Iowa.

2. George Rider; married Addie McDowell; lived Paston, Green County, Iowa.

3. Ella Rider; married William Simonmyer; lived Paston, Iowa.

DEWILD KINZEY and Sarah Wertz

Sarah Wertz, born 20 June 1822, daughter of Christian Wertz and Elizabeth Fisher; married Dewild/Dewalt or David Kinzey; four children:

1. John Kinzey, married Hester Banford.

2. Anna Kinzey, died before 1915.

3. Sarah Kinzey, married William Lambecker.

4. Catherine Kinzey, m. Warren Wakefield.

ANDREW WERTZ and MAGDALENA BERKEY

Andrew Wertz, born 2 May 1774, Quincy twp., Franklin Co., Penn., son of John Cunradt and Mary Wertz; married Magdalena Berkey, born 1 January 1779; moved to Ohio, probably before 1810, perhaps with his brother Daniel. This family was in Holmes Co., Ohio by 1830. Twelve children:

1. Elizabeth Wertz, born 9 June 1812; married Michael Swoveland; eleven children. Outline and records of this family begin on the next page.

2. Anna Wertz, born 8 October 1803; died in infancy.

3. Jacob Wertz, born 22 August 1805; died 1849; no heirs.

4. Andreas Wertz, born 2 July 1807; died in infancy.

5. George Wertz, born 25 May 1809/10; died 27 April 1877; married Amanda Myers; seven children. Outline and records of this family begin on page 68.

6. Catarina Wertz, born 21 March 1811; died 18 June 1879; married 16 Sept. 1830, Holmes Co., Ohio (E) to her 1st cousin, Jacob Wertz, born 14 June 1807; died April 1865, son of Peter Wertz. They had eleven children. See page 40 for outline and records of this family.

7. Christian Wertz, born 2 June 1813; died 5 Sept. 1854; married Mary Fairchild; seven children. See page 70 for outline and records of this family. Christian and Mary Fairchild Wertz were the grandparents of Estelle Ryan Snyder who wrote the 1915 chart which formed the basic outline for this family history.

8. Sarah Wertz, born 29 April 1815; died in infancy.

9. Heinrich Wertz, born 17 April 1817; married 5 Oct. 1843, Holmes Co., Ohio to Sofia Rudy. (E) No heirs.

10. Daniel Wertz, born 11 Feb. 1820; died April 1883; married 30 Dec. 1848 to Abby Anthony; three children. Outline and records of this family are on page 72.

11. Magdalena Wertz, born 6 Feb. 1822; died 18 July 1909; married 25 Jan. 1842, Holmes Co., Ohio to Jacob Hostleton (E); thirteen children. Outline and records of this family begin on page 72.

12. Wilhelm Wertz, born 2 June 1824; died in infancy.

MICHAEL SWOVELAND and ELIZABETH WERTZ

Elizabeth Wertz, born 9 June 1802, daughter of Andrew Wertz and Magdalena Berkey; married Michael Swoveland and had eleven children:

1. Anthony Swoveland, died unmarried.

2. Andrew Swoveland, born Sept. 1829, married 1st to Sarah Plough(?), born March 1838, died 28 March 1871; married 2nd to Elizabeth Rodegers. Seven children, four by first wife and three by second wife. See page 68 for outlines of these families.

3. Eva Swoveland, born 21 June 1821, died 13 Sept. 1889; married John Kaufman, born 13 March 1822, died 13 August 1889; seven children: (1) Isaac Kaufman, born 1 Sept. 1845, d. Sept. 1913, m. Mary Scarbrough, five children - Mary, Ida, Hattie, Thomas, and Benjamin; (2) Elizabeth Kaufman, born 26 Sept. 1846, married Morgan Dells(?), lived in Iowa; (3) Sofia Kaufman, born 9 Feb. 1849, married a Mr. Moran, lived at St. Paul, Minnesota; (4) Laura Kaufman, born 2 August 1851, died 22 Jan. 1897; (5) Henry Kaufman, born 21 Oct. 1854, married Mattie --?--, born 25 March

1860, lived Fairfield, Nebraska; (6) James Kaufman, born 4 July 1856, died 25 Dec. 185?; and (7) Jonathan Kaufman, born 10 May 1860.

4. George Swoveland; died before 1915, unmarried.

5. Sarah Swoveland; married David Weaver; seven children: (1) Milo Weaver, unmarried in 1915, living in New Paris, Indiana; (2) Rosie Weaver, married William Conrad, lived Goshen, Indiana; (3) Adaline Weaver, married Milton Rummel, lived Goshen, Indiana; (4) Laura Weaver, married Solomon Rummel, lived New Paris, Indiana; (5) Elizabeth Weaver, m. John Mishler, lived New Paris, Ind.; (6) Samuel Weaver, m. Elizabeth Warner, two children: Elmer and Clyde Weaver, lived at New Paris, Indiana; and (7) John Weaver, unmarried in 1915, living at New Paris, Indiana.

6. Elizabeth Swoveland; married Jonas Kaufman; eight children: (1) Matilda Kaufman, born 15 April 1855, married Mr. Zentz, lived Goshen, Indiana; (2) Lydia Ann Kaufman, born 10 Nov. 1862, married Mr. Christman, lived Indiana; (3) Blanch Kaufman, died by 1915, unmarried; (4) Noah Kaufman, born 23 Jan. 18?7, married twice; (5) Myette(?) Kaufman, born 8 Dec. 1860, lived Indiana; (6) Daniel Kaufman, born 3 Dec. 1864, lived Ind.; (7) Samuel Kaufman, m. 14 Feb. 18??, to Rosie(?) Hartman, lived in Ind.; and (8) Michael Kaufman, born 25 Sept. 18??, m. Hattie Fox, lived Indiana.

7. Lidy(?) Swoveland, m. John Ebby; no heirs.

8. Joel Swoveland, born 31 March 1840, married a Dess(?) Posta; no heirs.

9. Michael Swoveland, died before 1915; unmarried.

10. Jacob M. Swoveland, born March 1842; married 1st to Sofia Someftzer(?); married 2nd to Susie Detmeir(?); lived in Indiana.

11. Lewis Swoveland; married a Miss Smith; no heirs.

ANDREW SWOVELAND and Sarah Plough

1. Henry Swoveland, born 17 Oct. 1858, married Barbara Miller, born 20 Jan. 1867; lived at New Paris, Indiana.

2. Julia(?) Swoveland, married William(?) Penrod; lived New Paris, Indiana.

3. Hezakiah Swoveland, born Oct. 1863, married Nancy Brumbaugh; three children: (1) Charlie, died unmarried; (2) Sadie, m. M. Bainter(?), lived New Paris, Indiana; and (3) Earl, lived New Paris, Indiana.

4. Harvey Swoveland, born June 1866, married Phoebe(?) Detwiler; lived New Paris, Indiana.

ANDREW SWOVELAND and Elizabeth Rodegers

5. Emma Swoveland, born Feb. 1872; married James Whitehead; seven children, all living in Indiana in 1915: (1) Anna Whitehead, born 22 August 1894, m. M. Muhler; (2) Everett Earl Whitehead, born 24 Aug. 1895; (3) Hulda, born 8 Sept. 1897; (4) Glen Whitehead, born 17 July 1899; (5) Violet Whitehead, born 3 Jan. 1901; (6) Dorothy Whitehead, born 18 June 1902; and (7) Walter(?) Whitehead, born 23 June 1903.

6. Sarah Swoveland, born 30 April 1873; m. 1st to M. Bennett(?), married 2nd to Mr. Overhalt; lived at Three Rivers, Michigan.

7. Norman Swoveland, born 29 Oct. 1878; m. Miss Stouder; lived New Paris, Ind.

GEORGE WERTZ and Amanda Myers

George Wertz, born 25 May 1809/10, died 27 April 1877, son of Andrew Wertz and Magdalena Berkey; married 1 Oct. 1835, Holmes Co., Ohio to Amanda Myers,(E) born 31 May 1817, died 24 June 1904; seven children:

1. Jacob Wertz, born 9 June 183?; married Sarah B. Rood; one daughter; Grace Wertz, who married a Mr. Troy.

2. Sarah Ann Wertz, born 25 Dec. 1838; married Madero(?) Rood; three children: (1) Rolla(?) Rood, died before 1915, no heirs; (2) Noah Rood, lived Sparta, Ohio; (3) Thomas J. Rood, lived Fredericktown, Ohio.

3. Andrew Wertz, born 1841, died 24 May 1901; married Martha M. Vernon, born 23 July 1838, died 27 Dec. 1906(?); three children: (1) George H. Wertz, born 6 March 1875, married Nettie Larger, born 25 Nov. 1872, lived Ohio; (2) Leroy(?) Wertz, born ?5 Aug. 1878, married Mable Thompson, lived Ohio; and (3) Charles Fay Wertz, born 2 May 1883, died 4 March 1899.

4. Ezariah(?) Wertz, born 5 Sept. 1843; m. Louise Bucker(?); three children: (1) Carl G. Wertz, lived Mt. Vernon, Ohio; (2) Hattie Wertz, m. a Mr. Brown, lived Fredericktown, Ohio; (3) Luffie(?) Wertz, married a Mr. Merrill(?), lived Ohio.

5. Hessphelm(?) Wertz, born 16 June 1845, died 4 April 1913(?); married 1st to Lucinda Baughman(?), born 18 Oct. 1846, died 1 March 1897; married 2nd to Elizabeth Landers(?); four children, probably all by 1st wife: (1) Lamont Wertz, born Jan. 1871, married; (2) Orain(?) Wertz, born March 1873, married Rosa Hardin or Henderson(?), born 16 June 1876, died 6 Nov. 1910; (3) Bernard(?) Wertz, born 9 Oct. 1878, m. Viola(?) Friend(?), born March 1889; and (4) Matilda Wertz, born March 18??, m. Harry Way(?), born July 1878(?).

6. Mary Ellen Wertz, born 19 Sept. 1849, married Frank Foster, born July 1841; two children: (1) Charles H. Foster, born 22 Aug. 1873(?), m. Josephine Dunlop, one son:

Marion H. Foster, born 24 April 1894, lived at Freedom, Penn.; and (2) Ira G. Foster, b. Aug. 1876, m. Alma Gay(?), lived Columbus, Ohio.

7. George Henry Wertz, born 3 July 1852; married 3 Jan. 1875, Crawford Co., Ohio to Anna Mullons (E); two children: Ezariah(?) Wertz and Claude Wertz.

CHRISTIAN WERTZ and Mary Fairchild

Christian Wertz, born 2 June 1813, died 5 Sept. 1854, son of Andrew Wertz and Magdalena Berkey; married Mary Fairchild, and they had seven children:

1. William Wertz, born 16 Dec. 1839, died Nov. 1909; married Julie Waldeon(?); six children; lived in Iowa: (1) Roy Wertz, born 9 Jan. 1875, married 1st M. Peck(?), married 2nd --?--, lived Iowa City, Iowa; (2) Rhoda(?) Wertz, born 3 April 1877, married Edind(?) Lorn(?), lived Cedar Rapids, Iowa; (3) Minnie Wertz, born 7 May 1880, married S.Schleg(?), lived Wayborn(?), Canada; (4) Frank Wertz, born 27 Oct. 1882, married Amber Ganade(?), lived Iowa; (5) Vernon(?) Wertz, born 29 Jan. 1885, lived in Iowa; and (6) Elizabeth Wertz, born 16 Nov. 1887, died 14 April 1888(?).

2. Eliza Jane Wertz, born 4 June 1841; married William Cunningham; five children; lived Blair, Nebraska: (1) Mamie(?) Cunningham; (2) Charlie Cunningham, lived Kennard, Nebraska; (3) Frank Cunningham, unmarried in 1915, lived Blair, Nebraska; (4) Otto Cunningham; and (5) Emma Cunningham.

3. Rebecca Ann Wertz, born 13 April 1844, died 15 July 190?; married John Trimproly(?); lived in Nebraska: seven children: (1) Otis(?) D. Trimproly(?), born 31 July 1871, married Belle Green(?), lived Stanton, Nebraska; (2) Nellie Louise, born 1 Aug. 1873, married Cal(?) Menking(?), five children - Leroy Edward,

Shirley Louise, Earl, Gladys Mae, and Harold
Gilbert - all lived at Arlington, Nebraska;
(3) Judson W. Trimproly(?), born 24 Nov. 1874,
married Lara(?) Menking(?), three children-
Agnes Irene, Gladys Mae, and Edith - all lived
at Madison, Nebraska; (4) Adelle(?), born 18
Sept. 1876, married Cuthbert(?) Waterman(?),
three children - Pearl Darlene, John Noah(?),
and Nellie May; (5) Roy, born 21 Feb. 1878,
married Maggie --?--, lived Norfolk, Nebraska;
(6) Mary, born 21 Nov. 1880, married Ben(?)
Hasllinger(?), lived in Montana; and (7)
William W., born 16 April 1886, m. Zelda(?)
Farhoning(?), lived Madison, Nebraska.

4. Lavina Wertz, born 7 Jan. 1846, m. Frank
Baughman(?); two children; lived Rock Island,
Illinois: (1) Owen(?) Baughman, m. Mary Fritz,
two sons: Clay(?) and Ralph, lived Rock
Island, Ill.; and (2) Oliver Baughman, m.
Wanda(?) --?--, two children: Frank and Irma.

5. Sophia Wertz, born 2 May 1848, married John
Leslie; five children; lived at Rock Island,
Illinois: (1) Frankie Leslie, died in infancy;
(2) Edith Lora(?) Leslie, married Clarence(?)
Hibbard(?), two children: Myrtle and Irma,
lived Rock Island, Illinois; (3) Clyde E.
Leslie, m. Joanna(?) --?--, one child: Rose
Edith Leslie; (4) Earl Leslie, unmarried in
1915, lived Rock Island, Ill.; and (5) Mike
Leslie, unmarried in 1915, living in Indiana.

6. Lucinda E. Wertz, born 14 Nov. 1851;
married John Davidson; six children; all lived
at West Branch, Iowa: (1) Walter(?) Davidson,
married by 1915; (2) Harry W. Davidson; (3)
Clarence A. Davidson; (4) Pearl Davidson, m.
Glen E. Moore(?); (5) Herbert B. Davidson; and
(6) Frances Davidson.

7. Mary Louise Wertz, born 20 April 1854,
married 1st to Miles D. Ryan, two children;
married 2nd to Charles D. Williams; lived at
Maywood, Illinois: (1) Estelle Ryan, born 26
Oct. 1874, married William J. Snyder, two

children: Ryan Lowman(?) and Ethel Estelle;
living in Chicago, Illinois in 1915, author of
the charts that are the basic outline of this
family history; (2) Charles Ryan, born 16
August 1876, died unmarried.

DANIEL WERTZ and Abby Anthony

Daniel Wertz, born 11 Feb. 1820, died April
1883; son of Andrew Wertz and Magdalena
Berkey; married 30 Dec. 1848 to Abby Anthony,
died 10 June 1897; three children:

1. Ellen Wertz, born 28 May 1853; m. 1st J.
Carter or Castor(?); m. 2nd to a Mr. Cowan(?).

2. Henry Wertz, born June 1858.

3. a child whose name is impossible to read on
the charts, born 28 Feb. 18??, died Oct. 18??.

JACOB HOSTLETON and Magdalena Wertz

Magdalena Wertz, born 6 Feb. 1822, died 18
July 1909, daughter of Andrew Wertz and
Magdalena Berkey; m. 25 Jan. 1842, Holmes Co.,
Ohio to Jacob Hostleton; thirteen children:

1. Cintha(?) Hostleton, born 25 April 1842,
died 23 Jan. 1912; married John L. Gay; three
children: (1) Charles Loran(?) Gay, born 25
March 1869, m. Elmira(?) Hastleton, lived Des
Moines, Iowa; (2) Chester Auther Gay, born 22
May 1872, m. Mary Lessinger(?); and (3) Ada
May Gay, born 22 Sept. 187?, m. 1st Charles
Koppe, and married 2nd William Foster, lived
Kansas City, Missouri.

2. John Henry Hostleton, born 20 Aug. 1844;
married 1st Mary Tipton; married 2nd Minnie(?)
Hauriper(?); eight children, two by first
marriage and six by second marriage; lived
Rockford, Iowa: (1) Edna, born April 1872, m.
H. Gilbert, no heirs; (2) Roy Hostleton,

born Nov. 187?, died April 1912, married twice; two children by second marriage: Chris and Merridith; (3) Bessie Hostleton, born 23 Dec. 1891, married H. Allen, three children; Madge, Blanche, and Donald Allen; (4) Purdy or Birdy, born 20 March 1895, lived Kansas City, Missouri; (5) Lela, born 3 Nov. 1899, lived Iowa; (6) Hazel, born Sept. 190?, lived Rockford, Iowa; (7) Everett, born 16 Aug. 1905; and (8) Garrett, born 8 Feb. 1912.

3. Catherine Annie Hostleton, born 20 June 1846, died 2 July 1848.

4. William Allen Hostleton, born 1 Oct. 1847, died July 1848.

5. George Sylvester Hostleton, born 31 May 1849, died 1 Oct. 1850.

6. Minerva(?) Hostleton, born 14 April 1851; married Oliver VanVolkenburg(?); lived at Millersburg, Iowa.

7. Hulda E. Hostleton, born 15 March 1853, married William Snyder; lived Harlan, Iowa.

8. James Monroe Hostleton, born 14 Feb. 1855; m. Jewel(?) Downing(?); lived at Lamar, Colo.

9. Sara Margaret Hostleton, born 27 Nov. 1856; unmarried in 1915, living in Davenport, Iowa.

10. Laura Francis Hostleton, born 15 June 1859; married William E. Wilson(?); lived at Millersburg, Iowa.

11. Lillie Belle Hostleton, born 14 June 1862, died 10 October 1865.

12. Morilla(?) Ophilia(?) Hostleton, born 25 Sept. 1864; married J.J. Stepp or Steppe; one child: Hazel Steppe; lived Davenport, Iowa.

13. Cora Mary Hostleton, born 4 March 1867; unmarried in 1915, living Millersburg, Iowa.

DANIEL WERTZ and SARAH WEIMER

Daniel Wertz, born 20 Dec. 1781, Franklin County, Penn.; died 28 Sept. 1873, Montgomery County, Ohio, buried at Ellerton Cemetery, Ellerton, Montgomery County, Ohio; son of John Cunradt and Mary Wertz; m. Sarah Weimer, born 23 Nov. 1787, Somerset Co., Penn.; died 10 or 20 March 1854/9, Montgomery Co., Ohio, buried at Ellerton Cemetery; daughter of Frederick Weimer Jr. Daniel was a carpenter, and made windmills, until 1818 when the family moved to Montgomery Co. where he cleared and improved a farm. Daniel also served in the war of 1812. Information on this family was obtained from Mrs. Ester McAlister and Mrs. Naomi Hougham, by correspondence in 1974. This family can also be found in the 1850 Census of Montgomery Co., Ohio and all of them are listed in the IGI. Daniel and Sarah had fourteen children, the first two born in Franklin Co., Penn. and the rest born in Ohio.

1. Elizabeth Catherine Wertz, born 28 March 1804; died 1875 in Shelby Co., Indiana; married 24 Oct. 1822, Montgomery Co., Ohio to Jacob Mullendore. (E)

2. Anthony Wertz, born 15 Dec. 1805; died 1839, unmarried.

3. Mary E. "Polly" Wertz, born 25 August 1808, Warren Co., Ohio (E); married 14 March 1828 to George Getter (E); two children: (1) Henry Getter, who had a daughter, Hanna, living in Maywood, Illinois in 1915; and (2) a daughter who married a Mr. Shade, and lived in Ohio.

4. Sarah Wertz, born 4 August 1810, Warren Co., Ohio (E); married 25 Nov. 1830 (E), Montgomery Co., Ohio to Daniel Lambert.

5. Jacob Wertz, born 1 Sept. 1812/3, Warren Co., Ohio (E); died 16 Sept. 1876, Shelby Co., Indiana; married 16 June 1839 to Elizabeth Warble or Marble; three sons and at least

seven grandchildren.   Outline of this family begins on the next page.

6. Nancy B. Wertz,   born 12   Dec. 1814, Warren Co., Ohio   (E); died 16 Sept. 1858; m. 21 Jan. 1836 (chart) or 22   Jan. 1834   (E), Montgomery Co., Ohio   to Daniel Muck (chart) or Much (E).

7. Elizabeth Wertz, born 29 June 1818 (chart), or 12 June 1817 (E) at Middletown, Butler Co., Ohio; married 1st   Frederick Stine or Stone; married 2nd Jacob Warble.

8. Caroline Wertz, born   14 or   29 June 1822, (chart) or 16   April 1820 (E) at Montgomery Co., Ohio; m. 13 May (chart) or 14 March (E) 1844, Montgomery Co.,   Ohio to Peter Lambert (E); moved to Indiana.

9. Lavina or Lavine Wertz,   born 19 August 1822, Montgomery Co., Ohio (E); died 6 January 1904; m. 17 Sept. 1843, Montgomery Co., Ohio to Aaron Mullendore (E); six children. Outline of this family begins on the next page.

10. Harriet Wertz, born 7 Oct. 1824, (E) Montgomery Co.; m. 1 Dec. 1844, Montgomery Co., Ohio to Joseph Hartzel (E); lived at Anderson, Indiana.

11. Daniel Wertz, born 14 Feb. 1827, (E) Gettysburg, Montgomery Co., Ohio; died 28 Feb. 1910, Anderson, Indiana; married 1st 25 Nov. 1845/9, Montgomery Co., Ohio to Elizabeth Kuhns (chart) or Korns (E), two children; m. 2nd to Mariah Kuhns, two children; and m. 3rd to Sally McKinnon, nine children. Outline and records of this family begin on page 77.

12. John Wertz, born 14 March 1829, (E) Montgomery Co., Ohio; died 7 June 1885; married Anna Eliza Taylor; eight children. Outline of this family is on page 80.

13. Jerome Wertz, b.14 Sept. 1831, Miamisburg, Montgomery Co.,Ohio; is age 19 in 1850 Census,

Montgomery Co., Ohio (E); m. 9 June 1858 to
Sarah A. Schanook; one son: Alfred B. Wertz,
who was living at Middetown, Ohio in 1915.

14. Rachel Wertz, born 30 Oct. 1833/5,
Montgomery Co., Ohio (age 16 in the 1850
Census) (E); died at Anderson, Indiana;
married 15 Jan. 1854, Dayton, Montgomery Co.,
Ohio to Jacob Beachler (E).

JACOB WERTZ and Elizabeth

Jacob Wertz, b. 1 Sept. 1812, Warren Co., Ohio
(E); d.16 Sept. 1876, Shelby Co., Ind,; son of
Daniel Wertz and Sarah Weimer; m. 16 June 1839
to Elizabeth Marble or Warble; three sons:

1. Mathew Wertz, married Mary Malley(?).

2. John Wertz, m. Eliza Myers; seven children:
(1) Elizabeth Ann Wertz, m. Joseph Wilson(?);
(2) Minnie Wertz, m. Edward Anthony(?); (3)
Ida Wertz, m. J. W. Bamberg(?); (4) Philo(?)
Wertz, m. Katie Kuntzburg(?), lived in Ind.;
(5) Edna Wertz, m. Mert(?) Cahoy(?), lived
Ind.; (6) Clarence M. Wertz, m. Nellie Lucas,
one son – Clarence Kenneth Wertz – lived
Shelbyville, Ind.; and (7) Otis(?) Wertz,
unmarried in 1915, living in Shelbyville, Ind.

3. Daniel Wertz, married Martha Scott.

AARON MULLENDORE and Lavina Wertz

Lavina or Lavine Wertz, born 19 August 1822,
Montgomery Co., Ohio (E); died 6 Jan. 1904;
married 17 Sept. 1843, Montgomery Co., Ohio to
Aaron Mullendore (E); born 4 June 1824, died
13 Feb. 1907; six children:

1. David Mullendore, born 18 August 1844;
married Esther Polletak(?); seven children;
lived in Wisconson: (1) Eva, born 7 June 1869,
married by 1915; (2) Louanda(?), born 26 July
1871; (3) Wilda(?), born 2 May 1874, m. E.O.
Ayers(?); (4) Minnie, born 3 Sept. 1876; (5)

Anne(?) Mullendore, born 7 May 1880; (6) Dow(?) Mullendore, born Feb. 1883; and (7) Sylvia Mullendore, born 2 Oct. 1885.

2. Sarah J. Mullendore, born May 1846; married James Frint(?); four children; all lived in Wisconson: Bert, Harvey, Aaron, and Luke.

3. Daniel Mullendore, born 13 May 1848; married Ellen Mayhall(?); lived in Wisconsin.

4. Ellen Mullendore, born 11 April 1851; married Jacob Sand(?); lived in Wisconsin.

5. George Washington Mullendore, born 5 August 1855; m. Nell(?) Gasfton(?); four children; all lived in Colorado: (1) Mary L. Mullendore, born Oct. 1890, married Perry G. Lucas(?), one daughter, Ethelyn Rachel, b. 31 June 1913(?); (2) C.Ray Mullendore, b.26 Dec. 1891; (3) Cora Pearl Mullendore, born 30(?) July 1898(?); and (4) Francis L. Mullendore, born 29 March 1905.

6. Alice Mullendore, born 8 Aug.(?) 185?; married William O. McClintock, born 14 Dec. 1861; three children; lived Walnut, Colorado: John W. McClintock; Lawrence O. McClintock; and Lloyd A. McClintock.

DANIEL WERTZ and Elizabeth Kuhns

Daniel Wertz, born 14 Feb. 1827, Gettysburg, Montgomery Co., Ohio (E); died 28 Feb. 1910, Anderson, Indiana, buried at the Old City Cemetery in Anderson, Indiana. Daniel was married three times, and had thirteen children. Records of these families were obtained from a great-grandson of Daniel Wertz, Gerald W. Wertz, by correspondence in 1979. Daniel lived in Montgomery Co., Ohio where he was born, until 1860, when he moved to Madison Co., Indiana where his family lived in a log cabin on their 159 acre farm, until they built a house in 1883. Daniel married first 25 November 1845 (chart) or 1849 (E) in Montgomery County, Ohio to Elizabeth Kuhns or

Korns (E). They had two children before Elizabeth died 7 April 1852; she is buried at Ellerton Cemetery, Jefferson twp., Montgomery County, Ohio.

1. Francis M. Wertz, born 20 July 1850; died 17 April 1930 at Anderson, Indiana; married 1st to Isabelle M. Moss, four children; married 2nd 17 Jan. 1905 to Ora L. Rhynearson, two children.

2. George W. Wertz, born 27 Oct. 1851, Montgomery Co., Ohio; died 6 June 1947, Anderson, Indiana; married 1st by 1870 to Sarah Ellen Bowers, five children; and married 2nd about 1930 to Mary --?--. Outline and records of this family begin on the next page.

DANIEL WERTZ and Mariah Kuhns

Daniel Wertz married 2nd to Mariah Kuhns, a sister of his first wife. They had two children, before Mariah died 31 May 1859.

3. Sarah Wertz, born 1856; married Louis Spencer; one child (name not given).

4. William Wertz, born 1858; died in infancy.

DANIEL WERTZ and Sally McKinnon

Daniel married 3rd to Sally McKinnon, born 28 Sept. 1843, died 28 Jan. 1879; nine children.

5. Rosalind H. Wertz, born 1863; m. 3 April 1889 to William P. Jarrett; four children.

6. Joseph W. Wertz, born 1864; married 2 Sept. 1911 to Eliza E. Newton; one child.

7. Ella L. Wertz, born 24 Sept. 1865; married Thomas Eggman.

8. Alphonso Wertz, born 22 Nov. 1867; died 8 Jan. 1879.

9. Harriet A. Wertz, born 1869; married Arthur Davis; nine children.

10. Harry Wertz, born 1871; married 14 Sept. 1892 to Bertha E. Cox.

11. Alonzo or Elonzo Wertz, born 1872; married Cora May Perkins; three children.

12. Addie B. Wertz, born 1874; married 1913 to James A. Swinford; fourteen children.

13. Gertrude Wertz, born 1875, died 1913; married John A. Fisher. No children.

GEORGE W. WERTZ and Sarah Ellen Bowers

George W. Wertz, born 27 Oct. 1851, Dayton, Montgomery Co., Ohio; died 6 June 1947 at Anderson, Indiana, buried in the Old City Cemetery at Anderson, Ind.; son of Daniel Wertz and Elizabeth Kuhns; m. 1st about 1870 to Sarah Ellen Bowers, born 19 August 1855, Ind.; d. 8 April 1923, Anderson, Ind., buried in Old City Cemetery, Anderson; five children. After Sarah died George married about 1930 to Mary --?--, who died about 1941.

1. Flora E. Wertz, born 1871, Anderson, Madison Co., Indiana; died in infancy.

2. Otilia U. Wertz, born 1875, Anderson; died in infancy.

3. Larvy I. Wertz, born 20 Sept. 1878, Anderson; married 1st to Lillian B. Reynolds, born 1897, two children; married 2nd to Jessie J. Smith, four children.

4. Walter C. Wertz, born 1881, Anderson; died 1964; married 12 Dec. 1904 to Amy A.L. Reed; six children.

5. Chauncey Frost Wertz, born 3 Feb. 1889, Anderson, Madison Co., Indiana; died 19 Dec. 1935, Chicago, Illinois; m. 14 Nov. 1912, Fort

Wayne, Ind. to Clara Belle Gross, born 3 Jan. 1891, Anderson, Ind., daughter of Charles Lester Wilden Gross and Myrtle Quitera Hamer; one son: Gerald Wilden Wertz, born 23 Sept. 1913, Logansport, Ind.; m. 21 Sept. 1940, Chicago, Ill. to Anna Eva Guill, born 16 Jan. 1912, Chicago, Ill., dau. of Nicholas Guill and Louise Feller; three children: (1) Daniel Wilden Wertz, born 25 June 1941, Chicago, m. 26 Sept. 1970 to Sheila Petersen; (2) Patricia Ann Wertz, born 26 Jan. 1947, Chicago, m. 31 Oct. 1970 to Carroll Wayne Nafzger; and (3) Thomas Joseph Wertz, born 10 Sept. 1951, Chicago, m. 17 Sept. 1977 to Janice Kovitch.

JOHN WERTZ and Anna Eliza Taylor

John Wertz, born 14 March 1829, Montgomery Co., Ohio (E); died 7 June 1885; son of Daniel Wertz and Sarah Weimer; married Anna Eliza Taylor, who was living at Richland Center, Wisconsin in 1915. They had eight children:

1. Sarah A. Wertz; died before 1915; no heirs.

2. Manda E. Wertz, married Herman Burdick; two children: Fred Burdick and Laura Burdick.

3. Albert C. Wertz, married Belle Looker; one child: Gary(?) Wertz.

4. Della M. Wertz, m. William Bosaha(?); four children: Otto, Genevieve, Moses, and William.

5. John C. Wertz, m., one son: John Wertz Jr.

6. Daisy Wertz, m. Charles Waldock(?); two children: Ralph, who died before 1915; and Letha Waldock(?).

7. Josephine Wertz, married Harry M. Ide(?); one child: Onolee(?) Ide.

8. Charles Wertz.

Chapter 4

ABRAHAM KNEPPER and MARIA CATHERINA WERTZ

Maria Catherina Wertz, born 8/26 August 1738, and baptized 10 January 1739 at Coventry, Chester County, Pennsylvania, second child and eldest daughter of Hans Jacob Wertz and Anna Barbara Hoff/Huff. Mrs. Snyder's chart indicates only that she married a "Mr. Knipper" and had a son named Abraham.

However, by correspondence with Mrs. Shirley Jo Cunningham of Fort Wayne, Indiana in 1976, and 1988; and Bonnie G. Moats of Waynesboro, Penn. in 1988, both descendants of this Knepper family, we have obtained much more information on the family and descendants of Maria Catherina Wertz Knepper.

Sources of this information also include the Will of Abraham Knepper, written 21 May 1811; the Will of David Knepper, written 16 Sept. 1824; and the Will of Joshua Knepper, written March 1839. All of these wills are on file at the Chambersburg Courthouse, in Franklin Co., Pennsylvania. An excellent, well documented, article on this Knepper family also appears in the National Genealogical Society Quarterly, Volume 73, Number 2, June 1985, pages 83-92. (BB) Many Knepper deeds are also available at the Franklin Co. Courthouse. The DAR index, Volume 155, page 290, and the DAR papers of Clara Elden, also contain information on this family. And finally, many of the members of this family are listed in the IGI.

Abraham Knepper was the son of Wilhelmus Knepper and Veronica Bloom. Wilhelmus Knepper was bapt. 27 Oct. 1691 at the Solingen Reformed Church, Westphalia, Germany (BB); son of Peter Kneppern and Anna Maria Fischer; and grandson of Tilman Kneppern and of Johannes Fischer. Wilhelmus Knepper, a weaver, married

22 Feb. 1723 at Surhuisterveen, Friesland, Netherlands to Veronica (Ferona) Bloom or Bloem, daughter of Ludwig Bloem. Wilhelmus and Veronica Knepper came to America in 1729 on the ship "Allen" from Rotterdam, arriving in Philadelphia, 15 Sept. 1729.

They settled in what is now Quincy township, Franklin Co., Penn. Wilhelmus died there about 1755, and Veronica died 27 April 1769. Two land indentures made in 1821 and 1822 list five children of Wilhelm and Veronica Knepper: Peter, Mary, Elizabeth, Catherine, and Abraham. One or more of their daughters may have been born in the Netherlands, or in route to America, but both sons were reportedly born after their arrival in what was then Antrim twp., Cumberland Co., Penn., but is now Quincy twp., Franklin County, Penn.

Abraham Knepper was born 10 March 1734. The IGI (E) gives the date and place of marriage of Maria Catherina Wertz and Abraham Knepper as 1758 in Franklin County. During the Rev. War, Abraham served as a private in Capt. Samuel Rogers' company, 1st battalion, Cumberland County Militia. Abraham's will, written 21 May 1811, names five children: Catherine, David, Abraham, Joshua, and Samuel.

Abraham's Family Bible records the same five children, and also gives the death date of his wife, Maria Catherina Wertz, as 17 March 1823. (AA) Abraham died 8 Dec. 1823 in Washington twp., Franklin County. Abraham and Maria Catherina Wertz Knepper are buried at the Mt. Zion Cemetery in Franklin County. All of their children were born in what was then Antrim township of Cumberland County, and is now Quincy twp., Franklin County, Penn.

1. Catherine Knepper, born about 1758; died before her father wrote his will; married John Benedick. They had three children. This family is outlined beginning on the next page.

2. **David Knepper**, born 5 June 1759; died 18 Nov. 1824; married 20 December 1796 to Esther Foreman, born 27 March 1775, died 1826; daughter of Frederick and Mary Foreman. David's will, proved 16 Sept. 1824, names ten children: Andrew, Catherine, David, Esther, Frederick, George, Jonathan, Leah, Sarah, and Dekel. This family is outlined beginning on page 84.

3. **Abraham Knepper, II**, born 23 April 1766; died 25 August 1857; buried at Mt. Zion Cemetery, Quincy, Franklin Co., Penn.; married Elizabeth Benedict, born April 1767, died 23 Sept. 1834; buried at Mt. Zion Cemetery, Quincy; daughter of Peter Benedick. They had seven children. This family is outlined beginning on page 90.

4. **Joshua or Josiah Knepper**, born 23 March 1777; died 6 April 1839; buried at Mt. Zion Cemetery, Quincy; married Mary Short, born 31 August 1777, died 3 Jan. 1842. Joshua's will, written March 1839, names six children: Jacob, Ephraim, Conrad, Joshua, Catharine, and Lydia. This family is outlined beginning on page 96.

5. **Samuel Knepper**, born about 1780; died March 1839, Quincy twp.; married about 1814 to a Miss Biddinger or Bittinger. They had ten children, but both parents died before they were all grown, as their son Adam Knepper was appointed guardian over Frances, Susanna, Catherine, and Matilda. The other children were Hannah, Anthony, Wm.K., Dorothy, & Mary. Outline of this family begins on page 98.

JOHN BENEDICK and CATHARINE KNEPPER

John Benedick was born about 1750, probably a son of Peter Benedick, and a brother of the Elizabeth Benedick who married his brother-in-law, Abraham Knepper. John Benedick married 1st about 1775 to Catharine Knepper, who was born about 1755 in Cumberland (now Franklin) County, Penn.; died before 1823; daughter of

Abraham Knepper and Maria Catherine Wertz. John m. 2nd to Nancy Mack, daughter of Jacob Mack, and ggdau. of Alexander Mack (AA).

John Benedick and Catharine Knepper had three surviving children:

1. Susan Benedick married **Abraham Stoner**, son of Abraham and Mary Stoner of Washington twp., Franklin Co., Penn.; they had five children: (1) David or Daniel Stoner, born 21 Jan. 1826; died 23 March 1845; (2) Elizabeth "Lizzie" m. Louis Bonebrake; (3) Susan m. David Gordon and moved West; (4) John Stoner m. 1st Celia Martin, and m. 2nd Kate Smith; and (5) Mary Ann Stoner married Henry Bare.

2. Peter Benedick; married and had six children: (1) Elizabeth m. Mr. Deardorff; (2) Catherine m. Frederick Harbough; (3) Nancy m. Mr. Plowman; (4) Susan m. Mr. Bricker; (5) Rebecca m. Mr. Bryan; and (6) John Benedick.

3. David Benedick; married and had two daughters: Catherine m. Fred Lesher; and Sarah m. Mr. Snively.

DAVID KNEPPER and Esther Foreman

David Knepper, b. 5 June 1759, Antrim twp.; d. 18 Nov, 1824, Washington twp.; son of Abraham Knepper and Maria Catharine Wertz; m. 20 Dec. 1796, in Franklin Co. (E) to Esther Foreman, b. 27 March 1775, d. 31 Dec. 1826; daughter of Frederick and Mary Foreman. David served in the Rev. War as a private in the 5th Company, 1st battalion, Cumberland Co. Militia, under Lieut. John Stitt. They had ten children:

1. **Frederick Knepper**, born 10 Aug. 1797; died 1846, Bedford Co., Penn.; "Knepper Families", by Laura Knepper, shows Frederick with one son, Samuel, born 1822, whose wife's name was Judy, and they had eleven children. Other records show Frederick as a cripple who never married. (AA) (BB)

84

2. Jonathan Knepper, born 14 April 1799; died 1 August 1856; married 1st to Hannah Davis; married 2nd to Martha "Mattie" McFerron. Jonathan had at least three daughters: Rebecca married John Small; Lavina m. David Small; and Hannah married Mr. Wingert.

3. David Knepper, born 9 Feb. 1800, Quincy; died 11 Dec. 1860; married 25 Oct. 1827 to Mary Catharine "Polly" Geesaman, born 1 March 1809, Roxbury, Franklin County; died 25 May 1882; daughter of William Geesaman and Mary Catharine Meily. David and Mary are both buried at the Mt. Zion Cemetery in Franklin County. They had 14 children: Solomon, George, Hiram, Samuel, twins who died at birth, Mary Catherine, David, William, Kevin, Judith, Jacob, Joshua, and Obadiah. An outline of these families begins on page 87.

4. Andrew Knepper, born 12 March 1803, Quincy; died 23 Nov.1844 (X)(BB) or 20 Nov.1846 (AA), Washington twp.; "Andrew Knepper, son of David, deceased, married 4 March 1828 at the Zion Reformed Church of Chambersburg, to Maviern Reed, daughter of James of Washington township."(6) Mary Ann (K)(AA)(BB) or Maviern Reed was born 1806, died 7 Feb. 1880 (BB) or 1884 (X); buried at Nunnery Hill Cemetery, Snow Hill Cloister, Quincy twp. They had 10 children: twins = Mary Jane and Henrietta, Addie/Adelaide, Alexander, Albert, Andrew, Cyrus, Henry, John Albert, & James S. Knepper. Outline of these families begins on page 88.

5. Leah Knepper, born 19 March 1806; died 1 April 1896; m. by 1827 to Joseph Geesaman, born 1 Jan. 1802, died 10 (X) or 19 (AA) Nov. 1880 (X) or 1887 (BB), son of William Geesaman and Mary Catherine Miley. Joseph and Leah are both buried at Mt. Zion Cemetery. They had four children: (1) William Geesaman, born 24 Oct. 1827, Quincy; died 30 Oct. 1898; m. 1st to Elizabeth Monn; m. 2nd to Lydia Riddlesberger; (2) Findlay Geesaman, who died 15 Dec. 1917, and was never married;

(3) Josiah Ellsworth Geesaman, born 2 Feb. 1838, married to Anna Elizabeth Pentz, born 11 March 1842, Quincy twp., daughter of William M. Pentz and Mary Toms (see IGI) (E); and (4) James Geesaman, who died 24 Dec. 1838, unmarried.

6. George Knepper, born 13 Feb. 1809, died 16 July 1873; m. 1838/9 to Mary McFerren, born 1812, died 1899; three children: (1) Elizabeth "Lizzie" Knepper, born 1840, died 1914, m. 1862 to Melchor Elden, born 1840, died 1899. They had six children: George K., Mae, Corwin W., Jennie, Addie, and Clara B. Elden; (2) Clara K. Knepper married Wilson Reynolds and had four children: Harvey, George, Florence, and Lottie; and (3) David Knepper.

7. Dekel (IGI) or Theckla (X) or Zekiel (BB) Knepper, born 1 Jan. 1811; died 4 Feb. 1893, Warsaw, Koscuisko Co., Ind.; m. 25 March 1831 to Henry Goshert, b.6 April 1808, Lebanon Co., Penn.; died 5 May 1901, Warsaw, Ind.; ten children, the 1st 5 born Franklin Co., Penn., the next 3 born Lancaster, Fairfield Co., Ohio, and the last two born at Warsaw, Ind.: (1) Jemina Goshert, b. 18 April 1832, d. 4 March 1928, m. 22 Dec. 1850 to Dimmick Linn. (2) Elizabeth Goshert, b. 22 Nov. 1833, d. 29 Jan. 1928, m. 2 Dec. 1852 to Richard Ferguson. (3) George P. Goshert, b. 11 Aug. 1835, d. 14 Aug. 1927, m. 9 March 1858 to Saluda Dove;(4) David Goshert, b.8 Jan. 1838, d. 28 Oct. 1927, m. 24 July 1861 to Rebecca Dunnuck. (5) Henry Goshert, b. 22 Sept. 1839, d. 29 March 1920, m. 15 Jan. 1866 to Laural Hankerson; (6) Sarah Ellen Goshert b. 23 Oct. 1841, d.10 Feb. 1917, m. 11 March 1869 to Jacob Dillsaver. (7) John Goshert, b. 10 Oct. 1843, d. 16 April 1912, m. 16 Jan. 1870 Dicy Pinkerton. (8) William Goshert, b. 14 June 1847, d. 7 March 1917, m. Martha Ann Heeffer. (9) Jeremiah Goshert, b. 1 March 1850, d. 5 April 1923, m. 1 March 1879 to Martha E. Hoffer. (10) Harvey Goshert, b. 22 April 1853, d. 2 Feb. 1950, m. 16 Jan. 1878 to Mary Alice Hickman.

8. Esther "Hettie" Knepper, born 26 June 1813 (BB); m. Jacob Stites or Sites; 3 children: Isabelle m. Mr. Brumbaugh; Susan; and Elizabeth m. Mr. Barnhart.

9. Catharine Knepper, born 28 Oct. 1815 (BB).

10. Sarah Knepper, born 10 Sept. 1817 (BB); married Henry M. Meyers. (AA)

DAVID KNEPPER II & Polly Geesaman

David Knepper, born 9 Feb. 1800, Quincy; died 11 Dec. 1860, Quincy; son of David Knepper and Esther Foreman; married 25 Oct. 1827 to Mary Catharine "Polly" Geesaman, born 1 March 1809, Roxbury; died 25 May 1882, Quincy; daughter of William Geesaman or Geeseman and Mary Catharine Meily. David and Polly had fourteen children, all born at Quincy, Franklin Co.:

1. Mary Catherine Knepper, born 1 Sept. 1828; died 6 Feb. 1863; married George Gift, five children: (1) Daniel Gift m. Annie Heefner. (2) Jerre Gift, who had five children. (3) David Gift, who had six children. (4) Hiram Gift, born 1855, died 1926, married Elizabeth Fisher, born 1856, died 1903; they had twelve children. (5) Mary Catherine Gift, married Luther Mills, and had two children.

2. Solomon Knepper, born 7 May 1830; died 22 March 1865; married Esther Youkey.

3. David Knepper III, born 2 March 1832; died 15 July 1834, age 2 years.

4. William Knepper, born 30 Jan. 1834; died 5 August 1834, age 6 months.

5. George G. Knepper, born 15 May 1835; died 22 Oct. 1909; married Mary McFerran.

6. Samuel Knepper, born 1 Sept. 1837; died 21 Dec. 1923; married 21 Dec. 1863 to Mary Susan Nicodemus.

7. Kevin Knepper, born 1838.

8. Hiram Knepper, born 7 August 1839; died 30 June 1901; married Fredrica Stull; "went West"

9. Judith Knepper, born 29 June 1841; died 9 April 1850, age 8 years, 9 months.

10. & 11. twins, born and died 23 July 1843.

12. Jacob Knepper, born 21 July 1844, died 23 March 1863, age 18 years, 8 months.

13. Joshua Knepper, born 3 Oct. 1846; died 7 Sept. 1890; married Mary "Nettie" Harris; at least two sons: Edward and Seymore Knepper.

14. Obadiah Knepper, born 25 Sept. 1848; died 13 Feb. 1933; married Emma George; "went West"

ANDREW KNEPPER & Mary Ann Reed

Andrew Knepper, born 12 March 1803, Quincy; died 20/23 Nov. 1844 (X) or 20 Nov. 1846 (AA), Washington twp., Franklin Co.; buried in Snow Hill Graveyard, Quincy twp.; son of David Knepper and Esther Foreman. Andrew m. 4 March 1828 to Mary Ann or Maviern Reed, born 1806; died 7 Feb. 1884; daughter of James Reed (6). They had ten children, all born in Franklin Co. Their descendents include "Bob" Knepper, the noted baseballplayer (AA); probably the Charles Knepper, b. Anderson, Indiana, pitched for the Cleveland National League team in 1899. (See Official Encyclopedia of Baseball.)

1. Mary Jane Knepper, twin, born 24 Oct. 1828; died 22 March 1921; married John Funk, born 13 Oct. 1828; died 7 Jan. 1893; they had eight children: Upton; John; James who had seven children; Ben who had one son; Harvey who had five children; Margaret Smith who had one son; Amanda who married Jacob Decker and had two children; and Emma Keagy who had two children.

2. Henrietta Knepper, twin, born 24 Oct. 1828; died 11 April 1914; m. 30 August 1849 (E) to Abraham Baker, born 28 Dec. 1821; died 20 Sept. 1893; they had seven children: (1) Annie wife of John Rowe; (2) Emma, m. Daniel Fortney and had four children; (3) Henry Baker who had one son; (5) Samuel Baker; (5) Abraham Baker who m. Amanda Gater and had seven children; (6) Cyrus Baker who had four children; and (7) Mary, m. John Rock, and had four children.

3. Alexander Knepper, born 20 Dec. 1830; died 1 Sept. 1901; married 1st 8 April 1852, Waynesboro (E) to Nancy Mentzer, who had one daughter, Margaret, born 10 Dec. 1852, died 21 Oct. 1862, age 9 years and 10 months. Nancy probably died in childbirth, as Alexander m. 2nd in 1853 to Sarah Dunkle. Alexander and Sarah had four children: (1) Annie, born Sept. 1853, died 26 April 1873, age 19 years, 7 months, and 22 days, unmarried; (2) Daniel Knepper; (3) Henry Knepper; and (4) Mary Ann who married George Reed.

4. Addie or Adelaide Knepper, born 15 Feb. 1833; died 17 Sept. 1872; married 6 June 1850 to Levi Heefner, born 5 Oct. 1828; died 12 April 1895; six children: (1) Albert Heefner. (2) William H. Heefner, born 1857, died 1930, m. Mary E. Kauffman. (3) John Andrew Heefner, born 1858, died 1930; m. Charlotte R. --?--. (4) Mary Ann Heefner, died 3 Jan. 1932, m. 27 Aug. 1867 to Daniel Jacob Summers. (5) Emma Heefner m. a Mr. McCoy. (6) another daughter, not named, who also married a Mr. McCoy.

5. Henry Knepper, born a. 1841; m. 29 Nov. 1866, Waynesboro (E) to Malinda Knepper, born 1844, died 1924, daughter of Ephraim K. Knepper and Catherine Smetzer. Henry and Malinda had four children: (1) Ephraim S. Knepper, b.1867, d.1884; (2) James H. Knepper, born 1870, died 1933, m. Amanda McFerron; (3) Katie K., b. 1872, d. 1949, m. George Mickley, b. 1868, d. 1939; and (4) Margaret K. Knepper, born 1881, died 1933, married George Peters.

6. **Andrew Jackson Knepper**, born 22 Feb. 1842; married Mary E. Dickson or Jackson; nine children: (1) Ida B. Knepper married J. C. Dundor. (2) George A. Knepper, born 3 April 1873, married Eva Van Fleet. (3) Wm. Andrew Knepper, born 21 Dec. 1875, died unmarried. (4) Cyrus Eugene Knepper, born 21 August 1878, married Adella Myers. (5) Henry Roscoe Knepper, married Ada Garman. (6) Robert A. Knepper, born 15 April 1883, died 6 Jan. 1886. (7) Grover C. Knepper, born Jan. 1887, married Mae Hand. (8) Ruby R. Knepper, born 29 Jan. 1889. (9) Kitty May Knepper, b. 17 Oct. 1891.

7. **Albert Knepper**.

8. **Cyrus Knepper**, married 22 Sept. 1855 to Sarah A. Mentzer. (E)

9. **John Albert Knepper**.

10. **James S. Knepper**.

ABRAHAM KNEPPER & Elizabeth Benedick

Abraham Knepper II, born 23 April 1766, Antrim twp.; died 25 Aug. 1877 (X), or 27 Aug. 1857 (AA), Quincy twp.; son of Abraham Knepper and Maria Catharine Wertz; married by 1790 to Elizabeth Benedick, born 16 April 1767; died 23 Sept. 1834, Quincy twp.; daughter of Peter Benedick; both Abraham and Elizabeth are buried at the Mt. Zion Cemetery; they had seven children: Daniel, George, John, Peter, Susanna, Elizabeth, and Abraham III.

1. **Daniel Knepper**, born 1 or 4 July 1791; died 24 Sept. 1861; married Elizabeth Catherine Reed, born 28 Feb. 1793; died 11 April 1872; both are buried at Mt. Zion Cemetery; they had four children: Alex, James, Susanna, and Marguerite. This family is outlined beginning on page 92.

2. **George Knepper**, born 12 Nov. 1792; died 19 Feb. 1870; m. Elizabeth Lowry or Lowrey, born

15 May 1796; d. 11 Sept. 1869; both are buried at Mt. Zion Cemetery. They had five children: George L., Elizabeth, Hannah, John, & Abraham. Outline of this family begins on page 92.

3. John Knepper, b. 14 Dec. 1793, twin; name of 1st wife unknown; m. 2nd to Miss Smetzer. Four sons: Daniel, Samuel, John A., and Joseph. Outline of this family is on page 93.

4. Peter Knepper, born 14 Dec. 1793, twin; died 19 June (X) or July (AA) 1848; married 1st to Elizabeth Geesaman, born 21 Feb. 1804; died 16 May 1829; m. 2nd to Eliza Wagoman, born 8 Jan. 1811 or 1814; died 24 Sept. 1892. All are buried at Mt. Zion Cemetery. Peter had three children by Elizabeth Geesaman: Sarah Ann, Jeremiah, and Levi; and four children by Eliza Wagoman: Benjamin, Cyrus, Lizzie, and Amanda. Outline of this family begins on page 94.

5. Susannah Knepper, b. 11 August 1796; m. Josiah or Joseph Geesaman, b. 7 April 1796; buried 18 August 1841 at the White Church Cemetery, on Route 997 at Duffield; son of John Geesaman. Six children: (1) Rebecca m. 1 Feb. 1854 to Michael Long; (2) Anna Maria m. Jacob Bittinger; (3) Elizabeth m. Charles Thompson; (4) Lavina m. Jacob Baker; (5) Joseph Geesaman; and (6) Susannah Geesaman married Adam Cook.

6. Elizabeth Knepper, born 12 April 1803; married Samuel Reed. They had six children: (1) Henry Reed married Christiania Burger and they had eleven children; (2) Samuel Reed "went West"; (3) Emily, wife of William Burger; (4) Elizabeth, married Levi Heefner and had three children; (5) Mary Ann Reed, never married; and (6) Benjamin Reed, had four or five children and lived in Ohio.

7. Abraham Knepper III, born 3 Sept. 1809; died 14 Oct. 1883; married 1st to Catharine Sites; one son, Joseph; married 2nd to Mary

Anderson, born 1 August 1805; died 18 August 1870 after three children: William H., Ann Elizabeth, and Susanna; and married 3rd to Elizabeth (Hess) Stoner; no known children. Outlines of these families begin on page 95.

DANIEL KNEPPER & Elizabeth Reed

Daniel Knepper, born 1 or 4 July 1791; died 24 or 27 Sept. 1861; son of Abraham Knepper II and Elizabeth Benedick. Daniel married by 1819 to Elizabeth Catherine Reed, born 28 Feb. 1793; died 11 April 1872; both are buried at the Mt. Zion Cemetery. They had four children:

1. James Knepper, born 3 Sept. 1819; died 20 March 1860, buried at Mt. Zion Cemetery; married Martha --?--, born 1822. At least three children: (1) Maggie Knepper, married Mr. Mullen; (2) Henry Knepper, born a. 1846; and (3) James A. Knepper, born 12 Aug. 1848; died 15 Feb. 1870, at Mercersburg Academy. (See also 1850 Census of Franklin County.)

2. Susanna Knepper, born 1821; died 1910; married 22 June (E) or 3 July 1845, at the Lutheran Church of Waynesboro, Quincy twp. to Martin J. Beatty, born 1820; died 1859; both buried at Mt. Zion Cemetery. Two sons: Samuel R. Beatty, born 1847, died 1849; and Daniel A. Beatty, born 1849; died 1862.

3. Marguerite Knepper, born 1826; died 20 March 1911; m. George Benedict... ancestor of J. Glenn Benedict, and Donald Geesamen.

4. Alexander or Alex Knepper, born 1839, Quincy; three children: Dan, Jack, and Ida.

GEORGE KNEPPER & Elizabeth Lowrey

George Knepper, born 12 Nov. 1792; died 19 Feb. 1870; son of Abraham Knepper II and Elizabeth Benedick; m. by 1825 to Elizabeth Lowrey, born 15 May 1796; died 11 Sept. 1869; both buried Mt. Zion Cemetery; five children:

1. George L. Knepper, b. 1825, Quincy; d. 5 May 1895; m. Susan --?--, b. 1829; d. 5 June 1895; both buried at Mt. Zion Cemetery; seven children: (1) John Knepper,b.1858; (2) Ephraim Knepper, born and died in 1859; (3) Clarabell Knepper, b.10 Dec. 1860; d. 27 Feb. 1863; (4) Annie Knepper, b. 1863; (5) Mollie Knepper, b. 1865, m. Mr. Zody; (6) Harvey/ Harry Knepper; and (7) Amanda Knepper m. a Mr. Dunmore.

2. Elizabeth Knepper, born 10 April 1828, Quincy; died 8 January 1881; never married.

3. Hannah Knepper, born 23 Feb. 1832; died 20 Oct. 1890; never married.

4. John Knepper, born a. 1834; married Margaret --?--, born a. 1841; six children: (1) George Knepper, born a. 1866, Quincy; (2) Emma Knepper, born a. 1869; (3) Elizabeth or Lizzy Knepper, born a. 1870; (4) Frank Knepper, born a. 1872; (5) Lidy or "Pet" Knepper, born a. 1876; and (6) John Knepper, born a. 1877.(See 1880 Census of Franklin Co.)

5. Abraham Knepper, b. 1836, Quincy; wife = Sarah; one son known: John A.Knepper, born 21 Dec. 1861; d.15 Feb. 1862, buried at Mt. Zion Cemetery. Rest of this family moved West (AA).

JOHN KNEPPER & (2) Miss Smetzer

John Knepper, born 14 Dec. 1793; son of Abraham Knepper II and Elizabeth Benedick; married 2nd to a Miss Smetzer; four sons:

1. Daniel Knepper, b. a. 1808; wife in 1850 was Rebecca, b. a. 1809; eleven children by 1850: (1) John Knepper, born a. 1830; (2) Charlotte, born a. 1831; (3) David Knepper, b. a.1834; (4) Rebecca, born a.1837; (5) Matilda, b. a. 1838; (6) Ann, b.a. 1839; (7) Jerome Knepper, b. a. 1841; (8) Peter Knepper, b. a. 1843; (9) Eliza, b.a. 1845; (10) Henry, born a. 1848; and (11) William Knepper, born a. 1849. (See 1850 Census of Franklin Co.)

2. Samuel Knepper, born 6 August 1818.

3. John A. Knepper, born 1825; died 15 June 1890; never married.

4. Joseph Knepper, b.12 April 1826; d.10 April 1888; m. Elizabeth Smith; 5 children: Alfred, John, Harry, Charles, and Howard Knepper.

PETER KNEPPER & Elizabeth Geesaman

Peter Knepper, born 14 Dec. 1793; died 29 June 1848; son of Abraham Knepper II and Elizabeth Benedick; married 1st to Elizabeth Geesaman, born 21 Feb. 1804; died 16 May 1829; daughter of John Geesaman and Sabina Smith; both buried at Mt. Zion Cemetery; three children:

1. Sarah Ann Knepper, born 1825; married 9 Sept. 1845, Quincy twp. to Daniel Bricker; probably at least seven children, order unknown: (1) Harry Bricker; (2) George Bricker, born a.1849, died 10 August 1850, age 11 months and 9 days; (3) Annie Bricker; (4) John Bricker; (5) Daniel Bricker; (6) Levi K. Bricker, born a. 1857, died 17 August 1862, age 5 years, 2 months, and 27 days; (7) Mary Ray Bricker.

2. Jeremiah Knepper, born 1828; married 1 May 1849 to Harriet Sechrist; married 2nd to Eliza Wagoman; seven children: (1) Amanda m. Mr. King; (2) Edward Knepper; (3) Secrest Riley Knepper; (4) Emma m. Mr. Swartzmiller; (5) William Knepper; (6) James Peter Knepper; and (7) Loren Knepper.

3. Levi Knepper, born 1829; married Maria.

PETER KNEPPER & Eliza Wagoman

Peter Knepper, born 14 Dec. 1793; died 19 June 1848; son of Abraham Knepper II and Elizabeth Benedick; married 2nd to Eliza Wagoman, born 8 January 1811 or 1814; died 24 Sept. 1892, buried at Mt. Zion Cemetery; four children:

94

1. **Cyrus Knepper**, born a. 1836; married 22 Sept. 1855, Quincy, to Sarah A. Mentzer (E); three children: (1) Benjamin ... probably the Benjamin Franklin Knepper, born a. 1860, m. 15 Jan. 1885, Franklin Co. to Amanda Elberta Jones (E), with eight children recorded in the IGI; (2) Amanda Knepper m. a Mr. Bryan; (3) Alice Knepper m. a Mr. Blobaugh.

2. Benjamin Knepper, born 4 Dec. 1838; died 31 Jan. 1905; married 6 Feb. 1856 to Mary Ellen or Eleanor Reems. They lived in Seneca, Ohio and had eleven children: (1) Minnie Knepper, married John Loos; (2) Cyrus Knepper, married Mary Hunker; (3) Eva Knepper, born 1867, married Frank Beck; (4) Arletta Knepper, born 1869, married Charles Pomeroy; (5) Emma Knepper, born 1870, married Curtis Edwards; (6) Benjamin D. Knepper, born 1873, married Lillian Clara Smith; (7) William Irvin Knepper, born 1875; (8) Russell M. Knepper, born 1878, married Mamie Cune; (9) Clara Knepper, born 1880, married Ervin Zeis; (10) Mabel Knepper, married William Irvin; (11) Katie Knepper, born 1884, died in infancy.
Eva, Clara, Minnie and Cyrus Knepper all lived in the Tiffin-Findlay, Ohio area.

3. Elizabeth Knepper, married a Mr. Mentzer.

4. Amanda Knepper, b. a.1844; m. John Bonner.

ABRAHAM KNEPPER & Catharine Sites

Abraham Knepper III, born 3 Sept. 1809; died 14 Oct. 1883, buried Mt. Zion Cemetery; son of Abraham Knepper II and Elizabeth Benedick. Abraham married 1st to Catharine Sites and they had one son: Joseph Knepper, born 1829.

ABRAHAM KNEPPER & Mary Anderson

Abraham Knepper III, born 3 Sept. 1809; died 14 Oct. 1883, buried Mt. Zion Cemetery; son of Abraham Knepper II and Elizabeth Benedick. Abraham m. 2nd to Mary Anderson, born 1 August 1805; died 18 August 1890; three children:

1. William H. Knepper, born 6 January 1836; died 18 June 1888; married 22 Nov. 1860 to Rebecca Benedick, born 10 March 1842; died 1 Dec. 1917; both buried at Mt. Zion Cemetery. Four children: (1) Mary Alice Knepper, born 9 Nov. 1861, d. 18 Dec. 1861; (2) Anna Elizabeth Knepper, m. John Keller; (3) Emma or Erma Benedick Knepper, born 25 Feb. 1865, died 25 Sept. 1931; (4) Jennetta "Nettie" Knepper, born 26 June 1867, Quincy twp. (E), died 20 Sept. 1955, married to Welty G. Smith.

2. Ann Elizabeth Knepper, born 31 Oct. 1837; died 28 March 1841, age 3 years, 4 months.

3. Susanna Knepper, born 27 Nov. 1840; died 4 May 1906; married Peter Whitmore.

JOSHUA KNEPPER & Mary Short

Joshua Knepper, born 23 March 1777; died 6 April 1839; son of Abraham Knepper and Maria Catharine Wertz; m. by 1802 to Mary Short, born 31 August 1777; died 3 Jan. 1842; both buried at Mt. Zion Cemetery. Six children:

1. Catharine Knepper, b. 22 Sept. 1802; d. 2 March 1872; m.in 1824 to George Walk, b. 1792; d. 4 April 1839; son of Frederick Walk; three children: (1) Maria Walk, b.13 May 1826; d. 13 Dec. 1901; m. Jacob Rock, born 18 June 1816; died 7 Feb. 1900. (2) Samuel Walk, "moved West". (3) John Walk, born 15 June 1829; died 30 July 1911; married Elizabeth Kauffman or Coffman, born 12 March 1832; died 29 Jan. 1916; both buried at Mt. Zion Cemetery; three children: George, Samuel, and Catharine. (FF)

2. Jacob Knepper, b. 12 April or 24 Oct. 1804, baptized 24 Nov. 1804, Franklin Co.; died 27 Jan. 1888; m. Lydia Walk, who died 7 Sept. 1874; dau. of Frederick Walk; four children: (1) James Knepper. (2) Mary Knepper, born 20 April 1830, died 17 Feb. 1832, age 1 year, 9 months. (3) Caroline Knepper m. George W. McCleary. (4) Harriet K. Knepper m. Levi Row.

3. Lydia Knepper, born 17 Nov. 1808; died 30 Sept. 1883; m. Frederick Dull, born 23 May 1800; d. 2 Jan. 1881; one daughter: Malinda Dull, born 10 Nov. 1826, died 5 July 1865, m. Jess McCumsey or McGumsey, and they had three children: (1) Clayton A. McGumsey, b. 27 April 1852, died 27 July 1865. (2) Allison L. McGumsey, b. 6 March 1856, died 16 Dec. 1857. (3) Alice McFerren McGumsey, born 27 Oct. 1859, died 15 March 1864.

4. Ephraim K. Knepper, born 11 Oct. 1811; died 13 Nov. 1886; married Catharine Smetzer, born 4 Oct. 1813; died 24 Sept. 1897; both buried at Mt. Zion Cemetery; four children: (1) Harriet Knepper, born 1835, died 26 Sept. 1893, 59 years, 17 days; married Levi C. Row, died 7 Jan. 1914, 80 years, 4 months, 10 days; two daughters: Ida Row m. George Shaffer, and Mary Row m. George Heefner. (2) Mary Knepper, born 15 April 1838; died 14 Nov. 1856. (3) Henry Knepper, born 1841; died 5 Feb. 1842. (4) Malinda K. Knepper, born 1844; died 1924; married 29 Nov. 1866 to Henry Knepper (E), born 1842; died 1885; four children... outline of this family follows below.

5. Konrod or Conrad Knepper.

6. Joshua Knepper, married Elizabeth --?--.

HENRY KNEPPER & MALINDA K. KNEPPER

Henry Knepper, born 1842, died 1885 probably a son of Peter Knepper and Nancy Heller (see page 102; married 29 Nov. 1866, Waynesboro (E) to Malinda K. Knepper, born 1844, died 1924; daughter of Ephriam K. Knepper and Catharine Smetzer (see above). They had four children:

1. Ephraim S. Knepper, born 1867; died 1884.

2. James Knepper, born 1870; died 1933; m. Amanda McFerren, born 1867; died 1946; one daughter known: Esther Knepper, born 1906; m. Bruce E. Brubaker, born 1902; died 1966.

3. Katie K. Knepper, born 1872; died 1949; m. George Mickley, born 1868; died 1939; seven children: (1) Rosie Mickley, born 1889, died 1951, m. Ira W. Rock, born 1889; died 1951; a daughter, Mary Elizabeth, born 1906, died 20 Feb. 1919. (2) Bernice Mickley m. a Mr. Benchoof. (3) Ray Mickley. (4) Merbie Mickley m. a Mr. Kyler. (5) Miron B. Mickley. (6) Eva Mickley. (7) Ardella Mickley.

4. Maggie K. Knepper, married George Peters; five children: Vada, Rhoda, Albert, Zula, and Vergie Peters.

SAMUEL KNEPPER & Miss Bittinger

Samuel Knepper, born a. 1780, Franklin Co., died March 1839, Quincy twp.; son of Abraham Knepper and Maria Catharine Wertz; Samuel m. a Miss Bittinger, and they had ten children, at least four of whom (Frances, Susanna, Catherine, and Matilda) were still minors in 1839, when there brother, Adam was appointed their guardian. (See Franklin Co. deed book D, pages 212, 216, 226, and 238.)

1. Adam Knepper, m. in 1833 to Catherine Small; two sons: Samuel Knepper, born 1834, died 1 June 1936?; and William Knepper.

2. Hannah Knepper, born a. 1815; married David Grass.

3. Dolly or Dorothy Knepper.

4. Mary Knepper.

5. William K. Knepper, born a. 1821; m. Mary Smetzer; six children: (1) Josiah Knepper, born 1846; died 8 Sept. 1890; m. Mary Harris; five children: Ella, Clara, Lettie, Fanny, and Frank Knepper. (2) Jeremiah Knepper. (3) Samuel Knepper. (4) Adeline Knepper m. Harrison Bryant, two children: Viva and Cinthia. (5) William Knepper m. Christina Stump; five children: Samuel, Delia, Luella,

John, and Jessie. (6) Henry Knepper m. Alice Harris; two children: Charles and Estella.

6. Frany or Frances Knepper.

7. Susan Knepper, born 1825; died 2 May 1897, age 72 years, 4 months, and 10 days; m. Jacob Decker, who died 11 March 1895, age 73 years, 2 months, 2 days; eight children: (1) Abraham Decker, b. 11 Oct. 1852; died 22 March 1911. (2) Mary Ann Decker m. a Mr. Smetzer. (3) Martha Decker, born a. 1856, m. a Mr. Gossart. (4) Catherine Decker. (5) Susan Decker m. a Mr. Shockey. (6) Julia Decker m. a Mr. Mentzer. (7) Jacob Decker, born 4 Oct. 1855, died 13 Feb. 1938. (8) John Decker, born 13 March 1862, died 14 August 1865.

8. Catharine Knepper.

9. Matilda Knepper, born about 1827.

10. **Anthony Knepper**, born about 1829; married Catherine Sollenberger; five children: (1) Phares Knepper. (2) Catharine Knepper. (3) Susan Knepper. (4) William Knepper married Temperance --?--. (5) Margaret Knepper m. a Mr. Prentice.

THE OTHER FRANKLIN COUNTY KNEPPERS

As recorded at the beginning of this chapter, Wilhelmus Knepper or Knipper, and Veronica Bloem or Bloom had at least five children, two sons & three daughters (BB). According to the will, dated 18 March 1807, of their daughter Elizabeth Knepper, who never married, her sisters, were Mary and Catherine, and her brothers, Peter and Abraham. (See Franklin Co. Probates, Book B, page 319) Mary Knepper m. about 1745 to George Adam Martin; and Mary died 10 March 1770. Catharine Knepper married Johann Horn. More on these two families in (BB). We have just recounted the history and descendants of Abraham Knepper, who married Maria Catherina Wertz. Peter Knepper, born

99

1731 (X) or 1732 (BB), also left many Knepper descendants in Franklin County. Records of these families follow here.

PETER KNEPPER & ELIZABETH

Peter Knepper, born 1731/2; died by 15 Oct. 1791 at Ephrata (BB); son of Wilhelmus Knepper and Veronica Bloem; m. about 1755 to Elizabeth --?--; the "wife of Peter Knepper died at Ephrata on 10 Oct. 1794" (BB). They had eight children:Mary, Elizabeth, Feronica, Catherine, Susannah, Peter, Solomon, and William.

1. Susannah Knepper born 1757; died 2 Feb. 1832; m. 1784 to **Henry McFerren**, born 20 Jan. 1764, Cumberland Co., Penn.; died 19 April 1834, Franklin Co., Penn.; seven children: Jacob, John, Peter, Mary (Polly), Henry, George, and Susanna. Outline of this family begins on the next page.

2. **Peter Knepper**, born a. 1758; died 1829; m. a. 1790 to Regina Wolf (BB); seven children: David, Peter, Solomon, Joshua, Elizabeth, Samuel, and an unnamed daughter. Outline of this family begins on the next page.

3. **Solomon Knepper**, born 1759.

4. **William Knepper**, born a. 1761; died by 1829; four children: (1) Peter Knepper m. Rachel. (2) Solomon Knepper m. Elizabeth Foreman, three children... This family is outlined beginning on page 104. (3) Joshua Knepper. (4) Jacob Knepper.

5. Catherine Knepper.

6. Feronica (X) or Veronica (BB) Knepper m. Abraham Secrist.

7. Mary Knepper.

8. Elizabeth Knepper m. **George Smetzer**.

HENRY McFERREN & SUSANNAH KNEPPER

Henry McFerren Sr., born 20 Jan. 1764, Cumberland Co., Penn.; died 19 April 1834, Franklin Co.; married in 1784 to Susanna Knepper, born 1757; died 2 Feb. 1832; daughter of Peter and Elizabeth Knepper. Henry McFerren and Susanna Knepper had seven children:

1. Jacob McFerren, born 5 Sept. 1785; married Mary --?--. (Possibly the Mary Cook who married a "Mr. McFerren". See Cook Family Records by this author.)

2. John McFerren, born 28 Oct. 1786; died 17 July 1826; married in 1811 to Elizabeth Wertz. (Possibly the Elizabeth, b. 1786, daughter of Jacob Wertz and Hannah Emmons. See page 37.)

3. Peter McFerren, born 14 August 1792; married Elizabeth Fetterhoff.

4. Mary (Polly) McFerren, born 8 Feb. 1794; married William Mentzer.

5. Henry McFerren, born 14 Oct. 1796; never married.

6. George McFerren, born 27 Feb. 1803; married Rebecca Wertz (Possibly the Rebecca Wertz, born 1803, daughter of Conrad Wertz and Anna Maria Cook. See page 43.)

7. Susanna McFerren married Stephen Staley.

PETER KNEPPER & REGINA WOLF

Peter Knepper Jr., born a. 1758, Franklin Co.; died 1829; will proved 25 May 1829 (see Franklin Co. probate Book D, page 100); son of Peter and Elizabeth Knepper. Peter Jr. m. about 1790 to Regina Wolf, and they had at least seven children:

1. David Knepper, born 1801, Franklin Co.; married Catherine --?--, born 1812.

2. Peter Knepper III, born 2 Oct. 1802; died 7 March 1871; m. Nancy Mentzer or Heller... nine children: Lucy, Samuel, Amos, Henry,Elizabeth, Obed, Jeremiah, Solomon, and Peter IV. Outline of this family begins below.

3. an unnamed daughter.

4. Joshua Knepper, b. 1806; m. Susan, b. 1813.

5. Solomon Knepper, born 1807; m. Esther Youkey, born 1814; six children: (1) Sarah Knepper, born 1846. (2) Amanda Knepper, born 1848. (3) Charlotte Knepper, born 1849. (4) David Knepper... five children: William, Charles, Jerre, Scott, and Fred. Outline of this family is on page 104. (5) Aaron Knepper. (6) Peter Knepper.

6. Elizabeth Knepper m. David Moun.

7. Samuel Knepper, born 1810; m. Catherine, born 1814; six children: (1) Samuel Knepper Jr. born a. 1834. (2) Simon Peter Knepper, born a. 1835. (3) Sarah Knepper, born a. 1840. (4) David Knepper, born a. 1842. (5) Margaret Knepper, born a. 1846. and (6) John Knepper, born a. 1849. (See 1850 Franklin Co. Census)

PETER KNEPPER & Nancy Mentzer/Heller

Peter Knepper III, b. 2 Oct. 1802; d. 7 March 1854; son of Peter and Regena Knepper; m. by 1829 to Nancy Mentzer or Heller, born 2 March 1810 or 1814; d. 3 March 1885; daughter of Jonathan Mentzer (X). This Knepper family is outlined in Biographical Annals of Franklin County (F), p.457. But that record erroneously reports that Peter Knepper was born in Germany about 1810 and emigrated to America "when a young boy", settling and marrying in Franklin Co. about 1830. This article also states that Peter "married Nancy Heller of Lancaster Co." Their nine children and son Peter's three children are outlined in this article.

1. Lucy A. Knepper, born 1829, Quincy; married John Fahrney of Quincy twp.

2. Samuel H. Knepper, b. 5 Jan. 1836 or 1838, Quincy; died 15 April 1913; m. 1st on 21 Dec. 1863 to Mary S. Nicodemus. They moved West.

3. Amos Knepper, b.22 Nov 1840; d.29 Oct.1925; a farmer in Quincy twp.; m. Kate E. Loury, born 17 May 1848; died 21 March 1916; both are buried at Grindstone Church Cemetery in Quincy twp. They had one son: William Knepper.

4. Henry Knepper, born 1842; died before 1905. Probably the Henry Knepper married 29 Nov. 1866, Waynesboro (E) to Malinda Knepper, a daughter of Ephriam K. Knepper and Catharine Smetzer. Outline of this family is on page 97.

5. Peter Knepper, IV born 27 Sept. 1844; d. by 1885; m. 1st to Lizzie Sheller, and m. 2nd to Amanda Etter; three children: William, J.H., and Lydia May Knepper. Outline of this family follows below.

6. Elizabeth "Lizzie" Knepper, born 1845; married a Mr. McFerron (X) or McFern, a farmer in Guilford twp. (F)

7. Obed Knepper, born 1847; died 1928; married Agnes N. Keller. Lived in Guilford twp.

8. Solomon Knepper, a farmer in Quincy twp. Possibly the Solomon Knepper m. 6 Dec. 1874, Quincy twp. to Catherine Thompson. (E)

9. Jeremiah "Jerry" Knepper, married Emma Small; lived in Guilford twp.; farmer.

PETER KNEPPER & Amanda R. Etter.

Peter Knepper IV, born 27 Sept. 1844, Quincy twp.; died after 1905; son of Peter and Nancy Knepper. Peter IV m. 1st to Lizzie Sheller, daughter of Christian and Lydia Sheller. They had no children. Peter IV m. 2nd to Amanda R.

Etter, daughter of Jacob Etter and Susan
Miller; they had three children:

1. William L. Knepper, born about 1880; was a
farmer in Guilford twp. (F)

2. J. H. Knepper, born about 1882; was a
teacher, and then a telegrapher in Franklin
County. (F)

3. Lydia Mary Knepper, born about 1885. (F)

DAVID KNEPPER, son of Solomon

David Knepper, born a. 1851; son of Solomon
Knepper and Esther Youkey; name of wife
unknown; five sons known:

1. William Knepper.

2. Charles Knepper, name of wife unknown; ten
children: (1) Ned Knepper. (2) Joel Knepper.
(3) Anita Knepper. (4) Don Knepper, lived at
Fork Littlestown, Penn. and had two sons:
Rodney and Stephen Knepper. (5) Edith Knepper.
(6) David Knepper. (7) Phyllis Knepper. (8)
Robert Knepper. (9) Helen Knepper, twin.
(10) Harriet Knepper, twin.

3. Jerre Knepper.

4. Scott Knepper.

5. Fred Knepper.

SOLOMON KNEPPER, & Elizabeth Foreman

Solomon Knepper, born a. 1795; son of William
Knepper; name of William's wife in not yet
known. Solomon Knepper married Elizabeth
Foreman, daughter of Frederick Foreman; they
had three children and lived in Little Cove.

In the History of the Little Cove, of Franklin County, Penn.; by Harry E. Foreman; page 127 it states: "Solomon Knepper purchased the Beam lands in 1799 and 1804. When Frederick Foreman, executor, sold the Knepper lands to Henry Brewer in 1828, the acreage was given as 332 acres. William and Jacob Knepper were mentioned as heirs in 1828." on page 82, it states: "The Cooks, Beam, Knepper and Secrists came into the Little Cove from the southern part of Franklin County." also: "The Beam, later Solomon Knepper land, was the present Earl McClanahan — Grant Keefer places plus another place behind the ridge."

Other records of this family can be found in the Franklin County Courthouse, Orphan's Court dockets, volume B, page 463, which records the appointment of Frederick Foreman and John Dull as guardians for Elizabeth, William, and Jacob Knepper, all under 14 years of age, in 1822; thus all born between 1808 and 1822. Also Frederick Foreman's will, dated 3 March 1835, is found in Probate Book D, page 320.

1. Jacob Knepper.

2. William Knepper, born a. 1805, Waynesboro; died 1880; m. a. 1830 to Henrietta Rosan Houer, who died 1888. They had seven children: (1) Margaret Knepper, born a. 1831, Clear Spring, Washington Co., Maryland; died 1896; never married. (2) Alice Knepper, born a. 1833; died 1866; unmarried. (3) Catherine Knepper, born a. 1835; died 1890; married M.A. Hill. (4) Ann Knepper, born a. 1837; M. L. Anderson. (5) Susan Knepper, born a. 1839; m. Peter Sowers. (6) Elizabeth Knepper, born a. 1841; m. John Westerhouse. (7) Lewis Knepper, born a. 1843. (See 1850 Census of Maryland.)

3. Elizabeth Knepper m. Samuel Burgess.

OTHER FRANKLIN COUNTY KNEPPERS
"unattached"

from Franklin County Footnotes: Vol. 2, p. 28:
"Twenty First Cavalry of 1863: ... David
Knepper, Co. A., 21st Regt. Pa. Cav. 1844-1921
and Nettie L. Kuhn, his wife, 1848-1908. Both
buried in Green Hill Cemetery, Waynesboro."
This David Knepper, 1844-1921, might be a son
of Samuel and Catherine Knepper (see page 102)
or a son of Solomon and Esther Youkey Knepper
(see Page 104). Samuel and Solomon were both
sons of Peter and Regina Knepper.

Also in Franklin County Footnotes, Volume 1,
page 107: Marriages of the Zion Reformed
Church include: "13 Feb. 1827, Joseph
Geesaman, son of William, Washington twp.,
married to Leah Knepper, daughter of David,
deceased."

OTHER POSSIBLE DESCENDANTS

John Knepper and Elizabeth Stahl of Somerset
County, had a son, David Knepper, born 31
March 1826.

Chapter 5

JOHN WERTZ, 1742/3-1815

John Wertz, born about 1742/3, probably in York County, Pennsylvania, the fourth child of Jacob Wertz and Anna Barbara Hoff; died by 1815 in Franklin Co., when his administration papers were filed at Chambersburg. The name of his wife has not as yet been learned, but he is known to have had two sons: Jacob and Frederick; and at least one daughter: Susannah, b. 2 Sept. 1785; married John Baker (see page 150). (BB) (CC)

Jacob Wertz was born 1774, and died in 1848; he married by 1797, undoubtedly in Franklin Co., to Maria Snowberger. They had seven children. This family and their descendants are outlined beginning on page 109.

Frederick Wertz was born 1781; died 29 Oct. 1852, age 71 years. His obituary appeared in the Valley Spirit Newspaper on Nov. 18, 1852. (G) He married a Miss Baker, who may have been a sister to John Baker (see page 150) (BB). Frederick's will was proved 11 November 1852, and is on file at Chambersburg. It names six daughters: Christina, Francy, Betsie, Susan, Catherine, and Nancy; all of whom were born in then Washington, now Quincy twp., Franklin Co.

1. **Catherine** "Katie" Wertz, b.11 April 1808; d. 11 April 1885, No. Bloomfield twp., Morrow Co., Ohio; bur. Shauck Cem.,Perry twp., Morrow Co.; m. 22 June 1843, Franklin Co., Penn. to **Jonathan Rinehart/Rheinhardt** or Rhinehardt; one son known: Aaron Rheinhart, who lived at Johnsonville, Ohio; and had at least 4 children: Charles, George, Ella, and Cora Rinehart.

2. Francy (chart); Vrene (E); Irene (6); or Fanny (BB) Wertz, b.a.1811; d.13 Feb.1891, N. Bloomfield twp., Morrow Co., Ohio; bur. Shauck Cem., Perry twp.; m.19 Nov. 1853 at Second Evangelical Lutheran Church, Chambersburg (G) to David Detrick or Dietrich; chart says "no heirs". Their wills, on file in Morrow Co., Ohio, also indicate no children.

3. Christina "Ann" Wertz, b.a.1815; died 10 June 1890, Perry twp., Morrow Co., Ohio; bur. Shauck Cem., Perry twp.; married 16 March 1854, Franklin Co., Penn. to Josiah S.Cover, (BB); the chart says "no heirs". Her will, on file in Morrow Co., Ohio names three sisters and a nephew, but no children.

4. Elizabeth "Betsie/Betsy" Wertz, b.a.1815/7; m. 9 June 1836, Franklin Co., to John Light; living in Nebraska in 1890; four children: (1) David Light married Kate Burkett; (2) John Light married Miss Snyder; (3) Albert Light; and (4) Maria Light married Christ Annock.

5. Susan Wertz, born 19 March 1819; died 30 August 1893, age 74 years; married Dr. Charles Orlig/Olick/Ohlick; in 1850 this family was living in Middle Woodbury twp., Bedford Co., Penn.; they had seven children: (1) Kate, m. David Keagy, lived Altoona, Penn.; (2) Amanda, m. Andy Biddle, lived Johnson City, Texas; (3) Harry, m. Miss Bayers, lived Altoona, Penn.; (4) Sonnie, m. Dr. Klepser; (5) Cristy(?) Ann, m. Simon Replogle, and had a daughter, Alice who married James Weston(?); (6) Charles, died single; and (7) John, died single.

6. Nancy Wertz, born 1825; died 28 June 1891, Middle Woodbury twp., Bedford Co., Penn.; m. before 1847 to Michael Keagy, six children: (1) Frederick Wertz Keagy, married Annie Hagey and they had one son, David Keagy, and lived in Penn.; (2) Henry Keagy, married Millie Lindsey, lived at Newcastle, Penn.; (3) Manda Keagy, married George R. Replogle, lived Woodbury, Bedford Co., Penn.; (4) Elizabeth

Keagy, married W.S.Lee, lived Altoona, Penn.;
(5) William Keagy, married Rosa B. Hoffman,
lived Altoona, Penn., and had two children,
Alma and Michael Keagy; and (6) Jennie Keagy,
married L.Z.Replogle, lived Altoona Penn., two
children: Ida Replogle, married Charles R.
Flicka, Altoona, Penn.; and Keagy Replogle.

JACOB WERTZ and MARIA SNOWBERGER

Jacob Wertz, born 1774, died 1848; son of John
Wertz; married by 1797 to Maria or Martha
Snowberger, born 30 July 1774, died 22 Feb.
1844.(chart) Maria/Martha Snowberger Wertz,
died 23 Feb. 1844, 69 years, 3 months, and 30
days, buried at "The Nunnery" or "Snow Hill
Cemetery" in Quincy twp., near Waynesboro; she
was a daughter of Andrew and Barbara Karper
Snowberger. One tombstone record says Maria
Wertz, a second record says Martha Wertz (G).
Seven children: John, Nancy, Jonathan, Polly,
Susanna, Elizabeth, and Sarah. Jacob's will,
dated 12 March 1848, probated in 1848, is on
file at Chambersburg, and reads as follows:
"In the name of God, Amen. I Jacob Wertz, of
the township of Quincy, County of Franklin,
Commonwealth of Pennsylvania, being weak in
body, but of sound and disposing mind, memory,
and understanding; blessed by the Almighty God
for the same, considering the certainty of
death, and the uncertainty of the time thereof
and being desirous to settle my worldly
affairs and thereby be the better prepared to
leave this world when it shall be the will of
God to call me hence. I do therefore make and
publish this to be my last Will and Testament
in the manner and form following: "First and
principally I resign my soul to Almighty God
the author of my being and my body to the
earth to be decently buried by my executor
hereafter named. And with respect to the
things of this world wherewith it hath pleased
God to bless me with in this life, I do hereby
dispose of in the following manner: I do
hereby order and direct that all my just debts
and funeral expenses be paid by my executors.

"I order and direct my real and personal property to be sold at public or at private sale by my executors to the best advantage and it is further my will after my death, after my debts are paid to dispose of the surplus in the following manner: First I give & bequeath unto my housekeeper, Rebecca Cauffman, one bed and bedding, 3 chairs, one chest and $200 in money for her services to me rendered, and the remainder after my housekeeper is satisfied, I dispose of the remainder in the following manner: Secondly I give & bequeath unto my deceased daughter Nancy's children 1/7 part of the whole remainder. Thirdly I give & bequeath unto my son John Wertz's children 1/7 part of the whole remainder, & they are to be charged with what their father has already received. Fourthly I give & bequeath unto my daughter Susanna, intermarried with Jos. Kedinger the 1/7 part of the whole remainder. Fifthly I give & bequeath unto the children of my dau. Polly, intermarried with Thos. B. Cavan, 1/7 part of the whole remainder, and they are to be charged with what their father has already received. Sixthly I give & bequeath into my son Jonathan Wertz's children 1/7 part of the whole remainder and they are to be charged with what their father has already received. Seventhly I give & bequeath unto my deceased daughter Elizabeth's children 1/7 of the whole remainder. Eightly I give & bequeath unto my deceased daughter Sarah's children 1/7 of the whole remainder. And lastly I do hereby nominate, constitute, and appoint David Wertz and Emanual I. Stover, executors of this my last will and testament. In witness where of I have here unto set my hand and seal this 12th day of March 1848."
signed by mark by Jacob Wertz; witnesses: John H. Cordell and Fredrick Wertz.

Children of Jacob Wertz and Maria Snowberger

The order in which their children are listed on Mrs. Snyder's chart differs from the order they are listed in Jacob's will. Other records indicate that the order listed in his will is most probably the correct order of their birth, as follows. All were undoubtedly born in Franklin County, Pennsylvania.

1. **Nancy Wertz**, born 21 Nov. 1797, died 24 May 1832; married **Joseph Yockey**, born 25 Feb. 1796, died 10 June 1823; three children: (1) Abraham Yockey, born 15 March 1819, died 2 April 1819(?); (2) Susan Yockey, 1820-1894,(F) married 1840 to Dr. John Burkholder, eight children, outline of this family begins on the next page; and (3) Elizabeth Yockey, born 2 March 1824, died 21 June 1825.

2. **John Wertz**, born 2 Jan. 1799, Franklin Co., Penn.(E); died 30 Sept. 1854; m. 19 Feb. 1821, Franklin Co.(E) to Rebecca Reed, ten children. Outline of this family begins on page 113.

3. **Susanna Wertz**, married **Joseph Kittinger**; eight children: (1) John; (2) Tiszah(?) married Mr. Plauch or Plouck; (3) Nancy; (4) Aaron S.; (5) Ephriam; (6) Joseph; (7) Benj. F.; and (8) Jacob Levi. A Benjamin Kittinger married Amanda Diehl, see (F).

4. **Polly Wertz**, born 6 August 1801; died 22/23 Feb.1857/1887; m. Thomas Cavan; 11 children. Records of this family are on page 117.

5. **Jonathan Wertz**, born 10 June 1804/5, Franklin Co., Penn.; died 17 Jan. 1871, Wayne Co., Ohio; married Mary "Polly" Null; eight children. Outline and records of this family begin on page 118.

6. **Elizabeth Wertz**, married **Samuel Fisher**; four children: Andrew, Joseph, Nancy, and Susie Fisher.

7. **Sarah** or **Sara Wertz**, born 25 Oct. 1814, Quincy, Franklin Co., Penn. (E); married **Samuel Fisher**; two children: (1) Jacob Fahrney Fisher, 1838-1909, see page 118; and (2) Sarah Fisher, who died in infancy.

Dr. JOHN BURKHOLDER and Susan Yockey

Dr. John Burkholder was born 15 Jan. 1812 at Chambersburg, died 17 Feb. 1877 at Quincy, son of Ulrich Burkholder and Catharine Fahrney. He was a physician in Franklin County and his biography is included in the Biographical Annals of Franklin County, pages 642-3. (F) He married 3 March 1840 to Susan Yockey, b. 20 May 1820; d. 30 Sept. 1894, daughter of Joseph Yockey and Nancy Wertz. Eight children: Nancy, Benjamin, Catherine, John, David H., Joseph Alfred, Aaron W., and Susan Emma Burkholder.

1. Nancy Burkholder, born 9 Sept. 1842; died 12 April 1862. (F)

2. Benjamin F. Burkholder, born 27 May 1846.

3. Catherine Burkholder, born 10 Nov. 1847; died 11 March 1849. (F)

4. John Burkholder, born 30 Jan. 1850; died 5 Feb. 1850. (F)

5. David H. Burkholder, born 13 April 1854; m.4 November 1875 to Margaret Seilhamer; ten children. In 1915, this family was living in Chambersburg, Penn.; they are outlined below.

6. Joseph Alfred Burkholder, born 30 August 1856; died 8 May 1858. (F)

7. Aaron W. Burkholder, born 4 May 1858; died 30 March 1860. (F)

8. Susan Emma Burkholder, born 21 March 1860; married between 1905 and 1915 to a Mr. Funk.

DAVID H. BURKHOLDER and Margaret Seilhamer

David H. Burkholder was born 13 April 1854, Quincy twp., Franklin Co., Penn.; married 4 Nov. 1875 to Margaret Seilhamer, born 24 Nov. 1855, daughter of George Seilhamer and Catherine Ross. David was a pharmacist and groceryman at Staufferstown from 1876 to 1897 and then went into farming on the John R. Yockey farm on the Falling Spring in 1897. He was a member of the St. John's Reformed Church, Chambersburg. His biography is in the Biographical Annals of Franklin County, pages 642-3. They had ten children, all born at Staufferstown, Guilford twp., Franklin Co.(F)

1. Susan Burkholder, born 17 Oct. 1876, married 10 Dec. 1896 to J. Calvin Potter, son of John Potter and Rebecca Sourbaugh; one daughter, Rebecca, was born before 1905.(F)

2. Catherine Burkholder, born 19 Nov. 1878; married 21 Nov. 1900 to Charles W. Saum, son of John Saum and Anna Margaret George; two daughters, Margaret and Catherine, were born before 1905. (F)

3. Willis A. Burkholder, born 27 Oct. 1880; married 20 Nov. 1902 to Katie Wingert, daughter of John Wingert and Frances Wingert.

4. a daughter, born 5 Oct. 1884, died in infancy.

5. Paul Burkholder, born 13 March 1886.

6. John D. Burkholder, born 4 June 1888.

7. Ella Eva Burkholder, born 26 May 1891.

8. Maurice Burkholder, born 16 Feb. 1893.

9. Margaret Burkholder, born 9 Oct. 1896.

10. Mary Burkholder, born 25 July 1899.

JOHN WERTZ and Rebecca Reed

John Wertz, born 2 Jan. 1799, Franklin Co., Penn. (E); died 30 Sept. 1854; son of Jacob Wertz and Maria Snowberger; married 19 Feb. 1821, Franklin Co., Penn. (E) to Rebecca Reed, who died 8 March 1875. The Snyder chart lists ten children: Jacob, Elizabeth, Nancy, Jemima, Philip R., John, Susanna, Eva M., Joseph A., and Simon E. But the IGI includes records for twelve children. The first four children were born in Franklin County, the next six in Napier township of Bedford Co., Penn.; and the last two in Henry Co., Illinois.

1. Jacob Wertz, born 24 Jan. 1825; chart says "died young".

2. Elizabeth Wertz, b. 12/15 Feb. 1826; m. 1st 15 Sept. 1844, Franklin Co. (E) to Augustus Stickler; one daughter. Elizabeth m. 2nd to Joseph Boane or Doane; they had six children. This family is outlined on the next page.

3. Nancy Wertz, b. 21 April 1828; died young.

4. Jemima or Jamhna Wertz, born 21 Sept. 1829, Franklin Co., Penn.; died young.

5. Philip Reed Wertz, born 31 March 1831, Napier twp., Bedford Co., Penn.; married 14 March 1860, Sangamon Co., Illinois (E) to his 1st cousin, Barbara A. Cavan; three children. Their family is outlined on page 116.

6. John Wertz, born 3 Aug. (E) or 7 Oct. 1833; died young.

7. Susanna Wertz, b. 14 Oct. 1835; died young.

8. Eva or Eve Mary Magdalene Wertz, b. 21 Aug. 1837; m. 6 May 1862, Princeton, Bureau Co., Illinois (E) to Neal McAuthur; three children. This family is outlined on page 116.

9. Joseph Adam Wertz, b. 2 March 1840; d. young.

10. Rebecca Ann Catherine Wertz, born 2 July 1842, Napier twp., Bedford Co., Penn. (E)

11. Simon Ely Wertz, b. 17 June 1846, Henry Co., Ill. (E); m. 26 Nov. 1868, Bureau Co., Ill. to Mary Elizabeth Stoutenburg (E); lived in Texas.

12. Lydia Ann Wertz, born 31 Aug. 1844, Henry Co., Illinois; died in infancy. (E)

AUGUSTUS STICKLER and Elizabeth Wertz

Elizabeth Wertz, born 12/15 February 1826; daughter of John Wertz and Rebecca Reed; married 15 Sept. 1844, Franklin Co., Penn. to Augustus Stickler; one daughter:

1. Rebecca Stickler, married, but name of husband and records of children unknown.

JOSEPH DOANE and Elizabeth Wertz

Elizabeth Wertz Stickler married 2nd to Joseph Doane or Boane, and they had six children:

2. Samuel Doane, died in infancy.

3. Daniel C. Doane, married Rhoda --?--; eight children: (1) Augustus David, born 1 Feb. 1881, died 11 April 1881; (2) William Arthur, born 4 Feb. 188?, died 2 Oct. 1912; (3) Carrie Annie, born 24 Aug. 1884, died 27 Oct. 188?; (4) Louie Clement, born 30 Nov. 1885, died 26 Feb. 1886; (5) Leroy Alfred, born 27 April 1887, lived at Normal, Illinois; (6) Robert Oswald, born 25 Sept. 1890, lived Normal, Illinois; (7) Bertie Elmer, born 18 Aug. 189?, died 1 Feb. 1894; and (8) Elsie Louise, born 19 July 1895, lived Normal, Ill.

4. David A. Doane, born 1 May 1858; married Nancy Holland.

5. Anna M. Doane, born 8 April 1860; lived in Missouri.

6. Charles Anthony Doane, born 16 July 1862; died before 1915; no heirs.

7. Joseph C. Doane, born 18 August 1866; died before 1915; no heirs.

PHILIP REED WERTZ and Barbara A. Cavan

Philip Reed Wertz, born 31 March 1831, Napier twp., Bedford Co., Penn.; son of John Wertz and Rebecca Reed; married 14 March 1860, Sangamon Co., Illinois (E) to his 1st cousin, Barbara A. Cavan, born 15 Oct. 1830, daughter of Thomas Cavan and Polly Wertz (see next page). They had three children:

1. Merrian N. Wertz, born 1861, Sangamon Co., Illinois (E); (note: IGI says his parents were Philip Reed Wertz and Maria Cavan. This is probably an error, unless Barbara's name was Barbara Maria or Maria Barbara.); married Lidia(?) Chaptam(?); they had four children, all living in Penn. in 1915: Olive May Wertz; Emma Marie Wertz; Esther Barbara Wertz; and Thomas Wertz.

2. Mary Reed Wertz, born 12 Nov. 1862, Sangamon Co., Ill.(E); died 1887; no heirs.

3. Florella Wertz, born 26 Jan. 1866, Sangamon Co., Ill. (E); died 1873/93; no heirs.

NEAL McAUTHUR and Eva Wertz

Eva or Eve Mary Magdalene Wertz, born 21 August 1837, Napier twp., Bedford Co., died 1898(?); daughter of John Wertz and Rebecca Reed; married 6 May 1862, Princeton, Bureau Co., Ill. (E) to Neal McAuthur, died 1891(?); they had three children:

1. Louise or Laura McAuthur, born 11 March 187?; died 26 April 1904; married H. S. Minnich, born 5 June 1860; three children: Eva Maria, born 5 Sept. 1892; Cora Anna, born March 1894; and John George, born 18 Aug. 1896

2. Neal or Noel B. McAuthur; living in Little Rock, Arkansas in 1915.

3. Grace McAuthur, an adopted daughter, who died in infancy.

THOMAS CAVAN and Polly Wertz

Polly Wertz, born 6 August 1801; died 22/23 February 1857/1887; daughter of Jacob Wertz and Maria Snowberger; married Thomas Cavan, and had eleven children: Maria Anna, Barbara, Allison M., William H.H., Oliver A., Nelson R., Mary, Rosa Rosanna, Jacob, John A., and Joseph.

1. Mary Cavan, born 9 Jan. 1821; died young.

2. Rosa Rosanna Cavan, born 13 Nov. 1824; died in infancy.

3. Maria Anna Cavan, born 18 Dec. 1827; married A. J. Waugh(?); lived Springfield, Missouri.

4. Barbara Caven, born 15 Oct. 1830, died 7 Dec. 1912; married 14 March 1860, Sangamon Co., Ill. (E) to her 1st cousin, Philip Wertz; three children, see page 116.

5. Joseph Caven, born 10 March 1832; married a Miss Fisher.

6. John A. Caven, born 3 July 1833/5; died at age of seven years.

7. Jacob Caven, b. 21 March 1836; died young.

8. Allison M. Caven, born 12 May 1838; married Anna Rule(?); lived in Chicago, Illinois.

9. William H.H.Caven, born 10 March 1840; married Mollie --?--; lived Elwood, Illinois.

10. Oliver A. Caven, born 12 April 1842/3; married Sally Pleasant(?).

11. Nelson R. Caven, born 24 May 1850; married Eliza Bowen; lived Seattle, Washington.

SAMUEL FISHER and Sarah Wertz

Sarah Wertz, born 25 Oct. 1814, Quincy, Franklin Co., Penn.(E); daughter of Jacob Wertz and Maria Snowberger; married Samuel Fisher; two children:

1. Sarah Fisher, died in infancy.

2. Jacob Fahrney Fisher, born 21 March 1838, Quincy twp., Franklin Co., Penn.; died 24 May 1909, Quincy twp.; married 23 Sept. 1858, (E) Chambersburg to Mary Martha Rennecker, born 16 Nov. 1836, Quincy twp.; died 6 Aug. 1915, Quincy twp.; daughter of John D. Rennecker and Margaret Baulis. (H) Three children: (1) Susan Margretta Fisher, born 15 June 1859, Quincy twp.; died 14 Nov. 1941, Quincy twp.; married 20 Jan. 1881, Chambersburg to Joseph Flavius Biesecker (E)(H); lived at Allenwald, Franklin Co., Penn.; (2) John William Fisher, born 6 Feb. 1861, Quincy twp., died 6 June 1932, Guilford twp.; married 12 Sept. 1882, Greencastle to Mary Ellen Baker; (E)(H) lived Chambersburg, Penn.; and (3) Benjamin Samuel Fisher, born 9 May 1873, Quincy twp.; died 29 Dec. 1967, Waynesboro; married 12 June 1892, Hagerstown, Md. to Iva Loy Sellers; (E)(H) lived Greencastle, Franklin Co., Penn.

JONATHAN WERTZ and MARY NULL

Jonathan Wertz, born 10 June 1804/5, Franklin Co., Penn.; died 17 January 1871, Wayne Co., Ohio; son of Jacob Wertz and Maria Snowberger. Jonathan married by 1825 to Mary "Polly" Null, born 12 Feb. or March 1809/14; died 12 March or November 1871, Wayne Co., Ohio; Both Jonathan and Mary are buried at what was then known as the Yankeetown Cemetery, and is now called the Pleasant View Cemetery, in Plain twp., Wayne Co., Ohio. Records of this family and many of their descendants were compiled in 1978 by Mrs. Robert Ungerer of Wooster, Ohio. (D)

Jonathan and Mary moved from Penn. to Ohio sometime before 1850 when they are recorded in the Census in Plain twp., Wayne Co., Ohio. They had eight children:

1. Nathaniel Wertz, born 26 October 1825; died 12 February 1826.

2. Levi Wertz, born 17 April 1827; died 10 Nov. 1895; married Margaret McGregor; four children. This family is outlined below.

3. Sammuel Wertz, born 27 Feb. 1829; died 18 February 1840; no heirs.

4. Jacob Wertz, born 7 April 1830; died 23 August 1894/5, Wayne Co., Ohio; married 24 Oct. 1854, Wayne Co., Ohio to Charlotte Austen; nine children. Outline and records of this family begin on the next page.

5. Josiah Wertz, born 9 Dec. 1832; died 16 April 1884; married Mary Austen; ten children. Outline of this family begins on page 149.

6. Anthony Wertz, born 4 Jan. 1835; chart says "died young"; Mrs. Ungerer's records (D) say that Anthony died 1 Dec. 1888.

7. Frederick Wertz, born 23 Nov. 1838 (twin); died 7 Dec. 1838.

8. Sarah Wertz, born 23 Nov. 1838 (twin); died 7 Dec. 1838.

LEVI WERTZ and Margaret McGregor

Levi Wertz, born 17 April 1827; died 10 Nov. 1895; son of Jonathan Wertz and Polly Null; married by 1851 to Margaret McGregor, born 18 Sept. 1818/28; died 26 Feb. 1885; four children:

1. John W. Wertz, born 3 Jan. 1852; married Jessica McLucas Stuart; lived in Nebraska.

2. Alexander R. Wertz, born 19 Aug. 1853; married Althea(?) Crawford; lived Nebraska.

3. Orra H. Wertz, born 12 Sept. 1855; married Sadie Dugan(?); lived at Burlington, Iowa.

4. Sarah Ellen Wertz, born 13 Oct. 1858; died 23 January 1860(?).

JACOB WERTZ and Charlotte Austen

Jacob Wertz, born 7 April 1830; died 23 August 1894/5, Wayne Co., Ohio; son of Jonathan Wertz and Polly Null; married 24 Oct. 1854, Wayne Co., Ohio (E) by minister George Leiter, to Charlotte Austen, born 12 March 1830, died 5 June 1899/1900; daughter of John Austen and Susanna Newman, who were married 22 Feb. 1827, Wayne Co., Ohio (E). Jacob and Charlotte are both buried at the Pleasant View Cemetery, Plain twp., Wayne Co., Ohio. They had nine children, all born in Ohio:

1. Mary Susan Wertz, born 20 August 1855, Plain twp.; married 14 May 1885, Wayne Co., Ohio (E) to James B. Knox; two sons. Records and outline of this family begin on page 123.

2. Albert Jacob Wertz, born 4 Sept. 1857; married 8 Dec. 1881, Wayne Co. (E) to Mary Hare; seven children. Records and outline of this family begin on page 125.

3. Emily or Emma Jane Wertz, born 8/18 August 1859, Funk, Ohio; married 26 Sept. 1880, Wayne Co., Ohio (E) to Orrville Shafer; six children. Outline of this family begins on page 130.

4. Scott Winfield Wertz, born 17/21 June 1861/2, Funk, Ohio; married Ida Bell Tinsler; eight children. Outline of this family begins on page 131.

Jacob Wertz

Charlotte Austen Wertz

Jacob Wertz Homestead. Summer of 1910 or 1911.
Front row, left to right, Earl, Edna, Ethel.
Back row, Lillie, Tom, holding Grant.

5. Viola May Wertz, born 29/30 May 1864/9, Funk, Ohio; died 20 July 1937, Honeytown, East Union twp., Wayne Co., Ohio; married 14 May 1885, Wayne Co., Ohio (E) to Rolandus "Land" Milton Garn; four children. Outline of this family begins on page 143.

6. Sarah Ellen Wertz, born 10/11 June 1866, Funk, Ohio; married 22 Dec. 1887, Wayne Co., Ohio to James B. Snyder; one son. Outline of this family is on page 145.

7. Thomas Grant Wertz, born 18 October 1868, Funk, Ohio; married Lillie Mae Swain; seven children. Outline of this family begins on page 145.

8. Clara Anna Wertz, born 15 Sept. 1870, Funk, Ohio; died 8 Jan. 1934, Wooster, Ohio; married 14 May 1891 to Peter C. Rich; three children. Outline of this family begins on page 147.

9. Nettie Irine/Ieren Wertz, born 20 May 1872/3, Funk, Ohio; died 20 May 1954; married 24 March 1897, Lakefort, Ohio to William W. Bell; one son. Outline of this family begins on page 148.

JAMES KNOX and Mary Susan Wertz

Mary Susan Wertz, born 20 August 1855, Plain twp., Wayne Co., Ohio, died 26 July 1938; married 14 May 1885, Wooster, Wayne Co., Ohio to James Byron Knox, born 15 Nov. 1857, Springville, Wayne Co., Ohio, died 27 March 1938; son of John Knox and Catherine Donley. They had two sons, both born in Ashland Co., Ohio. They moved in 1893 to a farm north of Reedsburg, where they lived the rest of their lives. They are both buried in the Reedsburg Cemetery, Plain twp., Wayne Co., Ohio.

1. Russel Wayne Knox, born 18 Oct. 1890, Ashland Co., Ohio; never married; lived on the farm near Reedsburg until August 1977, when he retired, sold the farm and moved to Wooster.

The Albert Wertz Family. Taken 1892.

2. James Gail Knox, born 3 Oct. 1892, Ashland Co., Ohio, died 24 August 1948, Wooster, Ohio; married 3 June 1916 to Thais Brooks, born 21 July 1894, Delaware, Ohio, daughter of Earhart Brooks and Sarah Merrick. They had three children: Harold Galeman Knox, born 4 April 1918; Marjorie Marie Knox, born 5 July 1920; and Grace Glorene Knox, born 18 July 1926. James Gail Knox married 2nd in Oct. 1938 in Illinois to Mrs. Kathryn Mabel Baxter Ellen, who had two children by her first marriage.

ALBERT JACOB WERTZ and Mary Hare

Albert Jacob Wertz, born 4 Sept. 1857, Plain twp., Wayne Co., Ohio., died 19 Nov. 1924, son of Jacob Wertz and Charlotte Austen; married 8 Dec. 1881, Wayne Co., Ohio to Mary Roseann Hare, born 30 May 1863, Blachleysville, Ohio, died 21 Dec. 1944, Wadsworth, Ohio; daughter of Michael Hare and Elizabeth C. Fry. Albert and Mary are both buried at the St. Michael's cemetery near Marshallville, Ohio. They had seven children:

1. Shirley Wertz, born 21 August 1882, Lakefork, Ohio; died 24 Dec. 1952, Madisonburg, Ohio; married 20 Nov. 1905 at Marshallville, Ohio to William Elias Frase; three children. Outline of this family begins on page 126.

2. Flossie Wertz, born 8 Aug. 1883, Lakefork, Ohio; died 6 Feb. 1915, Marshallville, Ohio; married 12 April 1906, Marshallville, Ohio to Jacob R. Mussar; two children. Outline of this family begins on page 127.

3. Cloid Cline Wertz, born 18 Oct. 1884, Lakefork, Ohio; married Fannie Ellen Musser; four children. Outline of this family begins on page 127.

4. Gertie Wertz, born 31 Jan. 1890, twin, Lakefork, Ohio; died 15 March 1891.

5. an unnamed son, twin, stillborn 31 Jan. 1890, Lakefork, Ohio.

6. Florence Wertz, born 17 Oct. 1891, Marshallville, Ohio; died 12 Sept. 1916, Canal Fulton, Ohio; m. 6 July 1914 at Manchester, Ohio to Patrick H. Butzer; one son Delmar D. Butzer, born 24 August 1916 at Canal Fulton, Ohio; he was 19 days old when his mother died. Delmar married 2 March 1945 to Luella F. Geiser and they had two children: Amy May Butzer and Patrick D. Butzer.

7. Clarence Roderick Wertz, born 1 July 1901, Rittman, Ohio; married 14 March 1925, Wooster, Ohio to Ella Madelaine Rook; four children. Outline of this family begins on page 129.

WILLIAM ELIAS FRASE and Shirley Wertz

Shirley Wertz, born 21 August 1882, Lakefork, Ohio; died 24 Dec. 1952, Madisonburg, Ohio; daughter of Albert Jacob Wertz and Mary Hare. Shirley married 20 Nov. 1905, Marshallville, Ohio to William Ellis Frase, born 31 July 1882, Milton twp., Wayne Co., Ohio; died 7 Dec. 1961, Wadsworth, Ohio; both Shirley and Will are buried at the St.Michael's cemetery near Marshallville, Ohio. Three children:

1. Doris Idell Frase, born 29 July 1907 on the Frase farm south of Rittman, Ohio; died 30 August 1925, Wadsworth, Ohio; m. 6 Jan. 1925, Glenmont, Ohio to Charles Milan Drouhard, born 11 Aug. 1905, Glenmont, Ohio; one son: William Charles Drouhard, born 27 August 1925, lived Rittman, Ohio; married 1 Oct. 1947, Wooster, Ohio to Catherine Anne Cusack, born 7 Sept. 1928; two children: Linda May Drouhard, born 5 August 1948; and Milan Dale Drouhard, born 31 August 1951.

2. Honor Wertz Frase, born 23 January 1916, Rittman, Ohio; married 1 June 1940, at Doylestown, Ohio to Elnora E. Norton, born 27

June 1915, Wadsworth, Ohio; three children:
(1) Carol Ann Frase, born 22 Nov. 1942,
married 3 June 1962 to Dale Leo Tope, two
children: Diana Lynn Tope, and Cindy Ann Tope;
(2) Howard Stanley Frase, born 22 Nov. 1945,
married twice; (3) Beverly Frase, stillborn 31
Oct. 1950.

3. Thelma Maxine Frase, born 25 May 1924,
Rittman, Ohio; married 10 Sept. 1943,
Doylestown, Ohio to Russell Dwight Horner,
born 25 Oct. 1920, Smithville, Ohio; four
children: Larry James Horner, born 21 Sept.
1946; Thomas Keith Horner, born 6 Dec. 1949;
Deborah Lynn Horner, born 16 July 1951; and
Constance Jo Horner, born 16 Aug. 1953.

JACOB R. MUSSER and Flossie Wertz

Flossie Wertz, born 8 Aug. 1883, Lakefork,
Ohio; died 6 Feb. 1915, Marshallville, Ohio;
daughter of Albert Jacob Wertz and Mary Hare;
married 12 April 1906, Marshallville, Ohio to
Jacob R. Musser, born 29 Dec. 1885, Chippewa
twp., Wayne Co., Ohio, son of Daniel Musser
and Fannie Liechty; two children:

1. Fayetta Mae Musser, stillborn 13 Dec. 1908.

2. Faye Elizabeth Musser, born 16 August 1923,
adopted when 6 months old; married Raymond Leo
Butzer, born 24 April 1923; three children:
Dennie Lee Butzer, born 14 July 1944; Rebecca
Lynn Butzer, born 5 April 1951; and Kenneth
Ray Butzer, born 14 August 1953.

CLOID CLINE WERTZ and Fannie Musser

Cloid Cline Wertz, born 18 Oct. 1884,
Lakefork, Ohio; died 9 Jan. 1945, Kenmore,
Ohio; son of Albert Jacob Wertz and Mary Hare;
married 30 Nov. 1905, Marshallville, Ohio to
Fannie Ellen Musser, born 8 Jan. 1888,
Rittman, Ohio; died 29 Jan. 1954, Kenmore,
Ohio; daughter of Daniel Musser and Fannie
Liechty; four daughters:

1. Sylva Merideth Wertz, born 21 August 1906, Easton, Ohio; married 1st 27 Jan. 1923, Canton, Ohio to William Franklin Ashton, born 8 April 1902, Moffatt, Colorado; died 20 June 1953, Akron, Ohio; son of William Henry Ashton and Fannie R. Parsons; two children: Kenneth Cloid Ashton, born 5 Sept. 1923; and Meriem Fanny Ashton, born 13 Nov. 1926. Sylva married 2nd 12 July 1959 at Ormond Beach, Florida to Herbert Jack Stiltner, born 8 Dec. 1911, Virginia; died 28 May 1965, Barberton, Ohio. No children by second marriage.

2. Etha Marie Wertz, born 17 Jan. 1909, Easton, Ohio; married 7 April 1928, Canal Fulton, Ohio to Ray Marvin Jackson, born 3 Nov. 1904, Tar Fork, Kentucky; three children: Helen Pearl Jackson, born 30 Dec. 1928; Joyce Evelyn Jackson, born 13 August 1931; and Eugene Ray Jackson, born 8 Jan. 1935.

3. Ruth Arlene Wertz, born 2 August 1916, Rittman, Ohio; married 25 Dec. 1938, Akron, Ohio to Donald Alexander Cochoy, born 25 May 1915, Akron, Ohio; two children: Robert Edmund Cochoy, born 30 July 1942; and Dale Alan Cochoy, born 9 May 1949.

4. Betty Louise Wertz, born 14 June 1921, Canal Fulton, Ohio; married 1st 13 Nov. 1937 Covington, Kentucky to Nick Dan Boydanoff, born 20 Feb. 1918, Akron, Ohio; three children: Gary Boydanoff, born 12 March 1939; Neil Allen Boydanoff, born 23 June 1942(twin); and Phillip Lee Boydanoff, born 23 June 1942.

After Betty and Nick were divorced in 1942; Betty married 2nd 9 June 1943, Wadsworth, Ohio to Jack Edward Reed, born 29 June 1915, Penn.; two children: Nancy Oma Reed, born 9 Feb. 1949; and Edward Harry Reed, born 9 March 1950.

CLARENCE RODERICK WERTZ and Ella Rook

Clarence Roderick Wertz, born 1 July 1901, Pittman, Ohio; son of Albert Jacob Wertz and Mary Hare; married 14 March 1925, Wooster, Ohio to Ella Madelaine Rook, born 8 August 1904, Easton, Ohio; daughter of David Andrew Rook and Iva Myrtelle Barnes; four children:

1. Albert David Wertz, born 9 Nov. 1925, Easton, Ohio; married 3 April 1954, Wadsworth, Ohio to Evelyn Louise Martin, born 21 July 1930; five children: (1) Marcie Lee Wertz, born 9 Jan. 1955, Wadsworth, Ohio, adopted; (2) Denise Sue Wertz, born 23 August 1957, Doylestown, Ohio; (3) Rick David Wertz, born 24 Sept. 1958, Doylestown, Ohio, died 19 May 1962; (4) Jan Dean Wertz, born 31 Jan. 1960, Doylestown, Ohio; and (5) Donn Lee Wertz, born 16 Dec. 1964, Doylestown, Ohio.

2. Marion James Wertz, born 14 Nov. 1927, Hametown, Ohio; married 18 Nov. 1949, Loyal Oak, Ohio to Margaret Kolcun, born 6 Jan. 1925, Akron, Ohio; three children: (1) Gregory James Wertz, born 1 June 1958, Wadsworth, Ohio; (2) Richard Scott Wertz, born 17 May 1960, Wadsworth, Ohio; and (3) David Kevin Wertz, born 29 Sept. 1964, Wadsworth, Ohio.

3. Willey Anne Wertz, born 5 March 1932, Marshallville, Ohio; married 27 Aug. 1950, Doylestown, Ohio to James Warner Lemmon, born 9 Feb. 1931, Bareberton, Ohio; four children: (1) James Albert Lemmon, born 4 August 1951, Rittman, Ohio; (2) Guy Warner Lemmon, born 15 Nov. 1953, Rittman, Ohio; (3) Roderick Daniel Lemmon, born 12 August 1962(?), Rittman, Ohio; and (4) Elizabeth Anne Lemmon, born and died 11 March 1962, Rittman, Ohio.

4. Dennie George Wertz, born 10 Dec. 1936, Hametown, Ohio; Served in U.S.Army in Korea.

ORRVILLE SHAFER and Emily Jane Wertz

Emily Jane Wertz, born 8(D) or 18 August 1859, Funk, Ohio; died 3 Nov. 1936, Funk, Ohio; daughter of Jacob Wertz and Charlotte Austen; married 26 Sept. 1880, at McZena, Ashland Co., Ohio (D) or in Wayne Co., Ohio (E) to Orville (E) or Orville(D) Shafer, born 30 Sept. 1859, McKay, Ohio; died 28 Feb. 1937, Akron, Ohio; son of Peter S. Shafer and Susanah A. Black. Six children: Nellie May, Blaine, Guy Walter, Blanche Ferne, Orville Donn, and Mabel Chloe.

1. Nellie May Shafer, born 17 Sept. 1882; died 6 July 1962; married 1 Jan. 1902, Wayne Co., Ohio to John Clyde Raubenolt, born 23 Nov. 1888, Clinton twp., Wayne Co., Ohio; died 18 April 1971; son of William Raubenolt and Kathryn Hoy; four daughters: (1) Helen Margaret Raubenolt, born 3 June 1903; (2) Fae Vera Raubenolt, born 13 Sept. 1905; (3) Roxie Cathryn Raubenolt, born 30 Nov. 1908; and (4) Iona Emma Raubenolt, born 23 Nov. 1913.

2. Blaine Shafer, born 6 April 1884, Wayne Co., Ohio; died 3 May 1955; m. 1st 4 April 1907, Loudonville, Ashland Co., Ohio to Ada Pearl Murphy, born 1 Jan. 1885, Loudonville, Ohio; died 26 Feb. 1910; one son: Karl M. Shafer, born 23 Feb. 1910, died 24 Feb. 1910. Blaine m. 2nd 24 Nov. 1910 to Maude Elizabeth Criswell, born 29 April 1890, Green twp., Ashland Co., Ohio, died 24 Oct. 1970, Ashland Co., Ohio; daughter of Samuel Snyder Criswell and Cora Effie Hazlett; two daughters: Mildred Alleta Shafer, born 2 Oct. 1911; and Thelma Stearl Shafer, born 24 May 1920, married 7 June 1941 to Robert N. Ungerer. Thelma Shafer Ungerer is the compiler of most of these records on the descendants of Jacob Wertz and Charlotte Austin. (D)

3. Guy Walter Shafer, born 21 March 1888, Wayne Co., Ohio; died 19 Nov. 1970, Miami, Florida; married 23 Oct. 1910, Glenmont, Ohio to May Moores, born 1 April 1889, Ashland Co.,

Ohio, died 20 May 1949, Wayne Co., Ohio; daughter of Thomas Johnson Moores and Ada Shane; three daughters: (1) Naomi Blanche Shafer, born 12 April 1911; (2) Florence Irene Shafer, born 5 August 1912; and (3) Ada Maxine Shafer, born 11 April 1918.

4. Blanche Ferne Shafer, born 19 Sept. 1891, Clinton twp., Wayne Co., Ohio; died 18 Dec. 1977, Plain twp., Wayne Co., Ohio; married 23 Oct. 1910 to Clarence Wayne Nirode, born 16 July 1891, Wayne Co., Ohio, died 25 July 1976 Wayne Co., Ohio; son of William Franklin Nirode and Isadore Obenour; two sons: (1) Deloyne Shafer Nirode, born 17 Dec. 1917; and (2) Myron Wayne Nirode, born 24 July 1927.

5. Orville Donn Shafer, born 14 June 1893, Clinton twp., Wayne Co., Ohio; died 17 April 1899, Wayne Co., Ohio.

6. Mabel Chloe Shafer, born 17 Jan. 1898, Clinton twp., Wayne Co., Ohio; married 1st 25 Nov. 1915 Ashland Co., Ohio to Walter Clifford Lybarger, born 29 Sept. 1894, Lakefork, Mohican twp., Ashland Co., Ohio; died 18 August 1950, Akron, Ohio; one daughter: Margaret Anola Lybarger, born 8 July 1917, married Dec. 1937 to Reuben Mattingley; one son: Jerry Vincent Mattingley, born 5 July 1939. Mabel married 2nd in 1954 in Virginia to Norman Leroy Hoover, born 29 August 1912; died 11 July 1967, Barberton, Ohio.

WINFIELD SCOTT WERTZ and Ida Tinsler

Winfield Scott or Scott Winfield "Win" Wertz, born 17,18, or 21 June 1861/2, Funk, Ohio; died 28 Dec. 1942, Marshallville, Ohio; son of Jacob Wertz and Charlotte Austin; married 2 July 1891, Wooster, Ohio to Ida Bell Tinsler, born 7 Feb. 1873, Marshallville, Ohio; died 13 March 1915; daughter of George Tinsler and Mary Jane Ewing. Eight children:

131

Win and Ida Bell Wertz,
Oscar and Loyd.

1. Oscar Clyde Wertz, born 20 May 1892, Bauman twp., Wayne Co., Ohio; married Marie Gertrude Bachman; nine children. Outline of this family begins on the next page.

2. Loyd Delbert Wertz, born 27 Jan. 1894, Marshallville, Ohio; died 16 Oct. 1976, Baughman twp., Wayne Co., Ohio; never married.

3. Harold Scott Wertz, born 25 March 1896, Marshallville, Ohio; married Ruth Evelyn Edmonds; three children. Outline of this family begins on page 138.

4. Maude Eva Wertz, born 4 May 1898, Marshall-ville, Ohio; m. 27 Nov. 1918, Wooster, Wayne Co., Ohio to Raymond A. Baer; seven children. Outline of this family begins on page 139.

5. Ida Pearle Wertz, born 9 Feb. 1902, Marshallville, Ohio; died 9 Dec. 1971, Orrville, Ohio; married 5 June 1923 to Jay Buckwalter Rudy; two sons. Outline of this family begins on page 141.

6. Robert Clair Wertz, born 3 Sept. 1906, Marshallville, Ohio; married 1st to Helen Lucille Weaver, one son; married 2nd to Genevieve Taylor, five children. Outline of this family begins on page 141.

7. Esther Ruth Wertz, born 11 April 1909, Marshallville, Ohio; died 29 Jan. 1910, age 9 months and 18 days at Marshallville, Ohio.

8. Donald Dale Winfield Wertz, born 12 April 1914, Marshallville, Ohio; married 1st 21 August 1943 to Isabella M. Butterfield Imhoff, born 24 April 1921, Emsworth, Louisiana daughter of Charles Butterfield and Estella Fernhom; Donald and Isabella were divorced; no children. Donald married 2nd 14 Nov. 1947 in Wayne Co., Ohio to Myrtis Smith, born 1 Sept. 1912, Cromwell, Kentucky, daughter of John W. Smith and Maudra Render; Donald and Myrtis were divorced; no children.

Donald Wertz married 3rd 27 August 1955 at Canton, Ohio to Cora Marguerite Foutty Soliday, born 2 April 1923, Fly, Monroe Co., Ohio; daughter of George Wesley Foutty and Effie Luella West; two children: Donald Eugene Wertz, born 2 March 1956, Orrville, Ohio; and Ida Luella Wertz, born 24 March 1961, Massillon, Ohio.

OSCAR CLYDE WERTZ and Marie Bachman

Oscar Clyde Wertz, born 20 May 1892, Bauman twp., Wayne Co., Ohio; died 8 Feb. 1972, Rittman, Ohio; son of Winfield Scott Wertz and Ida Bell Tinsler; married 31 Jan. 1916 Columbus, Franklin Co., Ohio to Marie Gertrude Bachman, born 19 April 1897, Adamsville, Ohio; daughter of Herman H. Bachman and Clara Tussing; nine children: Lawrence Dillard, Vernon Dale, Harleth Clyde, Betty Jane, Leonard Byron, Richard Oscar, Dorothy Marie, Roger Roy, and Paul Gilbert Wertz.

1. Lawrence Dillard "Larry" Wertz, born 10 Dec. 1916, Marshalville, Ohio, died 6 Sept. 1973, Wadsworth, Ohio; married 1 Feb. 1941, Wadsworth, Ohio to Doris Marie Berlin, born 30 Dec. 1920, Wadsworth, Ohio; daughter of Loyal Delou Berlin and Savina Bell Oplinger; four children: (1) Bruce James Wertz, born 10 Sept. 1941, Marshallville, Ohio, married 2 Sept. 1967, Rittman, Ohio – a son, Travis James Wertz, born 22 Dec. 1971; (2) Thomas Lee Wertz, born 8 August 1942, Wadsworth, Ohio, married 7 Sept. 1962, Rittman, Ohio to Helen Angela Preattle –two children, Scott Thomas Wertz, born 25 April 1968, and Margaret Marie Wertz, born 14 March 1971; (3) Dolores Ann Wertz, born 15 June 1946, Wadsworth, Ohio, married 6 Nov. 1965 to Paul Dean Shrock; and (4) Bonita Kay Wertz, born 9 June 1947, Marshallville, Ohio, married 7 May 1966 to Danny Charles Stiltner.

2. Vernon Dale Wertz, born 21 Oct. 1918; died 8 April 1919, Marshallville, Ohio.

Oscar and Marie Wertz.

3. Harleth Clyde Wertz, born 17 Feb. 1920, Chippewa twp., Wayne Co., Ohio; married 2 Nov. 1940, Greenup, Kentucky to Opel Francis Burger, born 6 Feb. 1922, Doylestown, Ohio; daughter of Nathan Edward Burger and Gladys Jane Rohrer; seven children: (1) Terry Wayne Wertz, born 26 Oct. 1941, Wadsworth, Ohio, married 18 Sept. 1965, Creston, Ohio to Elaine Dian Nichols — two sons: Ryan Terry Wertz, born 1 March 1967, Wooster, Ohio; and Travix Christian Wertz, born 14 April 1971; (2) James Leonard Wertz, born 16 Jan. 1944, Wadsworth, Ohio, married 3 Sept. 1966 to Carol Louise Juersivich — two children: Timothy James Wertz, born 9 Dec. 1967, Orrville, Ohio; and Connie Ann Wertz, born 20 Feb. 1969, Orrville, Ohio; (3) Karen Lee Wertz, born 4 April 1948; married 20 Jan. 1968, Seville, Ohio to Robert Garfield Armbruster; (4) Robert Clyde Wertz, born 16 Oct. 1951; (5) Kenneth Glen Wertz, born 3 Sept. 1953; (6) Cynthia Sue Wertz, born 21 Oct. 1954; and (7) Michael Nicholas Wertz, born 15 April 1971, Orrville, Ohio.

4. Betty Jane Wertz, born 2 July 1922, Akron, Ohio; married 4 July 1946, Columbus, Ohio to Louis Harley Hinton, born 1 April 1917, Springfield, Ohio, died 15 Oct. 1969; son of Harley David Hinton and Flora Ann Myers; three daughters: Jenice Kay Hinton, born 14 April 1954, Springfield, Ohio; Donna Sue Hinton, born 14 July 1955, Springfield, Ohio; and Sandra Lou Hinton, born 9 May 1957, Springfield, Ohio.

5. Leonard Byron Wertz, born 24 Jan. 1925, Rittman, Ohio; served in the U.S.Navy, was reported "missing in action" on 16 Oct. 1943; officially declared dead on 21 Sept. 1944.

6. Richard Oscar Wertz, born 6 June 1927 at Rittman, Ohio; married 19 August 1949 to Glenna Jean Clapper, born 15 May 1929, North Lawrence, Ohio; daughter of Walter Glenn Clapper and Iris Lillian McFarlin; three children: (1) Theodore Allen Wertz, born 24

October 1950, Wadsworth, Ohio; (2) Pamela Sue Wertz, born 11 April 1954, Wadsworth, Ohio; married 1 Nov. 1975, North Lawrence, Ohio to Jon C. Null; (3) Mark Randal Wertz, born 16 May 1958, Wadsworth, Ohio.

7. **Dorothy Marie Wertz**, born 8 August 1929, Rittman, Ohio; married 1st 28 Nov. 1947, Marshallville, Ohio to **Richard Burrell Galehouse**, born 29 August 1926, Marshallville, Ohio; son of Daniel Leroy Galehouse and Florence Louise Waygandt; five children: (1) Sheryl Lynn Galehouse, born 9 Sept. 1948, married 21 Oct. 1967 to Melvin J. Miller, born 21 June 1943, one daughter - Melanie Marie Miller, born 19 March 1969; (2) Deborah Kay Galehouse, born 18 Dec. 1950, Wooster, Ohio; (3) Kim Eric Galehouse, born 7 April 1953, Orrville, Ohio; (4) Michelle Ann Galehouse, born 28 Feb. 1955, Orrville, Ohio; and (5) Tim David Galehouse, born 21 Oct. 1957, Orrville. Dorothy and Richard divorced Nov. 1965; and Dorothy married 2nd **Mr. Joseph** of Niles, Ohio.

8. **Roger Roy Wertz**, born 29 Oct. 1931, Rittman, Ohio; married 7 Feb. 1953, Smithville, Ohio to Dottie Marie Goody, born 18 Nov. 1935, WhiteCreek, West Virginia; daughter of Charley Goody and Ruth Jane Fowler; two children: Vickey Lynn Wertz, born 9 Jan. 1956, Wadsworth, Ohio, married 29 June 1974, Marshallville, Ohio to Don Allen Jameson; and Christopher Allen Wertz, born 7 Dec. 1959, Wadsworth, Ohio.

9. **Paul Gilbert Wertz**, born 5 June 1936, Rittman, Ohio; married 8 Feb. 1958 at Marshallville, Ohio to Catharine Jane McClain, born 8 Dec. 1936, Roane Co., West Virginia; daughter of Howard Franklin McClain and Lydia Kathryn Moss; three children: Melinda Joyce Wertz, born 8 Nov. 1959, Wadsworth, Ohio; Elizabeth Marie Wertz, born 24 May 1964, Wadsworth, Ohio; and Stephanie Jane Wertz, born 13 Nov. 1967, Barberton, Ohio.

HAROLD SCOTT WERTZ and Ruth Edmonds

Harold Scott Wertz, born 25 March 1896, Marshallville, Ohio; son of Winfield Scott Wertz and Ida Bell Tinsler; married 5 Jan. 1923, Wooster, Wayne Co., Ohio to Ruth Evelyn Edmonds, born 29 March 1902, Cleveland, Ohio; daughter of Byron High Edmonds and Eve Anne Royer; three children: Ida Evelyn, Vernon Floyd, and Miriam Lavonne Wertz.

1. Ida Evelyn Wertz, born 13 Oct. 1923, Wooster, Wayne Co., Ohio; married 11 Oct. 1940, Greenup, Kentucky to Allen Henry Cunningham, born 20 June 1917, Coleville, Washington; son of Proctor Cunningham and Cora May Shelt; seven children, all born at Marshallville, Ohio: (1) Daryl Wayne Cunningham, born 25 Sept. 1941, married, two children; (2) Carolyn Sue Cunningham, born 5 August 1943, married, two children; (3) Bruce Allen Cunningham, born 29 Oct. 1944, married, three children; (4) Harold Lee Cunningham, born 23 Oct. 1949; (5) Lois Evelyn Cunningham, born 25 Dec. 1950; (6) Kenneth Ray Cunningham, born 30 June 1956; and (7) Brent David Cunningham, born 14 Jan. 1963.

2. Vernon Floyd Wertz, born 14 Sept. 1925, Wooster, Ohio; married 29 August 1948, Dalton, Ohio to Margaret Mae Weisgarber, born 7 Feb. 1929, Massillon, Ohio; daughter of Raymond Ralph Weisgarber and Clarissa Grace Keller; six children: (1) Raymond Scott Wertz, born 1 July 1949, Massillon, Stark Co., Ohio; married 24 July 1976, Wayne Co., Ohio to Kathryn May Reichert; (2) Keith Allen Wertz, born 30 Jan. 1952, Orrville, Wayne Co., Ohio; (3) Gloria Jean Wertz, born 30 Sept. 1955, Orrville; (4) Wesley Vernon Wertz, born 4 Feb. 1960, Orrville; (5) Stanley Wayne Wertz, born 4 Nov. 1963, Orrville; and (6) Merlin Dean Wertz, born 31 Oct. 1964, Orrville, Wayne Co., Ohio.

3. Miriam Lavonne Wertz, born 23 March 1929, Marshallville, Wayne Co., Ohio; married 6 June

1948, Marshallville to Calvin Jearl Karlen, born 5 June 1926, Pickens, West Virginia; son of Delphia George Karlen and Ann Florence Sharp; four children: (1) Ila Jean Karlen, born 10 Oct. 1950, Wooster, married, one son; (2) Beth Ann Karlen, born 7 Jan. 1953, Wooster, married; (3) Eva Kay Karlen, born 6 Sept. 1954, Orrville; and (4) Jearl Wayne Karlen, born 1 Dec. 1958, Orrville, married.

RAYMOND A. BAER and Maude Eva Wertz

Maude Eva Wertz, born 4 May 1898, Marshallville, Ohio; married 27 Nov. 1918, Wooster, Ohio to Raymond Andrew Baer, born 23 August 1893, Marshallville, Ohio; son of Elmer Ellsworth Baer and Mary Graber; seven children: Wilmer Dale, Helen Lucille, Pearl Catherine, Ruth Eileen, Lester Raymond, Russell Winfield, and Larry Elmer Baer.

1. Wilmer Dale Baer, born 1 May 1920, Marshallville, Baughman twp., Wayne Co., Ohio; married 24 August 1941, Kidron, Ohio to Nettie Elizabeth Long, born 7 Oct. 1917, Peru, Indiana; daughter of Maxwell Long and Della Clara Brubaker; three children: Judith Ann Baer, born 3 Oct. 1942, married, two children; Karen Elizabeth Baer, born 6 April 1946, married; and Robert Michael Baer, born 18 May 1950, Wooster, Ohio.

2. Helen Lucille Baer, born 15 August 1921, near Marshallville; married 21 August 1939 Kernstown, Virginia to Ralph William Brown, born 3 May 1917, Stone Creek, Ohio; son of John Daniel Brown and Rozetta Julia Ott; four children: (1) Mary Helen Brown, born 11 April 1940, married, two children; (2) John Raymond Brown, born 20 Sept. 1943, married, two children; (3) Ruth Ann Brown, born 12 March 1946, married, two children; and (4) Robert William Brown, born 30 July 1952, Orrville.

3. Pearl Catharine Baer, born 19 Nov. 1923, near Marshallville; married 17 Sept. 1943,

Biloxi, Mississippi to Charles Emil Berlin, born 6 Feb. 1919, Wadsworth, Ohio; son of Loyal Delu Berlin and Sabina Bell Oplinger; five children: (1) Janet Pearl Berlin, born 1 Jan. 1946, married, one daughter; (2) Daniel Charles Berlin, born 29 Nov. 1947, married; (3) Jeanne Ann Berlin, born 28 Feb. 1953; (4) John Eric Berlin, born 3 March 1958; and (5) Jeffry Allen Berlin, born 4 April 1966.

4. Ruth Eileen Baer, born 18 Dec. 1924, near Marshallville; married 18 Feb. 1943, Marshallville to Lewis Henry Beech, born 13 August 1921, Massillon, Ohio; son of John Michael Beech and Carrie Lewis; three children: Constance Ruth Beech, born 10 Aug. 1945, Key West, Florida; Kathleen Lou Beech, born 7 Feb. 1953, Millersburg, Ohio; and Lewis Henry Beech Jr., born 25 June 1955, Millersburg, Ohio.

5. Lester Raymond Baer, born 20 June 1928, near Marshallville; died single on 25 Feb. 1974, Apple Creek, Ohio.

6. Russell Winfield Baer, born 31 July 1931, near Marshallville; married 9 Sept. 1959 in Fredericksburg, Ohio to Margaret Lucille Spencer, born 9 August 1931, Fredericksburg; daughter of Heber Spencer and Mary Kerr; four children, all born Orrville, Ohio: (1) James Edward Baer, born 5 May 1967; (2) Linda Sue Baer, born 28 August 1968; (3) Eva Jane Baer, born 28 May 1970; and (4) Thomas Raymond Baer, born 12 February 1975, Orrville, Ohio.

7. Larry Elmer Baer, born 24 Oct. 1940, near Marshallville; married 20 June 1964, Orrville to Roberta Francis Rutter, daughter of Robert Ray Rutter and Fern May Singer; three children, all born at Orrville: Shawn Michael Baer, born 21 May 1965; Heath Allen Baer, born 2 Sept. 1966; and Robyn Lynn Baer, born 1 May 1970, Orrville, Ohio.

JAY B. RUDY and Ida Pearle Wertz

Ida Pearle Wertz, born 9 Feb. 1902, Marshallville; died 9 Dec. 1971, Orrville; daughter of Winfield Scott Wertz and Ida Bell Tinsler; married 5 June 1923, Dalton, Ohio to Jay Buckwalter Rudy, born 8 March 1900, Dalton, died 1 March 1956, Cleveland, Ohio; son of Jacob B. Rudy and Mary Buckwalter; two sons: Dennis Dale, and Kenneth Jay Rudy.

1. Dennis Dale Rudy, born 11 March 1927, New Philadelphia, Ohio; married 27 June 1948, New Philadelphia to Beverly Jeanne Fritche, born 14 Nov. 1926, Bellaire, Ohio; daughter of Charles Henry Fritche and Wilma Mae Thorpe; four children: (1) Steven Dale Rudy, born 5 August 1949, New Philadelphia, Ohio; (2) Debra Ann Rudy, born 12 August 1952, Wilmington, Delaware; (3) Cynthia Jean Rudy, born 27 Nov. 1954, Wilmington, Delaware; and (4) Rebecca Gaye Rudy, born 13 Dec. 1956, Wilmington.

2. Kenneth Jay Rudy, born 28 March 1930, New Philadelphia, Ohio; married 29 June 1952, Marion, Ohio to Mary Helen Buckingham, born 6 June 1932, Marion, Ohio; daughter of Roy Clifford Buckingham and Grace Verhea Adams; two children: Cheryl Kay Rudy, born 3 May 1954, Marion, Ohio; and Jay Brian Rudy, born 14 March 1957, Cochocton, Ohio.

ROBERT CLAIR WERTZ and Helen Weaver

Robert Clair "Sonny" Wertz, born 3 Sept. 1906, Marshallville, Wayne Co., Ohio; died 24 August 1964, Orrville, Wayne Co., Ohio; son of Winfield Scott Wertz and Ida Bell Tinsler; married 1st on 18 Dec. 1923 to Helen Lucille Weaver, born 26 Feb. 1907, Benton, Ohio; daughter of Jonas J. Weaver and Mary Belle Snyder; one son: Robert Clair Wertz Jr.

1. Robert Clair Wertz Jr., born 27 June 1924, Marshallville; married 1st Pearl Amelia Kurtz, born 27 Sept. 1916, Wellington, Ohio; died 13

May 1967, Wooster, Ohio; daughter of Archie Kurtz and Alice Belle Ray; one daughter: Clair L. Wertz, born 1950. Robert Clair Wertz Jr. married 2nd 13 Sept. 1969, Holmesville, Ohio to Marcella McCullough Nolan, born 14 Oct. 1917, Millersburg, Ohio; daughter of Warren McCullough and Sarah Gey; no children.

ROBERT CLAIR WERTZ and Genevieve Taylor

Robert Clair Wertz and Helen Lucille Weaver were divorced May 1929; and Robert married 2nd 23 March 1931, Akron, Summit Co., Ohio to Genevieve Taylor, born 8 June 1910, Akron, Ohio; died 8 Aug. 1954, Barberton, Ohio; daughter of George S. Taylor and Charlotte Caroline Stovel; five children: Shirley Ann, Martha Gene, Evelyn May, David Clair, and John Winfield Wertz.

2. Shirley Ann Wertz, born 28 Jan. 1934, Marshallville, Chippewa twp., Wayne Co., Ohio; m. 7 June 1953, Dalton, Ohio to Harold Wayne Hauenstein, born 26 May 1933, Dalton, Ohio; son of Carl Oliver Hauenstein and Mary Wilma Edie; four children, all born at Orrville, Ohio: (1) Constance Sue Hauenstein, born 22 Nov. 1953; (2) Dean Allen Hauenstein, born 17 August 1956; (3) Richard Wayne Hauenstein, born 18 Nov. 1960; and (4) Annette Faye Hauenstein, born 21 June 1963, Orrville, Ohio.

3. Martha Gene Wertz, born 21 March 1936, Marshallville; married 4 March 1956, Marshallville to James Harry Wilson, born 10 Oct. 1935, Wayne Co., Ohio; son of Ashley Earl Wilson and Evelyn Blanche Waters; three children: (1) Vicky Sue Wilson, born 30 June 1959, Camp Irvin, California; (2) Genevieve Louise Wilson, born 27 Feb. 1963, Wooster, Ohio; and (3) Ernest James Wilson, born 30 June 1968, Wooster, Ohio.

4. Evelyn May Wertz, born 22 June 1938, Marshallville; m. 30 August 1958, Doylestown, Ohio to Mathew Joseph Kramer, born 31 May 1934

Barberton, Ohio; son of Matthew Lecas Kramer and Josephine Agnus; three children: (1) Matthew John Kramer, born 13 Sept. 1959, Marshallville; (2) Mary Jo Kramer, born 15 August 1960, Marshallville; and (3) Marie Kay Kramer, born 12 Feb. 1964, Burbank, Ohio.

5. **David Clair Wertz,** born 17 Dec. 1940, Wayne Co., Ohio; married 14 June 1958, Ashland, Ohio to Mary Irene Brown, born 6 March 1942, Orrville, Ohio; daughter of Clayton Oliver Brown and Margaret Vernell Zaugg; three sons, all born at Orrville, Ohio: (1) David Robert Wertz, born 22 Dec. 1958; (2) Rodney Dean Wertz, born 30 July 1960; and (3) James Lee Wertz, born 25 Nov. 1963, Orrville, Ohio.

6. **John Winfield Wertz,** born 29 Jan. 1944, Marshallville; m. 29 Feb. 1964 Wadsworth, Ohio to Sharon Sue Carpenter, born 9 Dec. 1946, Spencer, West Virginia; daughter of Lacoe James Carpenter and Dorothy Frances Reynolds; two children: (1) Cynthia Louise Wertz, born 25 June 1964, Orrville; and (2) Cari Lynn Wertz, born 7 Sept. 1967, Barberton, Ohio.

Robert Clair "Sonny" Wertz, married 3rd on 17 Sept. 1955, Canton, Ohio to Wilma Almeda Brown Henning, born 1 July 1908, Massillon, Ohio; daughter of William A. Brown and Clara E. Kuhns; no children.

ROLANDUS M. GARN and Viola May Wertz

Viola May "Lo" Wertz, born 29/30 May 1864/9, Funk, Ohio; died 20 July 1937, Honeytown, East Union twp., Wayne Co., Ohio; daughter of Jacob Wertz and Charlotte Austen; married 14 May 1885, Wayne Co., Ohio (E) to Ronandus or **Rolandus "Land" Milton Garn,** born 7 Oct. 1864, Reedsburg, Ohio; died 17 Oct. 1944; son of Henry Garn and Sarah Ewing; four children, all born at Reedsburg, Ohio: Ralph Rosco, Blanche Naomi, Jay Henry, and Park Albert Garn.

1. Ralph Rosco Garn, born 15 March 1888; died 28 Jan. 1978, Wooster, Ohio; married 17 Nov. 1915, Orrville, Ohio to Mayone "Mayme" Charlotte Huntsberger, born 8 March 1894, Dalton, Ohio; died 16 June 1959, Orrville; daughter of Abraham Huntsberger and Mary Brennamin; one daughter: Betty Irene Garn, born 8 August 1925, Dalton; married 12 Oct. 1947 to Leo Wilbur Leffel, born 5 Dec. 1925, North Manchester, Ohio; son of Walter Leffel and Blanche Lautzenheiser; two children: Lorin Jay Leffel, born 8 July 1956, Wooster; and Jedd Melvin Leffel, born 17 Oct. 1962, Wabash, Indiana.

2. Blanche Naomi Garn, born 16 Feb. 1981; married 1st 19 June 1909, Wooster to Franklin Earl Shelly, born 1 April 1884, Apple Creek, Franklin twp., Ohio; died 16 Sept. 1919, Akron, Ohio; son of Joseph Shelly and Rebecca Eberts; two children: (1) Stanley Garn Shelly, born 27 Nov. 1910, married, no children; and (2) Lucille Esther Shelley, born 1 July 1911, married, one son. Blanche married 2nd 19 Dec. 1924 to Benjamin Franklin McCann, born 28 May 1881, Bradford, Penn.; died 17 April 1949, Wooster; son of Franklin McCann and Anna Aletha Collins. No children.

3. Jay Henry Garn, born 12 May 1895, died 9 May 1971, Cuyahoga Falls, Ohio; married 1st, 24 Dec. 1918, Wooster, Ohio to Bessie Jean Carson, born 19 March 1889, Wayne twp., Wayne Co., Ohio; died 26 May 1923, Smithville, Ohio; two children: an unnamed son, born and died 1922, Smithville, Ohio; and Bessie Jean Garn, born 26 May 1923, Smithville.
Jay married 2nd 12 June 1929, to Mrs. Daisy Mae First Overholt, born 30 May 1905, Wooster, daughter of George W. First and Ida E. Cordray; no children.

4. Park Albert Garn, born 9 March 1900, Reedsburg, Ohio. Never married.

JAMES B. SNYDER and Sarah Ellen Wertz

Sarah Ellen Wertz, born 10/11 June 1866, Funk, Ohio, died 29 July 1940, Farmington, Michigan; daughter of Jacob Wertz and Charlotte Austen; married 22 Dec. 1887, Wayne Co., Ohio to James Buchanan Snyder, born 27 Dec. 1856, Ashland Co., Ohio; died 1 May 1937, Farmington, Mich.; son of Henry Snyder and Sarah Ann Black; one son: Floyd Lozene Snyder, born 24 Sept. 1888, Green twp., Ashland Co., Ohio; died 10 March 1974, Ormond, Florida; married 19 April 1919, Detroit, Michigan to Grace Kent Fisher, born 1898; died in 1977, Ormond Beach, Florida; three children: (1) Roy Wilbert Snyder, born 14 Feb. 1924, married, two children; (2) Joyce Beverly Snyder, born 21 Jan. 1929, married and divorced twice; (3) Cynthia Lee Snyder, born 28 Nov. 1947, married.

THOMAS GRANT WERTZ and Lillie Mae Swain

Thomas Grant Wertz, born 18 Oct. 1868, Funk, Wayne Co., Ohio; died 3 Nov. 1950, Funk; son of Jacob Wertz and Charlotte Austin; married 1 April 1900, MaZena, Ashland Co., Ohio to Lella Mae "Lillie" or "Lilly" Swain, born 1 Nov. 1881, Susten, Wayne Co., Ohio; died 4 May 1976, age 95 years, Ashland, Ohio; daughter of Matthew Elder Swain and Susanna Kiser; seven children: Ethel I., Ora Earl, Howard Jacob, Edna Leora, Thomas Grant, Doris Mae, and Clyde Dale Wertz, all born at Funk, Ohio.

1. Ethel I. Wertz, born 6 Feb. 1901; married 28 Jan. 1922, Wayne Co., Ohio to Dewey H. Otto, born 18 August 1898, Lakefork, Ashland Co., Ohio; died 21 April 1970, Funk, Ohio; son of George Lee Otto and Ida Stull; two daughters: (1) Imogene LaVaughn Otto, born 2 Nov. 1922, married 12 Nov. 1943, Shreve, Ohio to Robert Donald Murphy, born 3 Jan. 1920, Roscoe, Ohio; one daughter - Robin Jeanne Otto Murphy, born 29 April 1954, Ashland, Ohio; and (2) Dolores Irene Otto, born 28 June 1936, Wayne Co., Ohio; m. 26 June 1955, Ashland,

Ohio to David Cortland Johnston, born 2 April 1935, Ashland; son of David S. Johnston, and Doris Dilgard; two children — Larry David Johnston, born 24 Oct. 1957; and Sherry Lee Johnston, born 30 May 1961.

2. Ora Earl Wertz, born 4 July 1902, Funk, Ohio; married 14 June 1924, Mansfield, Ohio to Glenna May Elizabeth Seigfried, born 3 July 1905, McZena, Ashland Co., Ohio; daughter of Sylvester Joseph Seigfried and Ida Margaret Fisher; one son: Kenneth Eugene Wertz, born 7 Dec. 1930, Funk, Ohio; married 3 Aug. 1957, Kent, Ohio to Nancy Ann Barton, born 31 July 1931, Reedsburg, Ohio; daughter of Milton J. Barton and Kathryn Mowrey; one son — Eric Eugene Wertz, born 6 Sept. 1964, Akron, Ohio.

3. Howard Jacob Wertz, born 14 Oct. 1904, Funk, Ohio; died 15 Oct. 1905, age 1 year and 1 day, at Funk, Wayne Co., Ohio.

4. Edna Leora Wertz, born 21 Oct. 1905, Funk, Ohio; m.7 Nov. 1928, Nova, Ohio to Bruce Moody Seibert,born 14 Dec. 1901, Jeromesville, Ohio; son of Benjamin Franklin Seibert and Emma Jane Spaid; four children: (1) Thomas Dale Seibert, born 6 Sept. 1929, married, two children; (2) Janet Darlene Seibert, born 9 April 1935, married twice, one daughter; (3) Theodore Deane Seibert, born 31 March 1937, married, three children; (4) Judy Anne Seibert, born 12 April 1941, married, four children.

5. Thomas Grant Wertz, Jr., born 27 April 1909, Funk, Ohio; died 13 Feb. 1948, Ashland, Ohio; married 5 Oct. 1935 to Lois Marie Hendee, born 28 June 1914, Sullivan, Ohio; daughter of Ernest Alanzo Hendee and Alta Emmer Giar; one daughter: Julia Ann Wertz, born 17 July 1936, Ashland, Ohio; m. 5 August 1956, Ashland to Edward Darrell Skaggs, born 20 April 1935; son of Howard Thomas Skaggs and Verna Hart; nine children, the first eight born at Sundusky, Ohio: (1) Connie Sue Skaggs, born 2 July 1957; (2) Cindy Lou Skaggs, born 7

146

Oct. 1958; (3) Darrell Dean Skaggs, born 21
Feb. 1960; (4) Christine Marie Skaggs, born 22
August 1961; (5) Barbara Ann Skaggs, born 5
Dec. 1963; (6) Diane Carol Skaggs, born 1 Jan.
1966; (7) John Mark Skaggs, born 13 Nov. 1967;
(8) Linda Lee Skaggs, born 25 July 1969; and
(9) Rachel Kay Skaggs, born 1972, Huron, Ohio.

6. Doris Mae Wertz, born 8 Oct. 1911, Funk,
Ohio; married 19 June 1929, Wayne Co., Ohio to
Ray William Black, born 29 May 1908, near
Jeromesville, Ohio; son of George Wilson Black
and Emma Loretta Rush; one son: Clayton Dennis
Black, born 16 May 1933; married 1 Sept. 1951,
Mansfield, Ohio to Patricia Lou Foote, born 28
March 1934, Mansfield, daughter of Roy E.
Foote and Bessie Vivian Peters; two children—
Dennis William Black, born 30 May 1952,
Mansfield, Ohio; and Brenda Lynne Black, born
1 May 1957, Modesto, California.

7. Clyde Dale "Jack" Wertz, born 11 Sept.
1914, Funk, Ohio; married 26 Oct. 1950 to
Nellie Robinson Eskey, born 8 Dec. 1906; died
2 April 1977, Wayne Co., Ohio; daughter of
Charles D. Robinson and Mary Catherine Rogers;
no children.

PETER C. RICH and Clara Anna Wertz

Clara Anna Wertz, born 15 Sept. 1870, Funk,
Ohio; died 8 Jan. 1934, Wooster, Ohio;
daughter of Jacob Wertz and Charlotte Austen;
married 14 May 1891 to Peter Christian Rich,
born 10 August 1870, Green twp., Wayne Co.,
Ohio, died 1 Oct. 1936, Wooster; son of
Christian Rich and Catherine Roush; three
children: Hazel Charlotte, Rosco Wertz, and
Honor Clyde Rich.

1. Hazel Charlotte Rich, born 21 Dec. 1893,
Plain twp., Wayne Co., Ohio; died 28 Sept.
1969, Ashland; m. 10 May 1910 Wooster, Ohio to
George P. Buckingham, born 26 Jan. 1891,
Rowsburgh, Ashland Co., Ohio; died Jan. 1950,
Rittman, Ohio; son of Charles B. Buckingham

147

and Cora Morret; one son: Weldon Clyde Buckingham, born 24 Dec. 1910, Wayne Co., Ohio; married 19 June 1932, Ashland, Ohio to Helen Marie Gillespie, born 11 Oct. 1907, West Salem, Ohio; daughter of B.F.Gillespie and Mary Jane Repp; two daughters — Mary Ann Buckingham, born 29 Sept. 1934; and Jane Marie Buckingham,born 17 August 1942, Ashland, Ohio. Hazel married 2nd 18 April 1951, Ashland, Ohio to Horace Vinton Nelson, born 2 Sept. 1888, Ashland; died 16 Dec. 1960; son of Charles M. Nelson and Lorelda Wertman; no children.

2. Rosco Wertz Rich, born 9 Sept. 1902, Milton twp., Wayne Co., Ohio; died 13 Sept. 1959, Wooster; married 29 Nov. 1928, Wooster to Florence Estella Gerstenslager, born 25 April 1905; daughter of Henry Gerstenslager and Jennie Galehouse; three daughters: (1) Janet Elizabeth Rich, born 18 Nov. 1936, married, one daughter; (2) June Elaine Rich, born 15 May 1941, married, three children; and (3) Marilyn Kaye Rich, born 27 August 1942.

3. Honor Clyde Rich, born 7 Dec. 1907, Reedsburg, Ohio; died 23 Jan. 1957, Tuscon, Arizona; married 19 Nov. 1939, Wooster, Ohio to Frieda Elizabeth Zemrock, born 26 July 1916, Pittsburg, Penn.; daughter of Michael Zemrock and Ottillia Olsen; one son, born and died 25 February 1942.

WILLIAM W. BELL and Nettie I. Wertz

Nettie Irine or Ieren Wertz, born 20 May 1872/3, Funk,Ohio; died 20 May 1954, Michigan; daughter of Jacob Wertz and Charlotte Austen; married 24 March 1897, Lakefort, Ohio to William W. Bell, born 7 Nov. 1871, Holmes Co., Ohio; died 15 Oct. 1952, Ann Arbor, Washtenaw Co., Michigan; son of William D. and Anna Bell; one son: Ray Denver Bell, born 25 Feb. 1902, Wayne Co., Ohio; died 9 Oct. 1956, Novi, Michigan; married 1st 26 June 1920, Detroit, Michigan to Edna A. Draper; four children: (1) Winifred Edna Bell, born 24 April 1921, m.,

two children; (2) Ray Denver Bell, born 1 May
1923; (3) Donna June Bell, born 22 Feb. 1925;
and (4) Duane Eugene Bell, born 11 May 1927,
married, four children. Ray Denver Bell,
married 2nd 16 May 1942, Napoleon, Ohio to
Mrs. Flossie Ellen McEvers Townsbell, born 22
June 1907; daughter of William Albert McEvers
and Edna Cordella Alexander; one son: Ronald
Alvin Bell, born 13 Sept. 1945.

JOSIAH WERTZ and MARY AUSTEN

Josiah Wertz, born 9 Dec. 1832, died 16 April
1884; son of Jonathan Wertz and Polly Null;
married 28 Feb. 1854, Wayne Co., Ohio (E) to
Mary Austin/Austen, born 9 Nov. 1833; died 16
March 1884; ten children: Harrison, Colesta,
Austin, Mary Etta, Rose, Ambrose, Nathan,
Charlotte, William D., and Estelle Ethel.

1. Harrison Wertz, born June 1855; died 12
June 1861.

2. Colesta Wertz, born 15 Dec. 1856; married a
Mr. Simon; lived Ohio.

3. Austin Wertz, born 28 Nov. 1858; lived in
Ohio. Possibly the Austin Wertz married 3 July
1884, Medina Co., Ohio to Amanda Butarf (E).

4. Mary Etta Wertz, born 10 March 1860;
married a Mr. Baker; lived Ohio.

5. Rose or Rosella (E) Wertz, born 18 April
1862/3; married 19 Oct. 1882, Wayne Co., Ohio
to John Hoffelfenger or Heffelfinger (E).
Lived at Mansfield, Ohio.

6. Ambrose Wertz, born 15 Oct. 1865; lived
Ohio. Possibly the Ambrose Wertz m. 25 Oct.
1881, Auglaize Co., Ohio to Catherine Viet.(E)

7. Nathan Wertz, born 29 Dec. 1867; lived Ashland, Ohio.

8. Charlotte Wertz, born 13 Jan. 1870; married a Mr. Younker; lived Ohio.

9. William D. Wertz, born 25 March 1873; lived Ohio.

10. Estelle Ethel Wertz, born 26 April 1875; married a Mr. Gest; lived Cleveland, Ohio.

SUSANNAH WERTZ and JOHN BAKER SR.

Susannah Wertz, born 22 Sept. 1785, Franklin Co., Penn.; died 12 Sept. 1863, age 77 years, 11 months, 21 days; Washington twp., Richland Co., Ohio; buried at Crawford Farm Cemetery, Wash. twp., Richland Co., Ohio; an 1840 quit claim deed executed in Richland Co., Ohio and on file in Franklin Co., Penn. shows Susannah and her husband John Baker signing off their interest in the estate of "John Wertz deceased of the township of Washington now Quincy and County of Franklin and State of Penn." in favor of her brother, Frederick Wertz. This deed seems to prove that Susannah was in fact a daughter of John Wertz, 1742/3-1815. Other Hoover (Huber) records (CC) indicate that John Wertz possibly married Christena or Christiana Hoover, a daughter of John Hoover and Mary Watson. However complete proof that this Christena Hoover Wertz was the mother of Jacob, Frederick, and/or Susannah is lacking.

Susannah Wertz, 1785-1863, married by 1806/7, undoubtedly in Franklin Co., Penn. to John Baker, born 17 Oct. 1780, Franklin Co., Penn.; died 2 March 1853, age 72 years, 4 months, 13 days, Washington twp., Richland Co., Ohio; bur. Crawford Farm Cemetery. They had eleven children, the first six born in Franklin Co., Penn.: Christena, Elizabeth, John M., Daniel, Jacob, and Abraham; the last five born in Richland Co., Ohio: David, Isaac/Israel, Peter, and Timothy.

150

Stones of John and Susannah Wertz Baker

Crawford Farm Cemetery, Washington township, Richland County, Ohio; located in Southeast Quarter of Section 27. John Baker, died 2 March 1853, age 72 years, 4 months, 13 days. Susannah Wertz Baker, died 12 Sept. 1863, age 77 years, 11 months, 21 days.

Children of John and Susannah Wertz Baker

1. Christena Baker, b. 17 April 1807; d. 23 July 1870, age 63 y., 3 mo., 29 d.; m. Dec. 1830 to Jacob Andrews. They lived in Wash. twp, Richland Co., Ohio; seven children: John, Susannah, Nancy Frances, Jacob, Andrew Edward, Catherine, and a daughter who died in infancy.

2. Elizabeth "Betsy" Baker, married 17 Nov. 1836 to Daniel Fox.

3. John M. Baker, born 7 Oct. 1810; died 28 Feb. 1892, age 81 years, 3 months, 29 days; married 20 Nov. 1833 to Mary Magdalena Grove.

4. Daniel Baker, born 8 Feb. 1814; died 8 May 1875, age 61 years, 3 months; married 6 April 1837 to Catharine Hoover, daughter of Henry Hoover and Elizabeth Poffenberger; ancestors of Wanda C. Smith (BB).

5. Jacob Baker, born 6 Jan. 1816; died 9 Oct. 1902, age 86 years, 9 months, 3 days; married 23 March 1841 to Lydia Hoover.

6. Abraham "Abram" Baker, born 19 Dec. 1820, Franklin Co., Penn.; died 20 March 1912, age 91 years, 3 months, and 1 day; married 22 March 1849 to Leathea Huffman.

7. Frederick Baker, b. 5 May 1823, Richland Co., Ohio; d. 4 Feb. 1895, age 71 years, 8 mo., 29 days; m. 21 Sept. 1850 to Mary Thrush.

8. David Baker, born 16 July 1825; died 7 Jan. 1887, age 61 years, 5 months, 21 days; married 25 Dec. 1849 to Mariah Clever.

9. Isaac or Israel Baker, b. 1828; died 7 Jan. 1900; m. 13 Nov. 1855 to Lydia Mary Riggle.

10. Peter Baker, born 1831; died 1900; married 21 Dec. 1854 to Salina M. Charles.

11. Timothy Baker; no dates available.

Chapter 6

JOHANN GEORGE WERTZ and CATHERINE STONER

Johann George Wertz, born 31 Jan. 1745, probably in York County, Penn.; died 27 Nov. 1798, age 53 years, 9 months, 27 days, Quincy twp., Franklin Co., Penn.; 5th and youngest child of Hans Jacob Wertz and Anna Barbara Hoff. George Wertz probably married 19 Jan. 1778* to Catherine Stoner, born 27 Sept. 1758; died 16 April 1832, 76 years, 6 months, 19 days. Both are buried at Quincy cemetery. They had eight children: George, David, Jacob, Elizabeth, Barbara, Catherine, Eve, and Maria or Mary Wertz. Note: the date of 19 Jan. 1778* above, is given on the 1915 Chart as Catherine's death date, but she was clearly still living in 1798 when George wrote his will, and her tombstone says she died in 1832. Therefore it is probable that this other date on the chart is their marriage date, but proof is yet lacking.
George Wertz served in the Rev. War, as a Private in the Penn. Line, and is thus listed in the Pennsylvania Archives 3rd Series, Volume 23, page 817. Order of birth of their children is also uncertain, as the order (above) on the chart does not match the order named in George's will. The youngest son, Jacob, born only two and a half years before his father died, according to the dates on the chart, is not named in the will at all.

The will of George Wertz, written 16 July 1798, probated 3 Jan. 1799, and recorded at Chambersburg, Book B, page 67, reads as follows:
"In the name of God, Amen. I, George Wertz of Washington Township in the County of Franklin and State of Pennsylvania, being very sick and weak in body but of sound and perfect mind and memory, do by those present make and publish

this my last Will and Testament in manner and
form following: that is to say first I give
and bequeath unto my beloved wife Catherine
her choice of one of my horse creatures and
choice of one of my cows and my cloth piece
and a shirt and her bed. And I ordain that
the whole of my estate, both real and personal
shall be under my said wife's care so long as
she shall continue my Widow, or until my son
George shall arrive to the age of 21 years and
if then he wishes to enjoy the one half of my
plantation either he, himself, or my Executors
here after mentioned shall apply to the
Orphans Court for the Court to appoint six
proper men to divide my said Plantation in two
as equally as they can and value each part and
allow reasonable time to pay the money to the
rest of my Children in yearly payments and the
one half part where the house and barn is on,
my said son George shall have and the other
half my son David shall have again he arrives
to the age of 21 years, and they, my said
sons, shall hold the same to themselves, their
heirs, and assigns forever as fully and employ
as ever I did in my lifetime, and if my said
wife shall continue my Widow for nine years,
or during her natural life then my said sons
shall build her a sufficient house for her to
live in near the School house land and as
convenient to the Spring as she shall choose,
where she shall have four acres of land, two
acres upland and two acres of meadow, and five
acres of Woodland wherever she shall choose on
my said premisses which she, my wife, may
occupy as she pleases but if she shall marry
again she shall be excluded of the same, and
my personal estate shall be sold by my
executors at public sale, except what I have
herein first bequeathed unto her and each of
my daughters when they marry shall be
furnished out of my estate with one good
feather bed, spinning wheel, shirt, and a good
cow and household furniture at the discretion
of my Executors so that they shall be
furnished all alike, and the piece of Woodland

154

I have in the South Mountain, near Thomas Stoopers, shall be equally divided between my said two sons, George and David, and the same way as my other premisses. And all my children who have not yet got schooling shall be schooled as far as may be necessary and paid out of my estate. And I do hereby appoint my loving wife Catherine Executrix and Frederick Fisher and John Hastner, my trusty friends the executors of this my last will and Testament, and do hereby revoke all former Wills heretofore by me made, in witness whereof I have hereto set my hand and seal the 16th day of July in the year of our Lord 1798." George Wertz signed by mark, and the witnesses were Ludwig Noll, Christian Miller (who wrote their names in German Script) and Samuel Royer.

Following this will is recorded: "Adjacent to the last Will and Testament of George Wertz of Washington Township in County of Franklin, deceased and by an order of the Orphans Court of said County dated 17 Feb. 1809, John Huber, George Cook, James Johnston, John Johnston, Adam Small, and John Boyer are appointed to view, value and divide the lands of the said deceased as mentioned in his Will, between his two sons George Wertz and David Wertz and accordingly we went on the premises on the 17 day June 1809, and we do agree that George Wertz, the older son shall have the one half of said tract of land, including the buildings and improvements it being 12 acres and allowances, etc. (as this day laid off and a plot thereof made) at the sum of 1116 pounds 8 shillings, lawful in Pennsylvania, including his own part or share of said estate, at the yearly payments of $100 until the whole is paid fully up. The first payment to become due on the first day of May next. That David Wertz, the second son shall have the other half of said tract of land (as laid off) and as aforesaid denoted at the sum of 1016 pounds 8 shillings money of record including his own share or part of said estate at the yearly payments of $100 until the whole is fully paid up. The first payment to become due one year after the said David arrives to the full age of 21 years. And we further on the aforesaid day viewed 55 acres and allowances of Mountain Land going on the premises and do value the same at the sum of 80 pounds 18 shillings and nine pence money of record (being paid of said deceased estate) the sum to be equally divided between the two sons of said deceased, George & David Wertz, share and share alike, payments to be made as above directed in proportion as the $100 is to be paid, their own shares included, as above set forth. These are the valuations we make and the payments agreeable to said deceased's last Will, not taking into notice anything about the Widow's thirds or dowry which if she obtains these as options are that allowance ought to be made agreeable to what she received unto the aforesaid two sons of said deceased. In witness whereof we have hereunto set our hands and seals 17 day June 1807." Signed by John Huber, Geo. Cook, John Boyer, James Johnston, John Johnston, and Adam Small. All of them signing in German.

CHILDREN OF GEORGE AND CATHERINE WERTZ

1. Elizabeth Wertz, killed by a runaway team at age of 71 years; m. Michael Emminger; they had nine children: Ephraim, John, Michael, Margaret, Susan Ann, Barbara Elizabeth, Catherine, Marie, and Elizabeth. Outline of this family begins on the next page.

2. Barbara Wertz, m.John (DD) or Henry Keyler Kyler/Keeler or Kiler (DD); nine children: Jacob, Rudolph, Elizabeth, Jerry, Abraham, Lydia, Martha, Susan, and Henry Keyler Jr. Outline of this family begins on page 159.

3. George Wertz, born 8 Nov. 1785; died 2 Oct. 1805; married Catherine Emerick; at least eleven children: Martha Lana, Peter, George, Lewis, Henry, David, Charles, Jacob Augustus, Susan E., James Luther, and William Wertz. Outline of this family begins on page 160.

4. Catherine Wertz, m. Frederick Fisher; nine children: Francis, Sarah, Elias, Lydia, Frederick, Catherine, Amos, Elisa, and Belinda Fisher. This family begins on page 167.

5. David Wertz, b. 12 Nov. 1789; d. 17 Sept. 1866 (G); m. Elizabeth Emerick, born 15 Sept. 1793; died 19 July 1848 (G); both buried in Quincy Cemetery; six children: Matilda, Solomon, David Aaron, John Edwin, Catherine, and Hiram Emrick Wertz. Outline of this family begins on page 169.

6. Eve Wertz, b. 12 October 1793; d, 18 May 1880; m. John Bushman or Busman(DD); seven children: Margaret, Jacob, Catherine, Solomon, John, Henry, and Frederick Bushman. Outline of this family begins on page 170.

7. Jacob Wertz, born 2 May 1796; died 4 May 1877; married Margaret "Polly" Labe/Loeb/Lorb, born 1807; died 1869; both buried in Quincy Cemetery (G); three children: S. John Wertz, Augustus Luther Wertz, and Susanna Wertz. Outline of this family is on page 172.

8. Maria or Mary Wertz, married Henry Cordell; five children: Joseph, David, Samuel, Jacob, and Henry Cordell Jr. Outline of this family begins on page 173.

MICHAEL EMMINGER and ELIZABETH WERTZ

Elizabeth Wertz was probably born by 1780 (if her sixth child was born by 1814, see below.); she was killed by a runaway team at the age of 71 years; daughter of George Wertz and Catherine Stoner; married Michael Emminger; they had nine children:

1. Ephraim Emminger, died in Butler Co., Penn. leaving a family, but data on them is unknown.

2. John Emminger, died unmarried.

3. Michael Emminger, died unmarried.

4. Margaret Emminger, married John Renno or
Reneau; nine children: (1) Michael Renno, had
four children: Albert, Cora, Carrie, and
Catherine; (2) Regina Renno married Mr.
Elbel(?), lived Preston, Penn.; (3) Rebecca
Renno married Mr. Brink; (4) Mary Renno
married Mr. Burdette; (5) Elizabeth Renno
married Mr. Park, lived Pittsburgh, Penn.; (6)
Rose C. Renno, married Mr. Goodrich, lived in
Chicago, Illinois; (7) John Renno, died
without heirs; (8) Adam Renno; and (9) George
Renno, who also had nine children: Ida May,
Margaret, Alma, Emma, Rosamund(?), George,
Edward, Frederick, and James Goodrich Renno.

5. Susan Ann Emminger, married Mr. Weisman,
and had six children: (1) Henry Weisman; (2)
Mary Weisman, married Mr. Hamelton, lived at
Butler, Penn.; (3) Catherine Weisman, married
Mr. Haslet(?) and had four children: Mary,
Emma, Charles, and Bert Haslet; (4) Susan
Weisman; (5) Lena Weisman, married Mr. Roung;
and (6) Christina Weisman.

6. Barbara Elizabeth Emminger, born 1813/4;
married Mr. Smith, five children: (1) Henry M.
Smith, born June 1836, died 1865, unmarried;
(2) Charles F. Smith, born 2 Feb. 1838/9,
married Mary --?--, lived Penn.; (3) George W.
Smith, born 4 April 1841, died 8 May 1911,
unmarried; (4) Jacob C. Smith, born 25 Sept.
1850(?), unmarried; (5) Peter A. Smith, born
11 August 1856(?), married Ella(?) Anthony(?).

7. Catherine Emminger, married Mr. Zimmerman,
four children: (1) Jacob Zimmerman; (2)
Margaret Zimmerman, died unmarried; (3) Philip
Zimmerman; and (4) Annie Zimmerman, married
Mr. Wintard(?).

8. Marie Emminger, married Mr. Storm.

9. Elizabeth Emminger, married Mr. Miller,
moved to Ohio; family unknown.

HENRY KEYLER and BARBARA WERTZ

Barbara Wertz, probably born about 1782 (if her youngest child was born in 1818); daughter of George Wertz and Catherine Stoner; married Henry Keyler/Kyler/Keeler; nine children:

1. Jacob Keyler, died unmarried.

2. Rudolph Keyler, married Miss Null, family unknown.

3. Elizabeth Keylor. *

4. Jerry Keylor, died unmarried.

5. Abraham Keylor, died before 1915, left three children, names unknown.

6. Lydia Keylor, married Jacob Emminger, moved to Mansfield, Ohio; had four children: (1) Catherine Emminger, married Luther Garver, lived Wichita, Kansas; (2) James Emminger, died before 1915; (3) and (4) names unknown.

7. Martha Keylor. *

8. Susan Keylor. *

* One of the Keylor girls married George Riel.

9. Henry Keylor Jr., born 7 July 1818, married Mary Jane Cook, born 26 Aug. 1829, died 4 April 1893; seven children: (1) Eldridge V. Keyler, born 22 May 1850, married, lived Union Star, Missouri; (2) Francis Ashbury Keyler, born 21 Sept. 1851, died before 1915; (3) Elizabeth Keyler, born 31 May 1854, died before 1915; married Sprankle(?) Snyder, three children: Lee Roy Snyder, who lived in Alberta, Canada; Samuel Snyder; and Mural Snyder; (4) Wynette(?) Keyler, born 6 July 1857, died 2 Feb. 1875; (5) William S. Keyler, born 4 Sept. 1859, unmarried, lived Wagner, Colorado or California; (6) Anna Eliza Keyler, born 26 Jan. 1863, married Emmett F. Sanborn,

born 1 Oct. 1856, lived Alberta, Canada; and
(7) Mary Ida Keyler, born 9 Feb. 1867, lived
Fort Plazy(?), Colorado.

GEORGE WERTZ and CATHERINE EMERICK

George Wertz, b. 8 Nov. 1785 (chart) or 1788
(DD), Franklin Co., Penn.; d. 2 Oct. 1865, in
Oregon, Ill.; eldest son of George Wertz and
Catherine Stoner; m. Catherine Emerick, who d.
1858, Rockvale, Ill.(DD); twelve children.
This family is in the 1830 Census, Washington
twp., Franklin Co., Penn. "In 1840 they moved
to Illinois by land, with seven horses and two
wagons." They were 7 weeks on the road. (DD)

1. Martha Lana Wertz, born 4 April 1812,
Quincy; married John B. Snyder, who died 26
Jan. 1898 at Oregon, Illinois, age 87 years.
His obituary appeared in the Public Opinion
Newspaper of Franklin County, Penn. in Jan.
1898 (G). Nine children: (1) Kate Snyder,
m. Mr. Bennett, lived Rockford, Illinois; (2)
Alexine Snyder, m. Mr. Stewart, living in
California in 1896; (3) James Snyder, living
in Chicago in 1896; (4) Zack Snyder, living in
Ogle Co., Ill. in 1896; (5) Millard Snyder,
living in Rockville, Iowa in 1896 and 1915;
(6) John Edwin Snyder, wounded at Battle of
Shiloh and died in the Quincy, Ill. hospital;
(7) William Snyder, died in Oregon, Ill.; (8)
Emma Snyder, died in infancy; and (9) another
child who died in infancy.

2. Peter Wertz, born 1813, died 20 Sept. 1879;
married 1st to Mary Ann Secrest; married 2nd
to Aurila or Orela Austin; ten children, seven
by first wife, three by second wife: George
Albert, Mary, Upton C., Emma, Effa, Eugenia,
Riley; Lucy E., Ida R., and Alice C. Wertz.
Outline of this family begins on page 162.

3. George Wertz, m. Fannie Marshall; three
children: Rela and Kate Wertz, both living in
Calif. in 1896; and George Wertz, who died in
Calif. before 1896.

4. Lewis Wertz, died 29 Dec. 1897, at Rockvale, Ogle Co., Ill.(DD); m. Rebecca Bell; seven children: (1) Luther Wertz; (2) Frank Wertz, an attorney, lived Forreston, Illinois; (3) Arch Wertz; (4) Grant Wertz; (5) Blanche Wertz; and (6) and (7) two children who died in infancy, not named. All five surviving children lived in Ogle Co., Ill. in 1896. (DD)

5. Henry Wertz, born 13 April 1818; died 24 Oct. 1888; m. in 1843 (DD) to Susan Wagner, ten children: Benjamin F., Joseph H., Charles M., Newton, Ole R., Lulu M., Jane E., Margie, Eva, and Kate Wertz. Outline of this family is on page 163.

6. David Wertz, born 14 Dec. 1819; died 30 April 1900; married 25 Oct. 1848, Waynesboro, Penn. (E) to Eliza Elizabeth Fisher, born 20 Oct. 1828, died 21 May 1895; nine children: Morris H., Cora Fisher, Sarah Agnes, George R., Willard W., Eddie R., David A. Lincoln, Fred A., and Julie B. Wertz. Outline of this family begins on page 165. Author of (DD).

7. John Edwin Wertz, "died in infancy by pulling a cup of boiling water over himself."

8. William Wertz, married in Rockvale, Ogle Co., Ill. (DD) to Emma Jones, lived Des Moines, Iowa; six children: James W., William L., E.Claire, Louis A., Anna Louise, and Wilbur W. Wertz. Outline of this family begins on page 167.

9. Charles Wertz, died 1883; married 1st in Ill. to Catherine Sterret (DD); married 2nd to Fannie Patterson; four children, two by each wife: (1) Marshal Wertz, living near Lanark, Carrol Co., Ill. in 1896; (2) Lena Wertz, married Mr. Riddle or Ruddle; living in Missouri in 1896; (3) Addie P. Wertz, living in Bloomington, Ill. in 1896; and (4) Charles Wertz Jr., who died in 1888 in Indiana.

10. Jacob Augustus Wertz, married Lida Moore, of Byron, Ill.; two children: Harry Wertz, in 1896 he was a traveling salesman for the Omaha Packing Comm. Company; and Belle Wertz, who married Mr. Summers, lived Calendar, Iowa.

11. Susan E. Wertz, died 1892, Wichita, Kansas; no heirs.

12. James Luther Wertz, died 1886/8 in Minnesota (DD); married Mary (DD) or Margaret E. Redding or Reddy (DD) of Minnesota; four children: Emma A., George C., Harry E., and Mable Wertz. Outline of this family is on page 166.

PETER WERTZ and Mary Ann Secrist

Peter Wertz, born 1813, died 20 Sept. 1879, son of George Wertz and Catherina Emerick; married 1st to Mary Ann Secrist (DD) or Secrest (chart); seven children:

1. George Albert Wertz, "died in childhood" (chart); "was drowned in the Leaf River" (DD)

2. Mary Wertz, married William Mensor (DD) or Mentger (chart); living at Marion, Iowa in 1896, and at Sherryville, Iowa by 1915.

3. Upton C. Wertz, b. 1844; living in Banning, Calif. in 1896; died 14 Oct. 1913; no heirs.

4. Emma Wertz, married Fred Cooling; living at Wilton Junction, Iowa in 1896 and 1915.

5. Effa Wertz, married James Davis; living in Calif. in 1896.

6. Eugenia A. Wertz, born 23 March 185?; living at Wilber, Nebraska in 1896; died 10 June 1912; married J. A. Lowe; three children: (1) Emery Lowe; (2) Charles Lowe, lived Omaha, Nebraska; and (3) Mary Lowe, married Walter Sherman, lived Omaha, Nebraska.

7. Riley Wertz, "killed at the battle of Stone River", (DD) Nebraska or North Carolina?

PETER WERTZ and Aurila/Orela Austin

8. Lucy E. Wertz, m. Leonard Smith; living at Springville, Iowa in 1896 and in 1915.

9. Ida R. Wertz, died before 1896, no heirs.

10. Alice C. Wertz, died by 1896, no heirs.

HENRY WERTZ and Susan Wagner

Henry Wertz, born 13 April 1818; died 24 Oct. 1887 (DD) or 1888 (chart), in Missouri (DD); son of George Wertz & Catherine Emerick; m. in 1843 to Susan Wagner, born 27 Dec. 1823, died Feb. 1910; ten children:

1. Benjamin F. Wertz, born 1 Jan. 1852; m. Mary Campbell, born 1 Feb. 1860; living in Tex. in 1896, and in Oklahoma by 1915; seven children: (1) Ina Wertz, born 2 Nov. 1883, m. James Fitzgerald, lived Tulsa, Oklahoma; (2) Masra or Maria Wertz, born June 1885; (3) B. Harold Wertz, born 1886; (4) Fayette Wertz, born 27 Aug. 18??; (5) Lora Wertz, born 2 Sept. 1891; (6) Eunice Wertz, born 3 Oct. 1894; and (7) Miles Wertz.

2. Joseph H. Wertz, married 1st Ramona --?--; married 2nd Hariet --?--; living in Texas in 1896, and in California by 1915.

3. Charles M. Wertz, m. Roseanna --?--; living in Calif. in 1896, and in Oklahoma by 1915.

4. Newton Wertz, unmarried by 1915; lived in Nebraska in 1896.

5. Ole R. Wertz; living in Nebraska in 1896, and in Maryville, Missouri by 1915.

6. Lulu M. Wertz, married Mr. Robertson; lived Maryville, Missouri in 1896 and 1915.

David Wertz

Eliza Elizabeth Wertz

7. Jane E. Wertz, married Mr. Hammond; lived in Missouri in 1896.

8. Mary (DD) or Margie Wertz; lived Falls City, Nebraska with her mother in 1896.

9. Eva Wertz; died by 1896 in Missouri.

10. Kate Wertz, married Mr. Sprecher. Kate died before 1896 in Missouri.

DAVID WERTZ and Eliza E. Fisher

David Wertz, born 14 Dec. 1819, Quincy, Franklin Co., Penn.; died 30 April 1900, at Salem, Nebraska; son of George Wertz and Catherine Emerick; married 26 Oct. 1848, at Evangelical Lutheran Church, Waynesboro, Franklin Co., Penn. (E) to Eliza Elizabeth Fisher, born 20 Oct. 1828, Quincy; died 21 May 1895, Falls City, Nebraska; nine children: David Wertz wrote an autobiographical account of his own life up to 1864. His son, Willard, copied and published his journal in 1911. (DD)

1. Morris H. Wertz, born 16 March 1850, Beloit, Wisconsin; died 30 April 1851.

2. Cora Fisher Wertz, b. 14 Oct. 1851, Oregon, Ill.; m. 7 Nov. 1878 at Byron, Ill. to B.F.Jackman; lived in Alma, Nebraska in 1896; one son: Willis W. Fisher Jackman, born 8 July 1811, married Folena Castrup of Manson, Iowa.

3. Sarah Agnes Wertz, b. 7 April 1853, Oregon, Ill.; m. 7 April 1873 to John H. Timmerman; four children: (1) George C. Timmerman, born 28 Jan. 1874, m. 11 Oct. 1898 at Salem, Nebraska to Nannie M. Allen, four children: George Allen Timmerman, born 16 Dec. 1899; William Otto Timmerman, born 14 April 1901; Carrie Maurine Timmerman, born 30 May 1906; and Paul Edward Timmerman, born 4 Feb. 1909; This family living at Bethany, Nebraska in 1911; (2) Wilbur Otto Timmerman, born 12 March 1875, living with his parents in St. Joseph,

Missouri in 1911; (3) James Edward Timmerman, born 18 March 1877 and died 31 Jan. 1893 at Falls City, Nebraska; and (4) Linna E. Timmerman, born 23 August 1884, m. 17 Jan. 1911 at St. Joseph, Missouri to Charles Hunt, living in San Juan, Texas in 1911.

4. George R. Wertz, born 15 Nov. 1855, Oregon, Ill.; m. 22 Feb. 1883 at Mt.Morris, Ill. to Linna A. Webb; four children: (1) Winnifred Webb Wertz, b. 13 Jan. 1884, living with her parents in Alma,, Nebraska in 1911; (2) George Wertz, died 1887/8 at Maryville, Missouri, age "about two years"; (3) Anthony Wertz, died in infancy; and (4) another child who died in infancy, not named.

5. Willard W. Wertz, b. 13 Feb. 1859, Oregon, Ill.; married 19 Oct. 1886, Salem, Nebraska to Annie E. Smith; living in Lincoln, Nebraska in 1911. Compiled much of these records. (DD)

6. Eddie K. Wertz, born 20 Dec. 1861; died 5 January 1862.

7. David A. Lincoln Wertz, b.13 March 1863; m. 27 Aug. 1902, Dayton, Iowa to Nettie Umstead; living at Alma, Nebraska in 1911 and 1915; four children by 1915: (1) Alice or Allie Elizabeth Wertz, born 25 March 1903; (2) Cora Villa Wertz, born 6 Aug. 1904; (3) George David Wertz, born 5 Feb. 1906; and (4) Robert Umstead Wertz, born 8 Sept. 1910.

8. Fred A. Wertz, born 19 Sept. 1865, Oregon, Ill.; m. 20 Feb. 1901 at Beloit, Kansas to Villa Baker; living at Colby, Kansas in 1911 and 1915.

9. Julie B. Wertz, born 17 Oct. 1867, died 28 Oct. 1867.

JAMES LUTHER WERTZ and Margaret Redding

James Luther Wertz, born about 1824; died 1886 or 1888 (DD) in Minnesota; son of George Wertz and Catherine Emerick; married Mary (DD) or Margaret E. Redding. or Reddy (DD) of Minnesota; four children:

1. Emma A. Wertz, b. 1860; m. S. J. Fulton.

2. George C. Wertz, born 1868; died 1905.

3. Harry E. Wertz, born 1868; died 1900; married Lucy A. Munroe(?); two children: George S. Wertz, and Marion Wertz; both lived at Minneapolis, Minnesota.

4. Mable Wertz.

WILLIAM WERTZ and Emma Jones

William Wertz, born about 1826; son of George Wertz and Catherine Emerick; married Emma Jones; lived Des Moines, Iowa; seven children:

1. James W. Wertz, born Sept. 185?; lived Grand Junction, Iowa.

2. William L. Wertz, born March 1857/9; died August 1915.

3. E. Claire Wertz, born 16 August 1863; lived Sharf(?) River Falls, Kansas? or Minnesota?

4. Louis A. Wertz, born 15 August 1866, twin; lived Grand Junction, Iowa.

5. Anna Louise Wertz, born 15 August 1866, twin; lived Des Moines, Iowa.

6. Wilbur W. Wertz, born 16 Jan. 1868; lived Grand Junction, Iowa.

7. George Albert Wertz; died at age 2 years.

FREDERICK FISHER and CATHERINE WERTZ

Catherine Wertz, born about 1788; daughter of George Wertz and Catherine Stoner; married Frederick Fisher (probably the Frederick

Fisher, born a. 1790, son of Frederick and Susanna Fisher); nine children:

1. Francis Fisher, born 29 April 1809; died 10 Dec. 1862; married Jacob Leiter or Lester; one child: Levi Z. Leiter/Lester, married Mary Anna Carver, and had four children: Joseph, Nannie married Colin Campbell, Mary Victoria married Lord George Gurgar(?), and Daisy married Lord Suffolk.

2. Sarah Fisher, born 13 August 1810; died Holmes Co., Ohio; married Edward Lee.

3. Elias Fisher, born 24 August 1812; died 8 Sept. 1836; unmarried.

4. Lydia Fisher, born 28 Sept. 1814; died 10 August 1875; married Mr. Hamilton.

5. Frederick Fisher, born 11 June 1816; died 26 August 1870; unmarried.

6. Catherine Fisher, born 25 June 1820; died 10 June 1906; married John H. Meily or Mosly; nine children: (1) Catherine Anna Mosly(?), born 16 August 1840; died 15 Dec. 1900(?); married Coleman or Calvin S. Brice; five children: Helen Brice, lived New York; Stewart M. Brice, born 29 Dec. 1872, died 9 June 1910; Margaret K. Brice, born 1873, died 27 July 1911; Mark Patrick Brice, lived New York; and John F. Brice, lived New York; (2) Luther M. Meily(?), born 2 May 1842, died 21 Aug. 1894, married Miss Young, one son = Richard Young Meily(?), lived Los Angeles, Calif.; (3) Ann Eliza Meily(?), born 3 May 1844, lived Lima, Ohio; (4) Ringgold W. Meily(?), born 16/18 April 1846, died 29 Dec. 1911, married Julia E. Orphiam(?), two children = J.R. and Frederick R., lived Lima, Ohio; (5) George H. Mosly(?), lived Lima, Ohio; (6) Francis Mosly(?), born 17 Nov. 1850/2, died 26 Sept. 1909, married W.P.Orr, no heirs; (7) Harriet A. Mosly(?), born 23 Jan. 1857, married Mr. Moths or Motter, lived Lima, Ohio; (8) Mary V.

Meily(?), born 12 Feb. 1860, died 20 Jan. 1909, married A.J.Irwin, one daughter = Helen O. Irwin, lived Goshen, Indiana; and (9) Sarah Elizabeth Mosly(?), born 21 Sept. 1862(?), died 21 Sept. 1883(?), unmarried.

7. Amos Fisher, born 15 June 1822; died by 1915.

8. Elisa Fisher, born 14 Feb. 1823, died 25 March 1906; married Mr. Shickard.

9. Belinda Fisher, born 8 Oct. 1826, died Nov. 1829, age 3 years.

DAVID WERTZ and ELIZABETH EMERICK

David Wertz, born 12 Nov. 1789; died 17 Sept. 1866 (G); son of George Wertz and Catherine Stoner; married Elizabeth Emerick, born 15 Sept. 1793; died 19 July 1848; both buried in Quincy Cemetery (G); this family is in the 1830 Census, Washington twp., Franklin Co., Penn.; six children:

1. Matilda Wertz, born about 1820; married Dr. Henry Rosenburg; three children: (1) George Rosenburg; (2) Lucuis Rosenburg; and (3) Kate Rosenburg; all lived Knoxville, Ill. or Mo.

2. Solomon Wertz, born July 1821; died 16 Jan. 1824, age 2 years, 6 months, 24 days; buried at Quincy Graveyard (G).

3. John Edwin Wertz, born 1 Oct. 1825; died 9 April 1827, age 1 year, 6 months, and 32 days; buried at Quincy Graveyard (G).

4. David Aaron Wertz, born 14 Feb. 1826; died 13 April 1896, in Philadelphia; age 71 years, unmarried; buried at Quincy Graveyard (G). He is probably the David A. Wertz, who "in April 1858 with R.P. Hazelet, started a paper called "The Independent". In 1859 they sold it to W.I. Cook and P. Dock Frey, who changed its name to "The Times". (C), page 46; from an article on the Newspapers of Franklin Co.

5. Catherine Wertz, born about 1826; married a cousin, Jerome Wertz; no heirs. This couple was living in Springfield, Ohio in 1896. (G)

6. Hiram Emrick Wertz, born 25 Sept. 1829; died 20 Nov. 1918; in 1912 Hiram was living on the Wertz farm in Quincy twp., Franklin Co., Penn.; married Elizabeth Middour, born 25 Sept. 1841, died 4 Feb. 1889; both Hiram and Elizabeth are buried in the Quincy Graveyard (G); four children: (1) David Maurice Wertz, (see below); (2) Minnie Kate Wertz, born 13 June 1867, died 1953, buried Quincy (G), m. Les Ogler or Oyler, lived Chambersburg, Penn.; (3) Hermie Elizabeth Wertz, born 9 July 1869, died 19 July 1895, married 29 August 1895 to Grant Barnitz, of Carlisle; and (4) Edith Barbara Wertz, born 2 Feb. 1874, lived New York; died 1970; buried Quincy Cemetery (G).

DAVID MAURICE WERTZ and May B. Oller

David Maurice or Morris (E) Wertz, born 7 Oct. 1863, Quincy, Franklin Co., Penn., christened 21 May 1864, Evangelical Lutheran Church, Waynesboro, Franklin Co., son of Hiram E. and Elizabeth Wertz (E); married May B. Oller, born 14 April 1867, Waynesboro, daughter of Jacob F. Oller and Elizabeth Bonebrake (F); living in Waynesboro, Penn. in 1915; four children born by 1912:

1. A son born Nov. 1902, lived "a few hours".

2. Elizabeth Oller Wertz, born 13 March 1904.

3. David Maurice Wertz Jr., born 1 Nov. 1905, Waynesboro (E); died 20 August 1907.

4. Anna Ferndah(?) Wertz, born 6 July 1909.

JOHN BUSHMAN and EVE WERTZ

Eve Wertz, born 12 Oct. 1793; died 18/19 May 1880, age 86 years, 7 months, and 6 days; daughter of George Wertz and Catherine Stoner;

170

married John Bushman, born 4 May 1794; probably the John Bushman, born 4 May 1793, Littlestown, Adams Co., Penn., son of Jacob and Catherina Bushman (E); seven children:

1. Margaret Bushman, born 5 April 1819; died 10 Jan. 1907, age 87 years, 9 months, 5 days; married Baltzer Knoll, born 28 March 1811, died 13 August 1901, age 90 years, 4 months, 15 days; seven children: (1) Mary A. Knoll, born 16 May 1843, married 16 Oct. 18?? to Samuel B. Foreman; (2) Catherina Knoll, born 27 Nov. 1845, died 12 March 1849, age 3 years; (3) Margaret Knoll, born 11 Jan. 1848, married Jacob F. Foreman; (4) John Knoll, born 2 Sept. 1850, married Rebecca Dubrea(?); (5) David C. Knoll, born 14 July 1853, married Lizzie B. Dehart, lived Chambersburg, Penn.; (6) Susan Knoll, born 15 Dec. 1856, married William Miller; and (7) Rebecca J. Knoll, born 17 Feb. 1860, married C.C.Mowers, lived Chambersburg.

2. Jacob Bushman, b. 29 Nov. 1821; died young.

3. Catherine Bushman, b. 15 April 1822, d. 19 Jan. 1896, age 73 years; m. Peter George, b. 1 April 1821, d. 2 Jan. 1903, age 81 years; 8 children: (1) Adam George, b. 14 July 1842, m. Elizabeth Potter, born 21 June 1848; (2) Anna Margaret George, b. 8 Sept. 1846, m. John B. Simon; (3) David George, born 8 May 1852, m. Carrie Trytle, born 25 Sept. 1857, lived Chambersburg; (4) Jeremiah George, b. 27 Dec. 1854, m. Sarah Zook, both died before 1915; (5) Jacob F. George, b. 15 Dec. 1859, m. Mary Berkley, born 6 March 1861; (6) Charlotte E. George, born 16 May 1863, m. J. F. Cook; (7) Hiriam George, born 1 Jan. 1865, married Mary E. Holinger, born 14 July 1861(?); and (8) James George, died before 1915, dates unknown.

4. Solomon Bushman, born 2? Jan. 1824; m. 1st to Charlotte E. --?--, one son; m. 2nd to Eliza Wagner, one son: (1) James Bushman; (2) David E. Bushman, born 8 Feb. 1868, married Emma D.Danials, born 21 Nov. 1867.

5. John Bushman, born 1 Sept. 1826, died 15
Dec. 1908, age 82 years; married Mary
Clugeton(?), died 20 April 1896, age 68 years;
at least six children: (1) Samuel Bushman,
married Miss Hosfman(?); (2) John Bushman; (3)
Katie Bushman, died by 1915, married William
Frieger(?); (4) Annie Bushman, married
Alexander Small, lived Penn.; (5) Jennie
Bushman, married M.D. Jacobs; and (6)+ "other
children who died in infancy, names unknown".

6. Henry Bushman, born 8 Dec. 1830, died 14
April 1833, age two and a half years.

7. Frederick Bushman, born 21 May 1834, died 6
Nov. 1902, age 68 years; m. 8 Dec. 1859 to
Jane Crosmier or Crossiser, born 1 March 1836,
died 6 March 19?5, both buried Michawaka, Ind.
Eleven children: (1) George Andrew Bushman,
born 2 April 1860, lived Fayetteville, Penn.;
(2) Mary Cathernia Bushman, born 1 Sept. 1861,
m. Mr. Kelly, lived Michigan City, Indiana;
(3) Susan Bushman, born 21 March 1863, married
Mr. Baughman; (4) Margaret Bell Bushman, born
16 Jan. 186?, married Mr. Kling; (5) Ruthanna
Elizabeth, born 2? Jan. 186?, married Mr.
Kohler, lived Fayetteville, Penn.; (6) Edward
Frederick Bushman, born 3 Jan. 1869, lived
Ohio; (7) Solomon Davidson Bushman, born 23
May 1871, died 26 May 1908, age 37, five
children: Hazel, Norman, John, Lulu, and an
infant, name unknown, all living Michawaka,
Indiana in 1915; (8) John Jacob Aster Bushman,
born 8 June 1873; (9) Benjamin F. Bushman,
born 31 August 1875, lived Goshen, Indiana;
(10) Samuel Augustus Bushman, born 12 Sept.
1878, lived Thornton, Oklahoma; and (11) Emma
Jane Bushman, born 9 Oct. 1883, married Mr.
Hunter, lived Michawaka, Indiana.

JACOB WERTZ and MARGARET LABE/LOEB

Jacob Wertz, born 2 May 1796, died 4 May 1877,
son of George Wertz and Catherine Stoner;
married Margaret "Polly" Lorb or Labe, born
1807; died 1869; both buried at the Quincy

Cemetery (6). Probably the Jacob Wertz in the 1850 Census in Quincy twp., Franklin Co., Penn. (AIS) Three children:

1. S. John Wertz, born 31 Oct. 1825, Chambersburg, Franklin Co., Penn.

2. Augustus Luther Wertz, born 27 August 1832; died 17 Nov. 1910; married Catherine Colby; lived Newark, New Jersey; five children:
(1) Annie B. Wertz, born 10 August 1863.
(2) Charles C. Wertz, born 15 Oct. 1864.
(3) George D. Wertz, born 10 Nov. 1866.
(4) Margaret F. Wertz, born 3 Sept. 1870.
(5) William Augustus Wertz, born 20 Nov. 1872; married 11 February 1892 at Newark, New Jersey, to Lizzie Fleming, of White House, New Jersey (6).

3. Susanna Wertz, born 19 Dec. 1829, married David Neff, Neaof, Nerof, Neiof, or Nuof, lived Fayetteville, Penn.

HENRY CORDELL and MARIA/MARY WERTZ

Maria or Mary Wertz, born about 1798; probably youngest daughter of George Wertz and Catherine Stoner; married Henry Cordell; five children:

1. Joseph Cordell, born 24 April 1823; died 19 Jan. 1912; married Anna Hubbert, born 9 July 1837; six children: (1) Jennie Cordell, born 24 August 1858, married Mr. Carie or Crew, lived Normal, Illinois; (2) Eva Cordell, born 16 Nov. 1862, m. 1st Mr. Hunter; m. 2nd L.H. Lloyd; lived Hart, Michigan; one son: Earl D. Hunter, born 4 July 1883, m. Hattie Evans, lived Hart, Michigan, a daughter, Ruth Evans Hunter, born 6 Feb. 1911; (3) Scott Cordell, born 24 April 1867, died before 1915; (4) Ralph Cordell, born 5 Nov. 1869, died before 1915; (5) Grace Cordell, died before 1915; and (6) Blanche Cordell, died before 1915.

2. David Cordell, died without heirs.

3. Samuel Cordell, died without heirs.

4. Jacob Cordell.

5. Henry Cordell. Possibly this is the Henry Cordell who married Harriet Poper and had a son, Tell Philippy Cordell, born 17 June 1885, Antrim twp., Franklin Co., Penn. (E)

Map from 1868 Atlas of Franklin County, Penn. showing "H. F. Wertz" farm location just North of Quincy, in Quincy township.

Chapter 7

Unattached Maybe Related Wertz Families

The records in this Chapter are ones that may pertain to our Franklin County Wertz families, or their descendants, outlined in Chapters 1 through 6, or they may pertain to other Wertz families not immediately related to ours, such as those in Chapters 8 and 9.

These records are recorded here for the use of future researchers, in hopes that they may be able to prove links that we have as yet been unable to establish.

RECORDS from FRANKLIN CO., PENN.

From the 1850 Census, Peters township, Franklin Co., Penn.: family #923;

George Wertz, age 36, male, laborer,b.Pa.
Hetty   "   age 30, female, b.Pa.
William   "   age 10, male, b. Pa.
Isaac   "   age 8, male, b. Pa.
Elizabeth "   age 6, female, b. Pa.
Malinda   "   age 5, female, b. Pa.
Joseph W. "   age 2, male, b. Pa.
David   "   age 1, male, b. Pa.

This might be the George Wertz, born 1818, died 1881, who married Sarah Martin (see page 34); or it could be the George Wertz, born 1824, son of Henry and S. Witner Wertz (see page 39).

Obituary in the 14 March 1890 Peoples Register of Franklin County, for Mrs. John Wertz, age 57 years, died 10 March 1890 in Guilford, township ...survived by husband and two sons: Edw. and Harry... (6)

175

Marriage notice of 9 January 1891 for Harry J. Wertz and Florence E. Overcash, both of Franklin County, married at the Brides home on 18 Dec. 1890, by Rev. D. S. Lentz. (6)

Marriage notice in the 17 April and the 24 April 1891 Peoples Register of Franklin County for John A. Wertz of Oscela Mills, Clearfield County and Maggie B. Stewart of Fannettsburg; married at Fannettsburg on the 7th of April 1891 by Rev. A. D./S. Baldwin, assisted by Rev. H. Treverton. (6)

"Catherine Hoover, daughter of Joseph S. Hoover and Mary Small, married Edwin S. Wertz of Fayetteville, who died in August 1903." (F) page 670. Their marriage announcement appeared in the Democratic News of 2 June 1899, and states that "Anna K. Hoover of New Franklin married 1 June 1899 at the Reformed Church Parsonage, in Marion (Franklin County), Penn. by Rev. I. M. Beaver to Edwin S. Wertz of Altenwald." (6)

Webster Clay Wertz, married 7 May 1925 at Waynesboro, Franklin Co., Penn. to Ella May Sheeley. (E) Note: there was a Webster Clay Wertz, born 2 July 1882 at Johnstown, Cambria Co., Penn. (E), parents names not given. And a Webster Clay Wertz married in 1914 at Johnstown, to Maud Edith Reichard. (E)

Marriage notice of 23 May 1932 for Harry James Werts of Nanty Glo, Penn. and Ora Marie Wilkins, of Darragh, Penn. by Rev. W. G. Slifer of the St. Thomas Lutheran Church. (6)

Cemetery Record for John P. Wertz, born 1908, died 1950; buried at Catholic Cemetery, Chambersburg; in U. S. Navy, W. W. II. (6)

BEDFORD CO. WERTZ FAMILIES

The PAUL WERTZ family

Paul Wertz, born 19 Nov. 1745, Penn.; died 30 March 1825, Bedford Co., Penn.; son of Daniel Fahnstock Wertz (see Chapter 9 — page 244). Paul married 1787 to Catherine Stiffler; and was a Private, 5th Class, under Capt. William McCall, in the Bedford Co. Militia. (Z) Paul Wertz and his wife Catherine are buried in the Wertz Graveyard on the Hite farm in Cumberland Valley twp., Bedford County. Their tombstone reads: "Paul Wertz, born 1747, died 30 March 1826, age 79 years; wife, Catherine, born 1767, died 27 Feb. 1854, age 87 years." (Y)

Paul Wertz' will, dated 20 Oct. 1825, Bedford Co., Penn. names his wife, Catherine; four sons: John, Paul, Jacob, and Henry; five unmarried daughters: Elizabeth, Catharine, Sarah, Rebecca, and Ann... and one married daughter: Mary Wertz, married to George Lee.

Adding the Cemetery (Y) and Census records the family of Paul Wertz and Catherine Stiffler is probably as follows:

1. John Wertz, born 1789; died 3 June 1858; buried at Smith Cemetery; married Elizabeth Williams, born 12 April 1791; died 9 June 1846 (tombstone in Wertz Farm Cemetery) or died 9 June 1816 (tombstone in Smith Farm Cemetery); daughter of Henry and Rachel Williams. They had at least four sons: W.D., Banner, John J., and Scott A. Wertz. This family is outlined beginning on page 178.

2. Mary Wertz, married before 1825 to George Lee. Probably the parents of the Washington Lee, born 1822, died 1856, buried in the Wertz Farm Cemetery. (Y)

3. Elizabeth Wertz.

4. Catharine Wertz.

5. **Henry Wertz**, born 1794; died 16 May 1872, age 78 years; buried in Wertz Cemetery (Y); married Sara Oster, and according to the 1850 and 1860 Census records, they had at least six children: George F., Paul, Ann, David, Kehler, and Toliver Wertz. This family is outlined beginning on page 179.

6. **Paul Wertz**, born 1796; died 15 March 1869; buried at Bortz Cemetery (Y); married Mary M. --?--, born a. 1803; died 17 Dec. 1875, also buried at Bortz Cemetery (Y). They have eleven children listed in the 1850 and 1860 Census, Cumberland Valley twp.: Mary, William, Joseph, Rebecca, Jacob, Elizabeth, David, Sophia, Harriet, Martha, and Daniel. Outline on this family begins on page 180.

7. **Jacob Wertz**, born 10 May 1799; died 16 Dec. 1887; buried at Wertz Cemetery (Y); married Nancy Worley, born 1802; died 30 June 1871, alto buried at Wertz Cemetery (Y). The 1850 and 1860 Census, Cumberland Valley twp. show them with six children: Rebecca, John A., Ellen, Samuel, Eliza, and Ruth. Outline of this family is on page 181.

8. **Sarah Wertz.** Probably the Sarah Wertz, wife of J. Mahoney, born 1800; died 12 May 1839, age 39 years; buried in the Wertz Cemetery (Y).

9. **Rebecca Wertz.** Maybe the Rebecca Wertz whose marriage notice in the Bedford Gazette of November 30, 1832, states: "On Thursday, 22nd (of Nov.), by Thomas R. Gettys, Esq., William Work, of Adams County, was married to Rebecca Wertz, of Napier twp. in this county."

10. **Ann Wertz.**

JOHN WERTZ and Elizabeth Williams

John Wertz, born 18 Jan. 1789; died 2/3 June 1858; two tombstones, in the Smith Farm Cemetery, and in the Wertz Farm Cemetery give these dates (Y). The 1850 Census gives his age as 63 years. John was probably the eldest son of Paul Wertz and Catherine Stiffler. John married Elizabeth Williams, born 12 April 1791; died 9 June 1818 or 1845; daughter of Henry Williams, who died in 1815, and Rachel, born 1763, died 28 June 1852. Henry and Rachel Williams, and daughter Elizabeth Williams Wertz have tombstones in the Smith Farm Cemetery; and Rachel Williams and Elizabeth Williams Wertz also have tombstones in the Wertz Farm Cemetery (Y). In the 1850 Census, John Wertz is listed with Catherine, age 45, perhaps a second wife?; and two of his children. Other children are listed in the 1860 Census, and the Cemetery Records (Y):

1. W. D. Wertz, born 14 April 1815; died 19 April 1899; buried at the Wertz Farm Cemetery; along with his wife, Elizabeth, born 1814; died 1899 (Y).

2. Banner Wertz, born 23 Dec. 1819; died 5 March 1855; buried at Wertz Farm Cemetery.

3. John J. Wertz, born 1829; died 1913; with tombstones at both the Wertz and Smith Farm Cem. (Y); m. Mary E. Boor, born 1834; died 1922, buried at Wertz Farm Cemetery (Y). Two children born by 1860: (1) Samuel, age 5 = born a. 1855; and (2) James, age 2 = born a. 1858.

4. Rebecca Wertz, age 18 in 1850 (=b.1832).

5. Scott A. Wertz, born 6 July 1845; died 6 Feb. 1912; m. Rachel Smith, born 1848; died 1927; both buried at Wertz Farm Cemetery.

HENRY WERTZ and Sara Oster

Henry Wertz, born 1794; died 16 May 1872, age 78 years; buried Wertz Graveyard, Cumberland Valley twp. (Y); 1850 Census gives his age as 48; a farmer with $6000 real and $2000 personal property in Cumberland Valley twp. Henry was son of Paul Wertz and Catherine

179

Stiffler.   Henry married Sara Oster, and they
had at least six children:
1. George F. Wertz, born 1829/30. Probably
the George Wertz, born 1830, died 25 Jan.
1905, buried in the Bedford Cemetery.(Y)
2. Paul Wertz, born 1830.
3. Ann Wertz, born 1832.
4. David Wertz, born 1834.
5. Kehler Wertz, born 1836.
6. Toliver Wertz, born 1838.

PAUL and MARY M. WERTZ

Paul Wertz, born 1796; died 15 March 1869;
buried at Bortz Cemetery (Y); is listed in the
1850 Census as age 59, with $3000 in real and
$400 in personal property in Cumberland Valley
township.   Paul was son of Paul Wertz and
Catherine Stiffler. His wife, Mary M., was
born in 1803; died 17 Dec. 1875, and is also
buried at the Bortz Cemetery. Her age in 1850
is given as 47 years. The had eleven children
born by 1850, and probably all born in Bedford
County, Pennsylvania:

1. Mary Wertz, born 1827 (1850) or 1832 (1860)

2. Joseph Wertz, born 1829 (1850) or 1834
(60); probably the Joseph Wertz, born 1828,
died 11 Aug. 1818, buried at the Bedford Cem.

3. Rebecca Wertz, born 1831/36

4. Jacob Wertz, born 1833; probably the Jacob
Wertz, age 26, with wife Catharine, age 29,
and two children, Ida J., born 1859; and
Humphry, born Jan., 1860; in the 1860 Census,
Cumberland Valley twp.

5. Elizabeth Wertz, born 1837

6. William Wertz, born 1839/40; probably the
William Wertz, born 29 Oct. 1839; died 29 Feb.
1868; buried Bortz Cemetery (Y).

7. David Wertz, born 1841/44

8. Sophia Wertz, born a. 1843; probably twins

9. Harriet Wertz, born a. 1843   "   "

10. Martha Wertz, born a. 1845; perhaps the Martha Wertz McFerran, born 1846, died 19 Feb. 1941, buried in the Bedford Cemetery.

11. Daniel Wertz, born 1849.

JACOB WERTZ and NANCY WORLEY

Jacob Wertz, born 10 May 1799, age 50 in 1850, a farmer with $4000 in real and $100 in personal property in Cumberland Valley twp.; son of Paul Wertz and Catherine Stiffler; married Nancy Worley, born 1802; died 30 June 1871, age 69 years; both are buried at Wertz Graveyard, Cumberland Valley twp. They had at least six children and/or grandchildren:

1. Rebecca Wertz, born a. 1826; probably the Rebecca Heancy with husband Edward Heancy, born a. 1826, and two children; Alva. born 1857; and Bruce, born 1859... in 1860 Census, Cumberland Valley twp.

2. John A. Wertz, born 1827; died 28 June 1905; in the G.A.R.; buried at Bedford Cemetery. Probably the John W. Wertz, age 34, with wife Jane, age 24, and two children, Baron, age 4, and Fanny, age 2, in the 1860 Census, Cumberland Valley twp. Jane E. Wertz, born 1832, died 1905, is buried at the Bortz Cemetery (Y).

3. Ellen Wertz, born a. 1829. Probably the Ellen Wertz, born 26 June 1826; died 29 March 1885, buried at the Wertz Graveyard.

4. Samuel Wertz, born a. 1850... living with Rebecca and Edward Heancy in 1860.

5. Eliza Wertz, born a.1856.

6. Ruth Wertz, born a. 1859.

The GEORGE WERTZ family

George Wertz will was written 22 Feb. 1836, and proved 13 Feb. 1837 in Bedford County. He names five sons: John, George, Thomas, Daniel, and William... three married daughters: Mary Taylor, Elizabeth Kenton, and Rosenah Murray... and one unmarried daughter: Minlia or Mindia Wertz.

NICHOLAS and DIANA WERTZ

Nicholas Wertz, born about 1784, a farmer with $300 real and $50 personal property in 1850 and 1860 Census, Cumberland Valley twp.
wife = Diana, born about 1803.
Eight children listed:

1. Henry Wertz, born 1823/5

2. John Wertz, born a. 1828;probably the John Wertz, born 1827, died 28 Nov. 1905, in the G.A.R., buried at Bedford Cemetery (Y); and probably the John A. Wertz, age 32, with wife, Louisa, age 21, and two children: Clara A., age 3, and Oliver B. Wertz, born Feb. 1860; in the 1860 Census, Cumberland Valley twp.

3. Valentine Wertz, born 1830/2
4. Ellen Wertz, born a. 1832
5. Rebecca Wertz, born a. 1834
6. Elizabeth Wertz, born a. 1836
7. Nancy Wertz, born 1838
8. Emanul Wertz, born 1843/4.

PETER and Sarah WERTS

Peter Werts, age 65 in 1850 Census, Harrison twp. with wife Sarah, age 62, and four children. Peter thus born a. 1785.

1. Peter Werts, age 30 = born about 1820.

182

2. **Hugh Werts**, age 28 = born about 1822; probably the Hugh Wertz, born about 1830, in the Juniata twp. 1860 Census, P.O. = West End; wife = Susan, born about 1832; three children: Mary, born about 1855; Calvin, born about 1857; and Uriah Wertz, born April 1860.

3. **James Werts**, age 23 = born about 1827.

4. **Camilla Werts**, age 21 = born about 1829.

THOMAS WERTZ and EVE DIBERT

Thomas Wertz, probably born a. 1790; perhaps a son of the George Wertz who died 1836/7 (see page 178); "of Milligan's Cove", married Eve Dibert, daughter of Charles Dibert and Mary Steel; Eve married 2nd to Daniel May. Eve died June 1875, age 83 years old. (Q)
Thomas and Eve Dibert Wertz had four children:
1. **Joseph Wertz** "lived about Everett". (Q)

2. **Charles Wertz** "lived Pontiac, Illinois."

3. **Eliza Wertz**, m. Daniel Earnest, born 4 July 1818, died Sept. 1901; they had at least one son: William Earnest, who m. Kate Suters. (Q)

4. **Jane Wertz**, married Frederick Stuby, son of Elizabeth Earnest Stuby; four children: (1) Henry Heckerman Stuby; (2) Charles Stuby; (3) Maggie Stuby; and (4) Minerva Stuby. (Q)

WILLIAM and MARY E. WERTZ

William Wertz, born about 1812; could be a son of the George Wertz who died 1836/7 (see page 182); William is age 38 in 1850, a farmer with $3500 real and $750 personal property, in Union twp., P.O. = St. Clairsville. wife = Mary E., age 27 = born a. 1823. Eight children born by 1860:
1. Hannah Wertz, age 8 = born a. 1842
2. John Wertz, age 5 = born a. 1845; maybe the John A. Wertz, born 16 July 1845, died 22 June 1905, buried at Pavia Cemetery (Y).

3. William Wertz, age 3 (1850) = born a.1847
4. Mary Jane Wertz, age 1 & 12 = born 1848/9
5. Michael Wertz, age 7 months (1850) 9 years (1860) = born 1849/50.
6. Winfield S. Wertz, age 7 = born a. 1853
7. Sarah R. Wertz, age 3 = born a. 1857
8. Samuel R. Wertz, age 6 mo.= born Jan.1860.

WILLIAM and ELIZABETH WERTZ

William Wertz, born 16 Sept. 1815, died 21 Oct. 1876; buried at Mock Cemetery (Y); a farmer with $4000 real and $500 personal property in the 1850 and 1860 Census, Cumberland Valley twp., with wife, Elizabeth, born about 1817. They had six children by 1860.

Buried next to William Wertz in Mock Cemetery is Eve Wertz, born 1779, died 3 June 1835; who is perhaps William's mother? Also in the same cemetery is "Michael P. son of Wm. M.E. Wertz, born 14 August 1854, died 14 Sept. 1856."

Marriages from the "Bedford Gazette":
April 4, 1834: "On Thursday evening, 27th (of March), by Rev. Mr. Hall, William Wertz, of Washington City was married to Eliza Gilson, of this borough."

Children of William and Elizabeth Wertz:
1. Mary J. Wertz, born 1840/42
2. Mulvina Wertz, born a. 1844
3. Almedes or Almira S. Wertz, born 1845/6
4. Amanda Wertz, born 1847/8
5. Ann C. Wertz, born a. 1850
6. Rachel Wertz, born a. 1852
7. Michael P. Wertz, 1854-1856 (see above).

JOSIAH and ELIZABETH WERTS

Josiah Werts, born 8 Feb. 1820; died 6 Aug. 1891; buried at Everette Cemetery (Y); age 34 in 1850, a farmer with $150 personal property, in Harrison twp., and 1860 Census in Broadtop twp., P.O. = Hopewell. wife = Elizabeth, born about 1820; twelve children born by 1860:

1. Henry Werts, born 1842/3
2. Margaret Werts, born 1844
3. George Werts, born 1845/7
4. Sharlot/ Charlotte Werts, born 1845/6
5. Thomas Werts, born 1847/9
6. Ephram Werts, born 1849; perhaps died by 1860.
7. Eliza Jane Werts, born a. 1851
8. John Werts, born a. 1853
9. Sarah B. Werts, born a. 1855
10. Mary Werts, born a. 1856
11. Emiline Werts, born a. 1857
12. Louisa Werts, born Sept./Oct. 1859.

MICHAEL and MARY WERTZ

Michael Wertz, born about 1817; age 33 in 1850, a farmer with $1000 real and $300 personal property, in Union twp. in 1850 and 1860 Census, P.O. = St. Clairsville; wife = Mary/May, age 27 in 1850 = born a. 1821.
Six children:

1. Eveline Wertz, age 7 = born a. 1843

2. Samuel Wertz, age 4 = born a. 1846

3. Elizabeth Wertz, age 2 = born a. 1848

4. Hepziba Wertz, born a. 1853; Probably the Hephzibah Wertz, born 1852, died 1932; buried at Pavia Cemetery; married to Samuel B. Hartle, born 1845, died 1914; Pavia Cemetery; probably son of George Hartle, 1819-1882, and Catherine Burket, 1822-1908, also buried at Pavia Cemetery (Y).

5. Charlotte Wertz, born a. 1854

6. Elmira Wertz, born a. 1856

185

ZACHARIUS and Elizabeth WERTZ

Zacharius or Zacheus Wertz, born a. 1825; age 35 in 1860, a farmer with $800 real and $250 personal property in Colerain twp. (in Cumberland Valley twp. in 1850). wife = Elizabeth, born a. 1830. 5 children by 1860:
1. Campbell Wertz, born a. 1852
2. Alley Wertz, born a. 1854
3. Valentine Wertz, born a. 1856
4. Mary E. Wertz, born a. 1858
5. Emanuel Wertz, born a. 1859.

GEORGE WERTZ and SARAH NOGLE

Correspondence from Scheery L. Renken-Goekler, of Albuquerque, New Mexico in 1988 states that his ancestors were a George Wertz, born about 1820 at Hopewell, Penn.; married Sarah Nogle. They were parents of George Edgar Wertz, born 15 Feb. 1845, Hopewell, Penn.; died 11 March 1932, Williamsburg, Kansas; married 2 July 1869, at Hopewell, Penn. to Laanna Drollinger or Grollinger, born 25 Feb. 1852; died 27 Oct. 1883, buried Mt. Smith Cemetery (Y); daughter of Harry Grollinger, born 28 Feb. 1828; died 27 Nov. 1884, and Elizabeth L., born 16 May 18??; died 13 Aug. 18??, both buried at Mt. Smith Cemetery.
George Edgar and Laanna Wertz, were parents of Charles Wesley Wertz, born 18 July 1875, Bedford Co., Penn.; married 1st to Cora Roberts, and had two sons; married 2nd to Minnie Scott; and married 3rd to Ceila Adell Ryan, and had two daughters.
It is not known at present if this George Wertz, born a. 1820, is a son or perhaps a grandson of George Wertz who died in 1836/7 (see page 178.) Pictures of George Edgar and Laanna Wertz and some of their descendents are on the following pages.

George Edgar Wertz
1845-1932
his wife, Laanna, 1852-1883
and perhaps a daughter and grandchild

Charles Wesley Wertz I
1875-1947
and his daughter Doris Jean, born 1932

Charles Wesley Wertz II
1902-1942

Edgar Wertz
1904-1915

ENOS and EMALINE WERTZ

Enos Wertz, born about 1830; carpenter with $200 personal property; in 1850 Census in Napier twp., and in 1860 Census in Juniata twp.; wife = Emaline, born about 1836; three children living in 1860: Isaac C. Wertz, born about 1854; Mary Wertz, born about 1856; and a daughter, born about 1858 (name not legible). An "infant son of Enos and Emeline Wertz" also named Enos, is buried in the Old Union Church Cemetery, near the New Baltimore Road and Route 31, Bedford County. There are no dates on this infant's marker.

BALTZER or BOLSE WERTZ

Baltzer Werts, age 14 in 1850, age 22 in 1860, is listed in the 1850 Census in Cumberland Valley twp., and in the 1860 Census in Union twp. in the family of Baltzer and Mary Fletcher. Balser Fletcher, age 74 in 1850, 82 in 1860 = born 1776/8, in Maryland; farmer with $1400 real and $300 personal property; wife = Mary, age 73 & 81 = born 1777/9; with daughter, Harriet Fletcher, age 24; and Catherine Wertz, age 34 = born 1826; and Bolse Wertz, age 22 = born 1838. (perhaps Catherine is also a daughter of Baltzer and Mary Fletcher, who had a son born when she was only 14 years old, whom is named after her father?) Another Blatzer Wertz, born 14 April 1885, died 10 Dec. 1899, is buried at the Reformed Osterburg Cemetery (Y).

Some other Bedford Co. marriages:

Elizabeth Wertz, married 11 April 1868, at Saint Clairsville to Joseph S. Beegle. (E)

Evalina Wertz, married 6 Nov. 1865, at Saint Clairsville, to Adam Pressel. (E)

John William Wertz and Rebecca Ellen Bennett, parents of Theodore Ralph Wertz, born 24 Feb. 1905 in Bedford Co. (E)

Other Harrison township Wertz families

Henry Wertz, age 36 in 1850 = born a. 1814, with wife, Elisa, age 33, and five children:
1. Hannah, age 8 = born about 1842.
2. Mary A., age 6 = born about 1844.
3. George W., age 3 = born about 1847.
4. Jane C., age 2 = born about 1848.
5. Margaret, age 1 month = 1849/50.

Daniel Werts, age 50 in 1850 = born a. 1800, and wife, Mary, age 49 = born a. 1801; and three children:
1. Franklin, age 13 = born about 1837.
2. Mary Ann, age 9 = born about 1841.
3. Martin, age 6 = born about 1844.

Robert Wertz, age 24 in 1850 = born a. 1826; with wife Mary, age 20 = born a. 1830; and one son, Henry, age 1 = born about 1849.

Charles Werts, age 24 in 1850 = born a. 1826; with wife Sarah, age 23 = born a. 1827; and one son, Samuel, age 2 = born about 1848.

Valentine B. Wertz, age 37 in 1850 = born a. 1813; with wife Amanda, age 22 = born a. 1828; and one son, Vitillus, age 1 month. Vitilas B. Wertz, born 1850, died 1928, and his wife Lovenia, born 1852, died 1903, are buried at the Schellsburg Cemetery (Y).

Napier township Wertz families

Emanuel Wertz, age 22 = born about 1828, and Henryetta Wertz, age 24 = born about 1826, and Enos Wertz, age 20 = born a. 1830.

George Wertz, age 11, in 1850 in family of Jacob Dull, age 67, and wife Maria, age 49.

192

Levi Wertz, age 23, in 1850, in family of
Henry Horn, age 27, and wife Maria, age 28,
and children; also a Margaret J. Wertz, age 23
listed in this family.

East Providence twp. Wertz families

John Wertz, born about 1774, Penn.; wife =
Christina, born about 1785.

Fable ? Wertz, born about 1813, in Germany,
farmer, with $1200 real and $500 personal
property in 1860; wife = Murial, born about
1822, Penn.; six children, all born Penn.:
1. David Wertz, born a. 1845
2. Susana Wertz, born a. 1848
3. Jane Wertz, born a. 1850
4. Herman Wertz, born a. 1852
5. Samuel Wertz, born a. 1854
6. John Wertz, born a. 1856.

Isaac M. Wertz, born about 1785, Germany
Mathias Wertz, born about 1801, Germany,
farmer, with $300 real and $300 personal
property in 1860; wife = Mariah, born about
1822 in Germany; four children all born Penn.
1. Annie Wertz, born about 1844
2. John Wertz, born about 1849
3. William Wertz, born about 1854
4. Johannes Wertz, born about 1858.

George Wertz, born about 1827, Germany, farmer
with $700 real and $300 personal property in
1860; wife = Catherine, born about 1827 in
Germany; four children, all born in Penn.
1. Henry Wertz, born about 1854.
2. Solomon Wertz, born about 1856.
3. Mary E. Wertz, born about 1857.
4. Mariah Wertz, born January 1860.

Bedford township families

Elizabeth Wertz, born about 1787, Penn.

Philip Wertz, born about 1836, Penn.; farm
laborer, P.O. = Bedford, in 1860.

St. Clair township family

Jacob Wertz, born about 1829, Penn.; carpenter with $80 personal property in 1860; wife = Rebecca Ann, born about 1832; and three children:
1. Thomas Wertz, born about 1854
2. Susanah Wertz, born about 1855
3. Nicholas Wertz, born about 1858.

Middle Woodbury township family

George Wertz, born about 1834, Germany, farmer with $7650 real and $1353 personal property in 1860; wife = Fanny, born about 1836, Penn. Also living in the same household is a Jacob Buckhill, born about 1788, Penn., and his wife, Catharine, born about 1795, Penn.

From Bedford County Cemeteries

"Washington Lee Wertz, born 28 March 1822, died 1856", buried at Smith Farm Cemetery (Y); possibly a son of Jacob and Nancy Wertz (see page 181) or a son of John and Elizabeth Wertz (see page 178).

"John W. Wertz, born 25 Oct. 1824, died 18 Sept. 1872, and his wife, Jane E., born 9 Jan. 1832, died 20 Feb. 1905", both buried at Bortz Cemetery (Y). "Malvina Wertz, born 1843, died 1916, 1st wife of Sperry W. Oster, born 1856, died 1917" both buried at Bortz Cemetery (Y). John W. and Malvina could be children of Paul and Mary Wertz (see page 180).
"J. Nuner Wertz, born 1869, died 1966, and his wife, Rachel C., born 1874, died 1936", both buried at Bortz Cemetery (Y); possibly a grandson of Paul and Mary Wertz (page 180).

"Francis Wertz, born 23 Aug. 1828, died 21 Sept. 1912, and his wife, Matilda Haney, born 4 Feb. 1831, died 20 Oct. 1894; and Rufus Wertz, born 27 March 1859, died 23 May 1972; all buried at St. Thomas Roman Catholic Cemetery, Bedford County, Penn. (Y)

ADAMS COUNTY WERTZ FAMILIES

John George and Catherine Worth/Wertz had a daughter, Catherine, baptized 9 June 1783 at the St. Johns Evangelical Lutheran Church, Littlestown, Adams Co., Penn. (E)

Theobald and Molly Wirth had a son, Peter, baptized 29 June 1794 at Upper Bermudian Church, Huntington twp., Adams Co. (E)

Theobald and Magdalena Wirt had a son, name not given, baptized 28 Nov. 1795, at Upper Bermudian Church, Huntington twp. (E)

Adamus and Elizabeth Wertz had a daughter, Maria, baptized 24 Sept. 1797, at Conewago Sacred Heart Roman Catholic Church, Conewago township, Adams Co., Penn. (E)

Dewalt and Barbara Wert had a son, name not given, baptized 1 Sept. 1805, Upper Bermudian Church, Huntington twp., Adams Co. (E)

Michael and Magdalena Wurt had a daughter, Elisabeth, baptized 8 Oct. 1809, at Lower Bermudian Lutheran and Reformed Union Church, Adams Co., Penn. (E)

Bernhard and Lydia Wirt had a daughter, Sophia, baptized 27 March 1834 at St. John's Evangelical Lutheran Church, Gettysburg. (E)

Henry and Mary Magdalene Wirtz had a daughter, Sarah Catharine, baptized 27 March 1835, at Trinity Reformed Church, Gettysburg. (E)

Abraham and Elizabeth Wert had three children: Jacob, George, and Martha, all baptized 7 Oct. 1837 at the Lutheran and Reformed Church at Arendtsville, Adams Co., Penn. (E)

Marcus Wortz and Elizabeth Herbst had a son, George W. born 1 Sept. 1840 at McSherrystown, Adams Co., Penn. (E)

BERKS COUNTY WERTZ FAMILIES

Jacob Wuertz, had three children baptized at the Lutheran Church of Berks County: John Cunradt Wuerts, 25 October 1735; Maria Catharine Wuertz, 10 Jan. 1739; and Anna Margaretha Wuertz, 22 Sept. 1740. (E) This author notes that these are the same names and dates entered for the first three children of Hans Jacob Wertz/Wuertz/Worts and Anna Barbara Hoff, baptized at Coventry, in Chester County. Since it is not likely that another Jacob Wuertz had three children of the exact same names, baptized on the exact same dates at another location, it seems probably that these entries are erroneous. (See Chapter 2)

Johannes Wuertz had a son, Johannes, baptized 7 April 1754 in Bern twp., Berks Co. (E)

Georg Wilhelm and Elisabeth Werth had a son, Ludwig, baptized 28 March 1784 at the Altalaha Evangelical Lutheran Church, Rehrersburg, Berks Co., Penn. (E)

John and Catharine Wertz had a son, Benjamin, baptized 4 Nov. 1787 at the Little Tulpehocken or Christs Evangelical Church, Jefferson twp., Berks Co., Penn. (E)

Jacob and Elisabeth Wirtz had three children bapt. at the Altalaha Evangelical Luth. Church, Rehrersburg: Jacob, 11 Nov. 1787; Johannes, 21 May 1789; and Sara, 14 Nov. 1795. (E)

William and Elizabeth Wirth had two daughters baptized the Altalaha Evangelical Lutheran Church, Rehrersburg: Catharina, 30 March 1788; and Ann Maria, 6 May 1823 (her parents are given as William Schlessman and Elizabeth Worth, but her surname is given as Worth!).(E)

Christian Werth had a daughter, Catherine, baptized 10 Oct. 1802 at St. Johns or Hains Reformed Church, Lower Heidelberg twp., Berks Co., Penn. (E)

BUCKS COUNTY WERTZ FAMILIES

Jacob and Margaret Wirt had a son, John, baptized 12 August 1753 at the Lutheran Church at Tohickon, Bucks Co., Penn. (E)

Valentine and Maria Elizabeth Wirth had two children baptized at the Lutheran Church at Tohickon, Bucks County: John, 25 July 1766; Andrew, 7 Oct. 1767. (E)

Valentine and Elizabeth Wirth also had four children, baptized at the German Reformed Church, Tohickon, Bucks County: Margaret, 18 March 1770; Valentine, 16 August 1772; Christian, 17 August 1774; and John Adam, 20 Oct. 1782. (E)

John and Catharine Wirth had four children baptized at the Lutheran Church at Tohickon, Bucks Co.: Catharine Margaret, 25 Oct. 1770; John, 22 June 1783; Elizabeth, April 1789; and another John, 6 June 1790. (E)

CHESTER COUNTY WERTZ FAMILIES

Jacob Werts/Wertz, born about 1757 (age 61 in April 1818); died 15 March 1821, probably in Berks Co., Penn.; married 12 October 1777/8 "near Valley Forge", Chester Co., Penn. (E) to Catharine Shaffer, born about 1756 (age 79 in Sept. 1837); died between 1843 and 1845, probably in Robeson twp., Berks County. They had "several children". They lived near Churchtown, Lancaster from 1781 to ?; and were living in Berks County by 1818. Jacob Werts was a private from Vincent twp., Chester County, in Colonel Johnston's 5th Penn. Regiment, from 1777 to 1781. He was issued a pension April 1818, which his widow continued after his death. Rev. War pension claim #2980. Certificates #4415 or #4115.

John and Mary Worth had a son Thomas, born 1778, West Bradford twp., Chester Co. (E)

John and Catherine Wertz had a daughter,
Elizabeth, baptized 14 April 1799 in Chester
County, Penn. (E)

John and Lydia Worth had a son, Richard J.,
born 20 Dec. 1809, West Bradford twp. (E)

RICHARD J. WORTH & SOPHIA JEFFERIES

Richard J. Worth married 15 March 1838 at
Concord Monthly Meeting (Quaker), Chester Co.
to Sophia Jefferies. (E)
Richard J. Worth and Sophia Jefferies had
seven children, all born West Bradford twp.,
Chester Co.: Bennett J., born 21 Dec. 1838;
Rachel Ann, born 9 August 1840; Lydia H., born
3 Sept. 1842; Mary E., born 7 Oct. 1844; Annia
M., born 19 Dec. 1846; John R., born 1 Feb.
1849; and Thomas, born 25 Dec. 1852.

HUNTINGDON COUNTY WERTZ FAMILY

Mary Wertz, born 6 October 1746, died 4 Sept.
1822, Huntingdon County, Penn., daughter of
Adam Wertz; married 20 Dec. 1765 to William
Pringle, born 22 Jan. 1745, Scotland, and died
22 June 1829, Claysburg, Huntingdon Co., Penn.
They had nine children... one daughter, Susan
Pringle, born 1773, married John Garn. (This
data received by correspondence in 1969, from
Leslie H. Weber, of Saugus, California.)

LANCASTER COUNTY WERTZ FAMILIES

From the Orphans Court records of Lancaster
County: "John Hockethorn appointed guardian of
John Yeager, and Michael Tanner and Henry Wert
appointed Guardians over Henry and Barbara
Yeager, Orphan children of Henry Yeager,
deceased" The German will of Henry Yeager of
Catoris (Codorus) Twp., was dated 8 April
1748, and proved the same year. (I)

Conrad and Elizabeth Wirth/Werth/or Worth had four children baptized at the Zion Evangelical Lutheran Church, Manheim, Lancaster County: Joh. Michael, 27 Feb. 1776; Anna Christina, 25 Jan. 1778; Joh. Conrad, 6 May 1779; and Henry, 4 Nov. 1781. (E)

Jacob and Susanna Wurtz had a daughter, Elisabet, baptized 21 March 1790, at the Christ Evangelical Lutheran Church, Elizabethtown, Lancaster Co. (E)

Johann and Rosina Wertz had three daughters baptized at the Christ Evangelical Lutheran Church, Elizabethtown, Lancaster Co.: Susana, 1 January 1820; Sarah, 24 Feb. 1822; and Christina, 20 June 1830. (E)

John Peter Bener and Ann Justina had a daughter, Eve Barbara Wirz or Bener, baptized 1755 at the First Reformed Church, Lancaster, Lancaster Co. (E)

Lewis and Elizabeth Margaret Wurtz had four children baptized at the First Reformed Church, Lancaster: Ann Elizabeth, 1 March 1757; Elizabeth, 1 Dec. 1765; William, 8 May 1768; and Susan Elizabeth, 3 May 1772. (E)

LEBANON COUNTY WERTZ FAMILIES

Christian and Barbara Wirth: four children, one bapt. at the Quitapohila Hill Evangelical Lutheran Church, Lebanon twp.: Anna Christina, 9 Nov. 1790; and three baptized at the Hill Evangelical Lutheran Church, North Annville twp., Lebanon Co.: Johannes, 7 Feb. 1795; Joh. Georg, 12 March 1797; and Anna Catarina, 17 Nov. 1799. (E)

Ludwig and Elisabeth Worth had a daughter, Elisabeth, baptized 7 Feb. 1795 at the Hill Evangelical Lutheran Church, North Annville twp., Lebanon Co., Penn. (E)

Patrick **Wharte** had a son, Jacobus, baptized 3 Jan. 1796 at the Hill Evangelical Lutheran Church, North Annville twp., Lebanon Co. (E)

Peter **Werth** had a son, David, baptized Sept. 1810 at the Jerusalem Evangelical Lutheran Church, Annville, Lebanon Co. (E)

John **Wirth** had a son, Henry, baptized March 1814 at the Salem Evangelical Lutheran Church, Lebanon, Lebanon Co. (E)

LEHIGH COUNTY WERTZ FAMILIES

Daniel and Catherine **Werth** had thirteen children all baptized at Ziegels Lutheran and Reformed Church, Weisenberg twp., Lehigh Co.:
1. Josua Werth, 4 Oct. 1812 *
2. David Werth, 29 May 1821 *
3. Maria Wirth, 29 August 1830
4. Willoughby Werth, 6 May 1832
5. Daniel Werth, 5 January 1834
6. Carl William Werth, 25 Dec. 1835
7. Caroline Wirth, 20 June 1837
8. Emilia Werth, 28 April 1839
9. Catharine Werth, 7 June 1841
10. Anna Maria Werth, 2 July 1843
11. Elizabeth Werth, 11 May 1845
12. Edwin Werth, 12 June 1848
13. Levi Werth, 29 Dec. 1849
* mother's name is not given for these two children; could be another wife or family.

John **Werth** had two children baptized at Ziegels Lutheran and Reformed Church, Weisenberg twp., Lehigh Co.: Daniel, 22 April 1820; and Sara, 24 March 1822. (E)

Samuel and Maria **Wirth** had one son, George William, baptized 4 Nov. 1832 at Ziegels Lutheran and Reformed Church, Weisenberg twp., Lehigh Co., Penn. (E)

LUZERNE COUNTY WERTZ FAMILIES

John and Mary Wort married 8 August 1782, Kingston, Luzerne Co.; had five children, all born in Luzerne County: (E)
1. John Wort, born 22 Sept. 1789
2. Sarah Wort, born 9 May 1792
3. Elizabeth Wort, born 28 Feb. 1796
4. Rebecca Wort, born 25 Dec. 1801
5. Israel Wort, born 20 July 1804

John Wort and Jane Connor had four children all born in Luzerne County: (E)
1. William Wort, born 23 Sept. 1817
2. Joseph Wort, born 15 May 1820
3. Marilla Wort, born 14 Feb. 1822
4. Mary Wort, born 27 Dec. 1824

Israel Wort and Susan Miller had seven children born at Kingston, Luzerne Co.:
1. Charles Wort, born 6 Nov. 1828
2. Loyal B. Wort, born 6 Dec. 1830
3. Nancy B. Wort, born 23 Jan. 1833
4. John Wort, born 3 Nov. 1834
5. Louisa North Wort, born 31 August 1836
6. Mary Elizabeth Wort, born 25 Dec. 1838
7. Sarah Marlen Wort, born 27 Dec. 1840

MONTGOMERY COUNTY WERTZ FAMILIES

Jacob and Hindrance Wirth had three children: Sarah, Johann Jacob, and Thomas, all baptized 4 Feb. 1751, at Augustus Evangelical Lutheran Church, Trappe, Montgomery Co., Penn. (E)

Jacob and Anna Barbara Wirth had two sons baptized at Indianfield Lutheran Church, Franconia twp., Montgomery Co.: John George, 16 Jan. 1755; and John Jonas, 1 Jan. 1758. (E)

Andrew and Catharina Wirth had a son, Jacob, baptized 30 Oct. 1790 at the Indianfield Lutheran Church, Franconia twp.   (E)

Jacob and Maria Wert had a daughter, Maria, born 3 April 1823 and baptized at the Indianfield Lutheran Church, Franconia twp.(E)

John K. Wurtz married Naomi B. Kreamer. The family lived at Norristown, Penn. and they had five children: (1) Anna K. Wurtz, born 16 Sept. 1872; (2) Jacob K. Wurtz, born 14 Nov. 1873; (3) John K. Wurtz, born 5 Dec. 1875, died 10 May 1889; (4) Enos K. Wurtz, born 12 Dec. 1878, died 29 April 1881; and (5) David K. Wurtz, born and died 5 Feb. 1880.(U) p.412.

NORTHUMBERLAND COUNTY WERTZ FAMILIES

Johann Heinrich and Elizabeth Wirth had a son, John Wirth or Wirt, born 16 Nov. 1795.   (E)

Johannes Wertz had a daughter, Catharina, baptized 5 May 1822 at Trinity Evangelical Lutheran Church, Milton, Northumberland Co.(E)

John Wirt or Wirth and Barbara Witmer had a son, John, born 26 April 1825/6, Mandata, Northumberland County.   (E)

PHILADELPHIA COUNTY WERTZ FAMILIES

Servants bound and assigned at Phila. 14th Dec. 1772: "Theobald Cline, 9th June past, servant to George Wert of Phila." Servants bound and assigned at Phila. 1772-1773: "27 March 1773, Theobald Cline, servant assigned by George Wert to William McIlvain of Phila." (V) pages 188 and 215.

Joseph and Barbara Wert had two sons, both named Stephen, one baptized 27 May 1775, and one born 22 April 1778; both baptized at St. Josephs Church, Philadelphia.   (E)

Samuel Davis Page "one of the acknowledged
builders of Philadelphia", married 25 Sept.
1861 to Isabella Graham Wurts, of
Philadelphia. She died in France in 1867.
They had three children: (1) Ethel Nelson Page
married James Large; (2) Howard Wurts Page,
lawyer and editor of the Legal Intelligencer;
and (3) William Byrd Page, a mechanical
engineer. Samuel Davis Page died 11 Oct.
1921, age 81 years. (T) page 161.

Elizabeth White Robbins, born 29 May 1871,
daughter of William Bowdoin Robins and Anne
Bronson Reed; married 23 Sept. 1899 to Edward
Vanuxem Wurts. (N) Volume III, page 387.

Robert Kennedy Wurts of Philadelphia, married
Katharine Newbold, who died 10 Sept. 1927 in
Geneva, Switzerland. Three daughters survived
her in 1927: (1) Marian S. Wurts, married
George E. DeCoursey; (2) Eleonore T. Wurts,
married John H. Blye, Jr.; and (3) Rosamund
Wurts, married Benjamin R. Riggs. (N) Volume
III, page 143.

William Clark Hanna, born 23 Jan. 1909; a
lawyer in Philadelphia; married to Ann
Bissell, daughter of Ellison Perot Bissell and
his wife, Ann Wurts. William Clark and Ann
Bissell Hanna had three children: (1) John
Clark Hanna; (2) Sarah Anna Hanna; and (3)
Robert Bissell Hanna. (N) Vol.III, p.383.

SCHUYLKILL COUNTY WERTZ FAMILIES

Henrich and Rebecca Werth had two daughters,
baptized at Summer Hill, St. Pauls Church,
Wayne twp., Schuylkill Co.: Catharina Anna,
23 June 1833; and Rebecca, 5 Sept. 1841. (E)

Wilhelm and Elisabeth Werts had a son,
Jonathan, baptized 14 Feb. 1844 at Summer
Hill, St. Pauls Church, Wayne twp., Schuylkill
County. (E)

SNYDER COUNTY WERTH FAMILY

Adam and Margaret/Margeretha Werth/Worth had six children baptized at Grubb's (Botschaft) Lutheran Church, Chapman twp., Snyder County.
(1) an infant, baptized 22 July 1817, sponsors were Christian and Catherine Worth. (IGI says Jesaya Werth, a son, chr. 10 Aug. 1817.)
(2) Jamanuel or Imanuel Werth (E), a son, baptized 18 August or 9 Nov. (E) 1819, sponsors were Jacob and Margaret Roush.
(3) Frederick or Friederich Werth (E), baptized 10 Sept. or 7 Oct. (E) 1821, sponsors were Andrew and Anna Maria Shetterly.
(4) Martin Werth, baptized 8 March or 4 April (E) 1824, sponsors = Jacob and Margaret Roush.
(5) Joseph Werth, bapt. 18 May 1825 or 22 June 1826 (E), sponsors = Henry and Polly Zeller.
(6) William Werth, baptized 21 June or 27 Sept. (E) 1829, sponsors were Simon and Barbara Roush.

WESTMORELAND COUNTY WERTZ FAMILIES

John and Agnes/Hadnis Werth had three children born in Hempfield twp., Westmoreland and baptized there at the Harrolds Reformed Church: Philip Werth, born 19 May 1787; Anna Maria, born 19 May 1787; and Regina, baptized 21 May 1797. (E)

John Wertz married, probably in Westmoreland Co., Penn. to Barbara Stoner, born 1790, died 1845. This family lived at Scottdale, on the border of Fayette and Westmoreland Counties. Barbara Stoner was the daughter of Christian Stoner (1757-1814) and Barbara Shank (1765-1816), daughter of Tobias Shank. Christian Stoner was a Mennonite, migrated from Lancaster Co. about 1800 to East Huntingdon twp., Westmoreland County. Christian Stoner was the son of John Stoner (a.1728-1773) and Elizabeth Herr, Mennonites of Lancaster Co. (W) page 18.

YORK COUNTY WERTZ FAMILIES

Jacob Wirtz had a son, George, baptized 27 Nov. 1742 at St. Matthews Lutheran Church, Hanover, York County, Penn. (E)

Henry and Anna Wirt had a daughter, Catherine, born Jan. 1750, York County. (E)

Hans Martin and Catharina Barbara Wurtz, had a daughter, Anna Elisabeth Catharina, baptized 10 August 1769 at Strayers Salem Reformed Church, Dover twp., York Co. (E)

Jacob Wertz of Codorus twp. had letters of administration granted 14 August 1778, probated 26 August 1779; wife = Magdalena; three children (1) Elizabeth Wertz, born a. 1770 (age 8 years in 1778/9); (2) Mary Wertz, born a. 1773 (age 5 in 1778/9); and (3) John Wertz, born a. 1775 (age 3 in 1778/9). From York Co. Wills, Volume D., pages 115-118.

Johannes and Anna Christina Wertz had one son baptized at St. Pauls or Wolfs Reformed Church, West Manchester twp., York County:(E)
1. Johannes Wertz, baptized 16 August 1778.
And two children baptized at St. Pauls or Zieglers Lutheran and Reformed Church, North Codorus twp., York County. (E)
2. John Henry Wertz, baptized 17 Feb. 1787
3. Lydia Wirth, born 21 August 1803
And six children baptized at St. Jacobs or Stone Lutheran and Reformed Church, Brodbecks, York County: (E)
4. Sarah Werths, baptized 24 Nov. 1805
5. Jacob Werths, baptized 13 March 1808
6. Christina Wirtz, baptized 12 May 1810
7. Samuel Wertz, baptized 30 August 1812
8. Jesse Wertz, baptized 1 March 1815
9. Jhs. Werz, baptized 23 Oct. 1818

Daniel Wirtz had a son, John Michael, baptized 23 Nov. 1783 at St. Paul or Zieglers Lutheran and Reformed Church, North Codorus twp., York County. (E)

Henry and Catharine Wirt had two daughters baptized at St. Matthews Lutheran Church, Hanover, York Co.: Luisa Anna, 17 April 1816; and Catharine, 1 Feb. 1818. (E)

Jacob and Julianne Wert, had two daughters, Ludy and Henrietta, both baptized 7 May 1820 at St. Matthews Lutheran Church, Hanover. (E)

Samuel and Elizabeth Wertz, had a son, Abdiel, baptized 15 April 1832 at St. Jacobs or Stone Lutheran and Reformed Church, Brodbecks. (E)

Adam and Sarah Wirth had two sons baptized at Christ Lutheran Church, York, York Co.: (E)
1. William H. Wirth, baptized 19 Oct. 1832
2. Theodore Wert, baptized 29 July 1834.

Jacob and Mary Wortz/Wertz, had six children baptized at St. Matthews Lutheran Church, Hanover, York Co.: (E)
1. Ann Maria Wortz, 11 Dec. 1836
2. John Henry Wertz, 11 Dec. 1838
3. Wm. Henry Wertz, 20 Sept. 1842
4. Samuel Adam Wertz, 5 May 1844
5. Louisa Catherine Wertz, 21 June 1846
6. Margaret Jane Wortz, 29 April 1849

David and Rebecca Catharine Wortz had two children baptized at St. Matthews Lutheran Church, Hanover, York Co.: (E)
1. Juliana Baugher Wortz, 5 June 1845
2. Charles Augustus Wortz, 23 Oct. 1848.

OTHER PENNSYLVANIA WERTZ FAMILIES

Correspondence from James M. Kemer of Presque Isle, Maine in 1985 stated that his ancestor, Archibald William Wertz was born 1896 in Penn., the son of Carl Leslie Wertz. Nothing further is know of this family to date.

In 1978, Paul Getts, of Indiana, Penn. was seeking information on a Jacob Wert, born about 1803 in Penn., married Margaret Ross, who was born about 1811, in New Jersey.

Also in 1978, Mrs. Richard Wert of Holland, Penn. was seeking information on a Isaac Wert, who married about 1806 to Ruth Jones, born 12 Sept. 1786 in Chester or Berks Co., Penn.; died 12 Sept. 1857, and is buried at Douglessville, Berks Co., Penn.

In the 1760's there was "a family of Wirtz's living near Mexico" (Juniata Co., Penn.) who were probably descendants of Margaret Finley, daughter of John Finley and Elizabeth Harris. (J), pages 59-60.

FREDERICK & WASHINGTON CO., MARYLAND FAMILIES

Peter Wurtz, and Christina, parents of three children baptized at the Evangelical Lutheran Church, Middletown, Frederick Co., Maryland:
1. Jacob Wurtz, bapt. 18 Sept. 1768.
2. Anna Maria Wuertz, bapt. 15 Sept. 1771.
3. Johannes Wirtz, bapt. 22 June 1777. (E)
(Note that the surname is spelled differently for each child!)

Conrad Wuertz, Wurtz, or Wirtz and Maria Barbara, parents of two children baptized at the Evangelical Lutheran Church, Middletown, Frederick County, Maryland: (E)
1. Wilhelm Wurtz/Wuertz, bapt. 11 Dec. 1771.
2. Maria Elisabeth Wirtz, bapt. 6 April 1774.

Peter Wirt and Elisabetha, parents of two children baptized at the Salem German Reformed Church, Conococheague Dist., Washington Co.:
1. Vallentein Wirt, bapt. 19 Jan. 1772.
2. Eva Wirt, bapt. 30 March 1777. (E)

Michael Wertz and Catharina, parents of a daughter, Christina Wertz, baptized 1 May 1791, at the Evangelical Lutheran Church, Middletown, Frederick County, Maryland. (E)

Prince George Co., MARYLAND WIRT Family

Jasper Wirt, born about 1731 (age 45 in 1776), and wife, Catherine, born about 1729 (age 47 in 1776), are living in Prince George Co., Maryland in 1776 with six children: (1) a son, born a. 1751 (age 25 in 1776); (2) a daughter, born a. 1756, (age 20 in 1776); (3) a daughter, born a. 1758, (age 18 in 1776); (4) a son, born a. 1761, (age 15 in 1776); (5) a son, born a. 1766, (age 10 in 1776); and (6) a daughter, born a. 1770, (age 6 in 1776).

Perhaps the youngest three children are as follows (see Prince George Co. Marriage records and the IGI): (4) Christian Wirt or Wirtt, married 3 or 6 Sept. 1792, St. John's Parish to Mary Weaver. (5) Henry Wirt, married 15 Jan. or 30 April 1795, St. John's Parish to Jannett or Jennett Ferguson. (6) Barbara Wirt, m. 6 Jan. 1790 to John Tilley. Jasper Wirt took an oath of Fidelity in Prince George Co., Maryland; but date is not given. (see Maryland Records by Brumbaugh, Vol. II, pages 60, 160, 165, 170, 284.)

Midwestern States WERTZ FAMILIES

Rachael Wertz married 30 Sept. 1843, Preble Co., Ohio to Andrew Hoover (E), born 22 Nov. 1823, probably in Randolph twp., Montgomery Co.; died 1 May 1891; son of David Hoover, who went to Ohio in 1801/2 and became the first Justice of the Peace in Mont.Co. (P) page 10.

Correspondence from Mona Watkins of Omaha, Nebraska in 1888 seeks information on a John Wertz, born Dark Co., Ohio, who died near Schuyler, Nebraska; probably a son of a John Wertz; married at Fulton Co., Indiana to a Hesteran --?-- (surname unknown). Other Ohio records Mona has located show a John Wertz, age 26, carpenter, wife Anna, age 22, in the 1850 Peru twp, Miami Co., Ind. Census.
In Fulton Co., Indiana a John Wertz married 14 August 1884 to a Mary E. Bright.

CHARLES WERTZ and ALICE G. HAYMOND

Charles Wertz, born 19 Aug. 1863; married 5 July 1888 at Grundy, Ill. to Alice Gertrude Haymond, born 7 Aug. 1866, daughter of James L. Haymond and Melissa Hollenbeck (see the Genealogy of the Descendants of John Gar, pages 238 and 418). Charles and Alice had three children: (1) Arthur H. Wertz, born 4 April 1891; (2) Mabel Wertz, born 8 Aug. 1891; and (3) Charles Wertz Jr., born 14 March 1893.

HARRY C. STONEBRAKER and BESSIE WERTS

Harry C. Stonebraker, born a. 1874, Kansas, son of Samuel Asbury Stonebraker, 1832-1905) and Susan D. Strunck, of Warrior's Mark, Penn., and Black Jack, Kansas; married Bessie Werts... probably in Kansas. (See the Robeson Genealogy, pages 308 and 495.)
Harry and Bessie Werts Stonebraker had three children: (1) Eugene Stonebraker; (2) Herold Stonebraker; and (3) Vernon Stonebraker.

SIMON PETER WERTZ and ESTHER ANN SHERMAN

Simon Peter Wertz was b. 3 May 1819, possibly in Canada; died 20 January 1892 at San Jose, Santa Clara Co., California; and is buried at the Oak Hill Memorial Park Cemetery in San Jose. He m. Esther Ann Sherman, born 11 Sept. 1826; d. 19 January 1892, San Jose, Calif. They had five children, all born in Boone Co., Ill.: (1) Mary Ellen Wertz, b. 1846. (2) John Westly Wertz, b. 1847; d. 1936; m. 24 Dec.1876 to Mary C. Adams. (3) Emily M. Wertz, b.1848. (4) James A.Leonard Wertz, b. 1850; d. 22 Jan. 1926; m.16 Nov.1878 to Ida Jane Patrick. (5) Samuel Sanford Wertz, b. 1856; died 1928. (EE)

Chapter 8

A Parallel Wertz Family History

The following history is presented here, because there are several parallels in their story and the family traditions of our Bretten, Germany ancestors, although no proof is yet available that they are directly related. The possibility exists however, and must be seriously considered. Secondly, members of this Wurtz family emigrated to Pennsylvania about the same time as did our Bretten ancestors, and the given names are also very similar. Thus some records may have become confused or mixed, between the two families.

THE WIRZ FAMILY OF ZURICH, SWITZERLAND

Ulrich von Uerikon was the second son of Rudolph von Uerikon, and a knight and vassal of Rudolph of Hapsburg, who became Holy Roman Emperor of Germany. Ulrich married in 1280, to the Baroness von Wandelburg, daughter of the Lord High Steward of Rappenschwril, Zurich, Switzerland. Berkhardt von Uerikon, son of Ulrich von Uerikon, and his descendants for eight generations were Ammanns or chief magistrates and burghers of the town of Zurich in Switzerland. Burkhardt's son, Heinrich is believed to have been the first of the family to adopt the surname of Wirz. Two generations later, Heinrich Wirz, son of Burkhardt Wirz, and grandson of Heinrich (above), living at the time of the Reformation in Switzerland, became a convert of Zwingli. This Heinrich, and his two brothers, Jacob and Johannes, were known as the honorable and pious brothers, called the "Wirzen of Uerikon" and were granted the honor of knighthood by Albrecht von Bonstetten, Dean at Einsiedeln, in December of 1492. This Heinrich was chief magistrate of Uerikon and Almoner, of the Princely Abbey of Einsiedeln.

He married first in 1498 to Agnes Von Cham, and married second to Verena Wedischwiler. A son, by his second wife, Jacob Wirz, born in 1506, also held the office of chief magistrate at his death in 1536. Jacob Wirz married Margaretha Vachtigen, and a son of theirs, Casper Wirz, born 16 April 1532, became a burgher in Zurich in 1558, and married 9 Feb. 1553 to Anna Kleiner. Johannes Rudolph Wirz, eldest son of Casper and Anna Kleiner Wirz, was born in 1554. He married 1st 1 June 1577 to Verena Aeni, and 2nd on 30 June 1602 to Dorothy Richtmann. He was a weaver and a member of the weavers' guild. His third son, Franz Wirz, born February 1581, died 4 Oct. 1658; married 15 Oct. 1603 to Margaretha Horner. Franz was also a weaver. The eldest son of Franz and Margaretha Horner Wirz, Johannes Conrad Wirz, was born 20 May 1606, died 31 Dec. 1667. He was admitted to the ministry of the gospel March 1628, and became a preacher of considerable eminence. He married Juditha Knemm; and their son, also named Johannes Conrad Wirz, born 27 August 1631, died 30 Nov. 1682, also became a minister in 1654, and was pastor of churches at Rappenschweil in 1656; at Uerikon in 1658; at Richtenwell in 1661; at Zurich in 1668 and 1680. He married 17 Jan. 1660 to Ursula Holzhalb, and their eldest son, also named Johannes Conrad Wirz, was born 5 May 1661 at Zurich. He also became a minister of the gospel and was pastor of St. Peter's Church in Zurich; and later pastor at Kerensen, Switz., where he died 20 April 1730. He married 3 Nov. 1685 to Magdalena Klinger, born 14 Sept. 1664, died 1729, and they had six sons and six daughters. Their fifth son was also named Johannes Conrad Wirz, and was born 30 Nov. 1706 in Zurich. As a young man he entered the service of the King of the Netherlands, as a cadet. But he soon abandoned the military profession, returned to his native city of Zurich, engaging in the practice of law. In 1735 he emigrated to America.

1735 EMIGRANT JOHANNES CONRAD WIRZ

Rev. Moritz Goetschy or Goetschius, born 26 Sept. 1686, in Zurich, a son of Rudolph and Magdalena Kolloker Goetschy, who had been a minister at Salentz in the Canton of Zurich, but was deposed from the ministry in 1731, began to organize a colony of Swiss to go with him to America. In 1734 advertisements in the Zurich newspapers described the American colonies as "a second Canaan" and enticed many to emigrate. Goetschius succeeded in his efforts, and on 4 October 1734, three large boats floated down the river Zimat containing a party of from 174 to 256 Swiss men, women, and children, including Goetschius, his wife and eight children, and Johannes Conrad Wirz or Wurtz, who was the commissary of the party. They were bound for Rotterdam, and then America. At Neuwid, on the Rhine, four couples went ashore and were married by a Reformed clergyman. Among them was "Commissari Hans Conrad Wirtz and Anna Goetschi", daughter of the leader of the expedition.

Rev. Moritz Goetschius, his wife, and eight children, including daughter, Anna, and her husband, Conrad Wurtz sailed from Rotterdam in the ship "Mercury" on 24 February 1735 and arrived in Philadelphia 29 May 1735. On the day of their arrival, the men took the oath of allegiance at the Philadelphia State House, and the name of Conrad Wuertz heads the list. Rev. Goetschius was not well when they arrived in Philadelphia, and was carried ashore the next day, so weak that he could not walk unaided, and died later that day, 30 May 1735. His seventeen-year-old son, John Henry Goetschius soon became a minister (by 1739 he was a Pastor) (N) and under his leadership the family and most of the colony settled near Skippack.

Johannes Conrad Wurtz is believed to have remained with the remnant of his wife's family near Germantown for a time. Their first child, Anna Maria Magdalena Wurtz was baptized

at Christ Church in Philadelphia on 20 August
1735 at three days of age. Later he became
a school master at Old Goshenhoppen (N) (now
Montgomery County) and then at Conestoga (now
Lancaster County. A land warrant in Phila.
Co. for 150 acres to Conrad Wurtz is dated 14
September 1738. This land was probably in
what became Montgomery County in 1784 and
later Berks County in 1752. In 1742 Conrad
Wurtz became pastor of the Egypt Church, in
Whitehall twp., in then Bucks (now Lehigh) Co.
In 1744 he became pastor of Trinity Reformed
Church, Schuggenhaus, Springfield township,
Bucks Co., and in 1747 he added responsibility
for congregations at Saucon, (O) Forks of
Delaware, and Lehigh. By 1750 he had removed
to near Lebanon, New Jersey where he lived
until 1762. He was not officially ordained to
the ministry until 5 June 1752 in New Jersey,
and then became the first Reformed minister in
the Province of New Jersey. (O) He was pastor
for ten years of the church near Ringoes,
Larison's Corner, New Jersey, and also took
charge of the congregations at Fox Hill,
Alexandria, Rockaway, German Valley, and
Amwell. Then on 9 May 1762 he was installed
as pastor at the Zion Reformed Church, York,
Penn. and officiated there until his death 21
Sept. 1763. During his brief pastorate there,
a new stone church was erected and eighty-
three children were baptized by him. At his
death, the floor of the church was not yet
laid, so he was buried under the alter.
Several sessions of the Continental Congress
were later held in this church.

Rev. Johannes Conrad Wurtz and Anna Goetschius
had one daughter and five sons: Anna Maria,
Conrad, John, George, Peter, and Maurice.

1. Anna Maria Magdalena Wurtz, born 17 August
1735, bapt. 20 August 1735 at Christ Church.

2. Conrad Wirtz, probably born about 1740;
died 1787 in Roxbury, New Jersey, leaving a
wife, Anna, and several daughters.

3. John Wirtz. born 30 June 1744, Springfield twp., Bucks Co., Penn.; died 14 Sept. 1793, Mt. Pleasant, Morris Co., New Jersey; married 8 June 1773, Morris Co., New Jersey to Sarah Grandin. The had eight sons. More on this family below.

4. George Wirtz, born about 1748.
A George William Wirt married 20 June 1779 at Tulpehockon, Berks Co., Penn. to Elizabeth Schmidt. (E)

5. Peter Wirtz, born about 1750.
A Peter Wirz married 3 Feb. 1774 at Oldwick, Hunterdon County, New Jersey to Eleonora Rudolfs. (E)

6. Maurice Wirtz, born about 1752.
A Maurice Morris Wurts married 19 August 1779 at Amwell twp., Hunterdon Co., New Jersey to Sarah Williamson. (E)

JOHN WIRTZ and SARAH GRANDIN

John Wirtz, born 30 Sept. 1744, Springfield twp., Bucks Co., Penn.; died 14 Sept. 1793 Mt. Pleasant, Morris Co., New Jersey, and also buried at Mt. Pleasant; son of Johannes Conrad Wurtz and Anna Goetschius; married 8 June 1773 at Flanders, Morris Co., New Jersey to Sarah Grandin, daughter of Samuel Grandin and Susanna Johnston. They had eight sons, but only six are named: Samuel, George, Maurice, William, Charles, and John.

1. Samuel Grandin Wurtz, "the eldest son", probably born about 1774/5. After a brief career at sea, he settled down as the manager of an iron furnace in New Jersey, where he died.

2. George Wurtz, born 29 June 1777, Limington, New Jersey; died 8 March 1835; a Doctor; married Abigail Pettit. More on this family on the next page.

3. Maurice Wurtz, a merchant in Philadelphia.
There is a Maurice Werts in the 1810 Census,
High Street Ward, Philadelphia Co., Penn.

4. William Wurtz, a merchant in Philadelphia;
and living in New York City in 1835. There is
a Wilhelm Wurtz Jr. and Sr. in Philadelphia in
1754; and a William Wurtz in the 1810 Census,
North Ward, Philadelphia Co., Penn.

5. Charles Stewart Wurts, a merchant in
Philadelphia.

8. John Wurts, "youngest son", graduated from
Princeton; admitted to the bar in Philadelphia
in Oct. 1816. Member of the Penn. State
legislature and the 19th Congress as a
representative from Philadelphia. John went
abroad for his health in 1859, and died in
Rome, Italy.

GEORGE WURTS and ABIGAIL PETTIT

George Wurts, born 29 June 1777, Lamington,
New Jersey; died at the home of his brother
William, in New York City, on 8 March 1835;
son of John Wurts and Sarah Grandin. George
married Abigail Pettit, daughter of Amos and
Esther Pettit. Two sons are identified:

1. John Jacob Wurts, a lawyer at Easton, and
Wilkes-Barre, Pennsylvania.

6. William Wurts, "sixth child", born 25 Nov.
1809, Montville, Morris Co., New Jersey;
lived Carbondale and Wilkes-Barre, Penn.; died
15 July 1858, Carbondale, Penn. Married 17
March 1836 to Lucretia Jeannette Lathrop,
daughter of Salmon Lathrop and Aurelia Noble.
A son, Theodore Frelinghuysen Wurts, born 31
May 1844 at Wilkes-Barre, Penn.; married 8
April 1868 to Anna Vanuxem, born 7 Jan. 1846,
Lambertville, New Jersey, daughter of Edward
Vanuxem and Elizabeth Krusen. One of their
sons, John Sparhawk Wurts, born 18 June 1876,
Carbondale, Penn. was a prominent attorney in

Philadelphia, Penn. and the subject of the article from which most of this data was obtained.

JOHN SPARHAWK WURTZ, Phila. Attorney

John S. Wurtz, born 18 June 1876, Carbondale, Penn.; son of Theodore F. and Anna Vanuxem Wurts. He was educated at the West Jersey Military Academy, where he graduated in 1893. he engaged in Civil Engineering with his father in field, railroad, and mine surveys; started in the insurance business in Philadelphia in 1894; and was admitted to the Philadelphia bar in 1904; admitted also to practice before the Supreme Court of the United States, specializing in organizational and property management. He also served for thirty-five years as Commissioner of Deeds, appointed by President Theodore Roosevelt in 1902. He had an absorbing interest in Colonial families, their pedigrees and traditions. He was for a time associated in genealogical compilations with several noted authors. He was president of "Descendants of the Continental Congress" and a member of other historical societies and patriotic hereditary orders. His picture is on the next page, and a short biographical sketch is on the following page.

John C. Wurtz

John S. Wurts

Lawyer, Author, Editor, born in Pennsylvania in 1876; a member of the Philadelphia Bar, admitted also to practice before the Supreme Court of the United States, specializing in organization and property management; he served for thirty-five years as Commissioner of Deeds, his initial appointment being made by President Theodore Roosevelt in 1902.

Since youth Mr. Wurts has had an absorbing interest in Colonial families, their pedigrees and traditions. He was for a time associated in genealogical compilations with each of the noted writers, Frank Willing Leach, Warren S. Ely and Charles H. Browning.

Mr. Wurts is widely known for his leadership in the Daily Vacation Bible School movement, of which he was a Founder in 1907 with Robert G. Boville and Floyd W. Tomkins, and succeeded the latter as President.

A Delegate repeatedly to The Indian Rights Conference, he has also actively served his own locality in Rescue Missions, Relief Societies, care of the aged, and local reform politics; a member for many years of the Executive Committee of the Pennsylvania State Y. M. C. A.

Pending the restoration of St. George's Chapel, the shrine of the Knights of the Garter at Windsor Castle, Mr. Wurts served as American Treasurer of The Garter Chapel Fund at the request of the Duke of Somerset. He is President, Descendants of the Continental Congress and a member of other historical societies and patriotic hereditary orders.

Other Records of Probable Descendants
of this Wurtz Family

"Rev. John Conrad Wirtz, born in Zurich, Switzerland, was the first German Reformed preacher in Lebanon and German Valley, before 1750. A great-great-grandson, George Theodor Werts, was governor of New Jersey from 1893 to 1896." (L) Vol. I, page 154 (O)p.103

"In 1754, Rev. Conrad Wirtz and wife were sponsors for an Isler family baptism at the First Trinity Reformed Church at York, York County, Penn." (K) p. 504.

William Wirt, died in 1834, Baltimore, Maryland; was appointed by Pres. Thomas Jefferson as prosecuting attorney in the 1807 trial of Aaron Burr, Vice President of the United States. William Wirt's father was born in Switzerland, and his mother was born in Würtemberg; William was admitted to the bar in 1792; had a law office at Culpeper Court House, Virginia; and in Richmond in 1799; in 1816 he was appointed U. S. Dist. Att. for Virginia by Pres. Madison; and in 1817 to 1829, he served as U.S. Attorney General, under Presidents Monroe and Adams. (L), Volume 2, pages 143 and 181; (M), Vol.6, page 86.

Chapter 9

OTHER PENNSYLVANIA WERTZ FAMILIES

A Dauphin County Family

"John Adam Wirt was born in the year 1727 in Germany, emigrated to America in the ship Mascliffe-Galley, George Durell, commander, from Rotterdam, last from the port in Dorsetshire, England. On the same ship were Philip Ludwig Wert and John Jacob Wertz, possibly his brothers. John Adam Wirt first settled in Montgomery County, Penn. thence removed to the Tulpehocken settlement, and finally to Lykens Valley." (J) He was warranted 300 acres of land 6 June 1774, and made other purchases from time to time, "amounting to sufficient acreage to give each of his children, twelve in number, a large sized farm." All of this land was in the vicinity of St. David's Reformed Church, Dauphin County, Penn. John Adam Wirt married probably about 1760, to Eva Elizabeth Schnug or Snoke, born 1730, in Germany; died 1800, Lykens Valley. John Adam Wirt died in 1830, Lykens Valley, Dauphin Co., Penn. (J)

FAMILY OF ADAM AND ELIZABETH WIRT

1. **Adam Wirt.** "He left Dauphin County when single and settled in Virginia, where he married and raised a large family." See Chapter Eleven for possible descendants.

2. **Jacob Wirt/Wert**, born 21 May 1764, Lancaster County, Penn.; died 1 Jan. 1833, Dauphin County; married Anna Maria Sophia Miller, born 2 August 1776; died 22 Oct. 1832; they had "six sons, four daughters, and 22 grandchildren". (J) Outline of this family begins on page 223.

3. a daughter * who married **Michael Radel**, who resided near Mahontongo Mountain, Dauphin Co., and are both buried at the St. John's Church there. They had five sons: David, Joseph, William, Philip, and Jacob Radel.   (J)

4. **Christian Wirt**, probably born about 1767; died near Schnee's Mills, Snyder Co., Penn.; married about 1787 to Catherine Bretz, daughter of Ludwig Bretz; eleven or twelve children.   Outline of this family begins on page 225.

5. **Anna Catharine Wirt**, married **Sebastian Metz**; they "resided and died in the Lykens Valley". They had ten children.   Outline of this family is on page 227.

6. **George Wirt**, born 10 May 1770; died 13 Feb. 1845; married Anna Catharine Miller.   They lived and died in the Lykens Valley and had five or six children. Outline of this family begins on page 228.

7. **Margaretha Wirth**, christened 25 June 1771 at the Salem Evangelical Lutheran Church near Killinger, Dauphin Co., Penn. (E)   Perhaps she is the daughter who married Michael Radel (#3 above) *.

8. **Henry Wirt**, born 22 Nov. 1771; married Elizabeth Enterline; daughter of Rev. John Michael Enterline, born 1726, died 16 March 1800. Henry and Elizabeth had at least seven children.   Records of this family are on page 229.

9. **Peter Wirt**, probably born about 1772; died near Carlisle Springs, Cumberland Co., Penn.; married "Miss Sheesly", probably Elizabeth Sheesly.   They had at least three children: Peter, Philip, and Eve.   Outline of this family begins on page 229.

10. **Johann Philip Wirt**, christened 6 April 1773, Salem Church, Killinger; was married in Union Co., Penn. and had at least three children: Eve, John, and another son, not named. (J) No further records of this family have been clearly identified to date, but some possibilities exist in the Dauphin and Cumberland Co. records cited at the conclusion of this chapter.

11. **Joseph Wirt**, christened 9 May 1775, Salem Church, Killinger; wife = Barbara; lived at Carlisle, Cumberland Co., Penn. and later they removed to Crawford Co., Ohio. Probably had at least four children. Outline of this family begins on page 231.

12. **Mary Elizabeth Wert**, born 8 May 1784, baptized 29 May 1784 at Bindnagle Lutheran and Reformed Church, Derry twp, Dauphin Co.; sponsors at her baptism were John and Anna Margaret Snoke Jr. (E) (J) Perhaps she was the daughter who married Michael Radel * (see #3 above.)

13. **John Wirt**, born 25 January 1788; died 8 Feb. 1858, at the Wirt settlement, Lykens Valley, Dauphin Co., Penn. and is buried at Killinger; married Anna Maria Elizabeth Miller. They had at least eleven children. Outline of this family begins on page 233.

JACOB WIRT and ANNA MARIA SOPHIA MILLER

Jacob Wirt/Wirth, born 21 May 1764, Lancaster Co., Penn. (K); died 1 Jan. 1833, Upper Paxtang twp., Dauphin Co. (J); buried 3 Jan. 1833 at Wirth's Church Lutheran graveyard near Killinger, Dauphin Co. (J)(K); son of John Adam and Eva Elizabeth Wirt; married* Anna Maria Sophia Miller, born 2 August 1776, died 22 Oct. 1832. (*There is a marriage record at St. Paul's Church, Philadelphia dated 15 Sept. 1777 for a Jacob Wirth and Mary Miller. (I) However, either this date is incorrect, or this record is for a different Jacob Wirt and

Mary Miller, as this couple were probably married about 1794.) They had "six sons, four daughters and 22 grandchildren" (K), but to date we have found records for only nine children and 16 grandchildren, all of whom were baptized at the Salem Evangelical Lutheran Church, Killinger, Dauphin Co. and are listed in the IGI (E).

1. Anna Christina Wirth, baptized 1 Sept. 1795. Nothing further in known of her.

2. Eva Elizabeth Wirth, baptized 1 Sept. 1795.

3. Johannes Wirth (E) or Johan Wirt (J), born 7 Dec. 1796, married Magdalena Shupp. "Removed to Huron County, Ohio and died there leaving a family." (J)

4. Daniel Wirth/Wirt, born 7 Dec. 1796; died 20 Oct. 1858, at Killinger; married Susanna Shupp, born 2 March 1797, died 12 March 1873, daughter of George Shupp, born 4 August 1759, died 27 August 1839, and Maria Elizabeth Deibler, born 10 Jan. 1776, died 8 April 1846. Daniel and Susanna had five children baptized at Salem Church, Killinger:
(1) Elisabeth Werth, baptized 17 March 1819
(2) William Wirth, baptized 25 Feb. 1821
(3) Catharina Werth, baptized 20 April 1823
(4) Isaac Werth, baptized 7 August 1825
(5) Emanuel Werth, baptized 16 March 1828

5. Anna Maria "Mary" Wirth/Wirt, baptized 17 March 1799; married Ludwig Paul. "Resided and died near Pumpkin Hill, Dauphin County." (J) They had at least two children.

6. Jacob Wirth, baptized 20 July 1804; married Betsy Fauver. "Resided and died in Paul's Valley. Had issue." (J)

7. Solomon Wirth, born 25 Dec. 1805; married 2 May 1826, Lykens Valley Lower Church, Killinger, to Maria "Mary" Noll, daughter of Johannes Noll Sr. (K). "Resided and died in

Center County, Penn." (J) Had at least two children baptized at Salem Church, Killinger. (1) Elias Werth, baptized 28 Sept. 1828; and (2) Josias Werth, baptized 31 May 1830. They probably had other children, perhaps after moving to Center County.

8. Isaac Wirth, born 22 March 1808; married 17 August 1826, Lykens Valley Lower Church, (K) Killinger, to Elisabeth Badeiger (K) or Potteiger (J), daughter of Johannes Badeiger. "Resided near Killinger" (J) Seven children were baptized at Salem Church, Killinger:

(1) Jonas Werth, baptized 18 Feb. 1827
(2) Joseph Werth, baptized 24 Nov. 1828
(3) Sarah Werth, baptized 24 May 1838
(4) Catharina Werth, baptized 5 April 1840
(5) Anna Maria Werth, baptized 27 June 1841
(6) Susanna Wirth, baptized 21 May 1843
(7) Samuel Werts, baptized 12 August 1847

9. Henrich or Henry Werth/Wirt, born 16 May 1810, baptized 8 July 1810; died 13 April 1880. "Resided and died near Berrysburg" (J) Married Miss Harmon. "Left issue" (J)

CHRISTIAN WIRT and CATHARINE BRETZ

Christian Wirt, son of John Adam and Eva Elizabeth Wirt, died near Schner's Mills, Snyder Co., Penn. He married probably about 1787 to Catharine or Catharina Magdalena Bretz, daughter of Ludwig Bretz. They had twelve children, all baptized at the Salem Evangelical Lutheran Church near Killinger, Dauphin County. It is not known if they had any other children after removing to Snyder County, but Engle (J) names only eleven children and all of them were baptized at Killinger. Birthdates are from Engle (J), and baptismal dates from the IGI (E) Engle spells the surname Wirt, the IGI uses Wirth, Wirt, and Werth. The IGI spellings are given here.

1. **Anna Maria Wirth**, born 8 June 1788, baptized 15 June 1788; married John A. Miller; "Removed from Snyder Co., Pa. to Crawford Co., Ohio. Had issue." (J)

2. **Johann Adam Wirth**, born 17 Jan. 1790, baptized 7 Feb. 1790. The IGI shows six children baptized at the Botschaft Lutheran and Reformed Church, Chapman twp., Snyder County to Adam and Margareth/Margeretha:
(1) Jesaya Werth, male, 10 August 1817
(2) Imanuel Werth, baptized 9 Nov. 1819
(3) Friederich Werth, baptized 7 Oct. 1821
(4) Martin Werth, baptized 4 April 1824
(5) Joseph Werth, baptized 25 June 1826
(6) William Werth, baptized 27 Sept. 1829

3. **Susanna Margaretha Wirth**, born 16 June 1791, bapt. 10 July 1791; m. Casper Miller; "Removed to Crawford Co., Ohio in 1830, and finally to Springfield, Ohio, where he died. They had issue twelve children, of whom the ninth was Catharine, born 20 Feb. 1827, died 12 Sept. 1878. She married Ross Mitchell, born 14 Nov. 1824, in Landisburg, Perry Co., Penn. and resides in Springfield, Ohio." (J)

4. **Catharine or Catharina Magd. Wirth**, born 11 Jan. 1793, baptized 24 Feb. 1793; married Mr. Wise; removed to Crawford Co., Ohio.

5. **Johann Ludwig Wirth**, born 21 July 1794, baptized 31 August 1794; died 12 July 1845 at Baskin's Island, Dauphin Co., Penn.

6. **Elizabeth Wirth**, born 29 May 1796, baptized 31 July 1796; married 1st to Isaac Diddy; removed to Crawford Co., Ohio; had a "large family." (J)

7. a daughter, not named, baptized 1 April 1798. Perhaps died young.

8. **Christina Wirth** (E) or **Christian Wirt** (J), baptized 12 Nov. 1799. "married twice, and many of his descendants in Susquehanna and

L.P. townships." (J)   (Note: Engle claims this is a son, but the baptismal record is for a daughter!)

9. Sarah Wirt (J) or Salome Wirth (E), born 26 Sept. 1801 (J),bapt. 22 Nov. 1801 (E); m. John Shive. "They lived and died at Twin Locks, near Halifax, Penn.; are buried at Long's Church in Halifax twp., and have a number of children residing in the Lykens Valley." (J)

10. George Werth, b. 1 Nov. 1803; bapt. 4 Jan. 1804; "resided in Northumberland Co." (J)

11. Rachael/Rahel Wirth, born 17 August 1806 (J)(E); "married Wendel Row, and resided in Lykens Valley; are buried at St. John's church, Berrysburg, Penn. They have numerous descendants in the Upper End." (J)

12. Ann Eve Wirt (J) or Anna Eva Werth (E), born 10 Oct. 1808, baptized 8 Nov. 1808; died 10 Sept. 1831; "married Martin Shaffner, son of Martin Shaffner and Fanny Halderman, of Dauphin County; and had (1) John Frederick Shaffner, a practicing physician of Willshire, Ohio, and (2) a daughter who resides at Van Wert, Ohio." (J)

SEBASTIAN METZ and ANNA CATHERINE WIRT

Anna Catherine Wirt, daughter of John Adam and Eva Elizabeth Wirt; married Sebastian Metz; both lived and died in Lykens Valley, Dauphin County, Penn. They had ten children:
1. Adam Metz.
2. Jacob Metz.
3. Michael Metz m. Lizzie Geeseman; two children: (1) William Metz, born 28 May 1812, died 10 May 1866, Berrysburg, Penn., married Catharine Forney, "had issue"; and (2) George Metz, born 14 June 1814, died 7 Nov. 1878, Rutherford Station, Dauphin Co., Penn., married 1st Miss Hoke, married 2nd Sarah Fisher, daughter of Daniel Fisher and Catherine Parthemore, "had issue".

4. Christian Metz married Fannie Geeseman.
5. Henry Metz married 1st Elizabeth Weaver, and married 2nd to Anna Weaver.
6. John Metz married Eliz. Harmon.
7. Anna Metz.
8. Catharine Metz, born 20 Nov. 1790, died 12 Nov. 1873, married John Jacob Swab, born 6 Sept. 1792, died 5 Feb. 1867; one son, Eli Swab was commissioner of Dauphin Co.
9. Eva Metz married Mr. Sweigert.
10. Elizabeth Metz married Peter Werner.

GEORGE WIRT and CATHARINA MILLER

Johann George Wirt/Wirth/Werth, born 10 May 1770, died 13 Feb. 1845, Lykens Valley; son of John Adam and Eva Elizabeth Wirt; married Anna Catharine/Catharina Miller, daughter of John Adam Miller, born 25 July 1775, died 27 April 1842. They had six children baptized at Salem Evangelical Lutheran Church near Killinger, Dauphin County, Penn. Five are recorded by Engle (J) and all six are in the IGI (E).

1. Elizabeth Wirth, baptized 29 Oct. 1798; married Jacob Ulsh; "resided in Wild Cat Valley, Perry Co., Penn. Left issue." (J)

2. Anna Catharina Wirth, baptized 22 March 1801; married Jonas Hocker; "settled and died in Crawford Co., Ohio. Left issue." (J)

3. Lydia/Lidia Wirth, born 26 Jan. 1805; died 8 April 1864; married Daniel Feedt, son of George Feedt, 1771-1829, and Rachel.

4. Johann George Werth, baptized 7 March 1807; died 1891, Dauphin Co.; "had a large family". (J) Probably the Johann George Werth who had the following daughters baptized at Salem Church, Killinger. Mother of the first three is Catharina, and of the fourth, Hannah.
(1) Sarah Amanda Werth, baptized 5 April 1835.
(2) Marianne Werth, baptized 13 Nov. 1836.
(3) Delila Werth, baptized 12 Jan. 1840.
(4) Nancy Amanda Werth, bapt. 23 March 1847.

5. Johannes Werth, baptized 4 Nov. 1809; married Sarah Sheaffer; "removed to Crawford Co., Ohio and had issue". (J)

6. a male child baptized 9 Sept. 1811, name not given; perhaps died young.

HENRICH WIRT and ELIZABETH ENTERLINE

Henrich or Henry Wirt/Werth, born 2 Nov. 1771; son of John Adam and Eva Elizabeth Wirt; married probably about 1793 to Elizabeth or Elisabeth Enterline, daughter of Rev. John Michael Enterline, born 1726, died 16 March 1800. They had seven children baptized at the Salem Evangelical Lutheran Church near Killinger, Dauphin County.

1. Elisabeth Wirth, baptized 20 April 1794.

2. Johannes Wirt, born 16 Nov. 1795.

3. Michael Wirth, baptized 1 April 1800.

4. Catharina Wirth, baptized 13 July 1800.

5. Johann Philip Wirth, baptized 23 Oct. 1802.

6. Anna Maria Werth, baptized 16 March 1805. Probably the Anna Maria Werth married 8 June 1824, at the same church as she was baptized, to Philip Heckart, son of Casper Heckart. (K)

7. Anna Barbara Werth, baptized 30 Oct. 1809.

PETER WIRT and ELIZABETH SHEESLY

Peter Wirt, born about 1772, a farmer who died near Carlisle Springs, Cumberland Co., Penn.; son of John Adam and Eva Elizabeth Wirt. Engle (J) says Peter married Miss Sheesly and had three children, Peter, Philip, and Eve. A Baptismal record at the Salem Evangelical Lutheran Church near Killinger, Dauphin Co. shows a Peter Wirth, baptized 6 Oct. 1793, son of Peter Wirt and Elizabeth. Other baptisms

at the First Evangelical Luthern Church,
Carlisle, Cumberland Co., Penn. for parents,
Peter and Elizabeth, show two sons, Jacob and
William, both baptized in 1821. These could
be sons or grandsons of this Peter who married
Miss Sheesly. The following probable outline
of this family is given here, although
complete proof is lacking.
The three children of Peter Wirt and Miss
Sheesly named by Engle are:

1. Peter Wirt "resides in Trumbell Co., Ohio."
Probably the Peter baptized at Killinger 6
Oct. 1793; possibly the father of the Jacob
Wert and William Wert, both baptized at
Carlisle 29 Jan. 1821. Maybe also the father
of the Peter Wert, born 1815, outlined below.

2. Philip Wirt "resided in Trumbell Co.,
Ohio."

3. Eve Wirt "resided in Trumbell Co., Ohio."

     PETER WERT, born 1815, married four times

Information on this family was received by
correspondence with a descendent, Edith Wirt,
of Cypress, California in 1987. Proof that
this Peter descends from this Dauphin County
Wirt family is not definite yet, but names,
dates and places seem to indicate a tie.

Peter Wert, born 1815, probably in Cumberland
County, Penn.; died 3 March 1885, age 70
years, 1 month, and 23 days old; buried at
Grant Cemetery near Garden City, Cass Co.,
Missouri. Peter married 1st to Cecelia
Litrell, born 16 May 1818, and died when their
first child, Margaret, was born, about 1841.
Peter married 2nd to Lydia McClasky, born
about 1826, died about 1853, they had four
sons, Robert, Joshua, James and Charles.
Peter married 3rd on 2 Nov. 1854, to Mary Ann
Kayler, they had one son, Samuel, before she
died. Peter married 4th 29 Jan. 1857 to
Isabel Magee Ferney, born 6 March 1822, died

24 March 1907; they had one son, William.
In the 1860 Census this family is shown living
in Jackson County, but the record is on the
Crawford County, Ohio microfilm. 7 children:

1. **Margaret A. Wert**, born about 1841, died at
birth.

2. **Robert Francis Wert**, born 1 Jan. 1844,
Leesville, Carroll Co., Ohio; died 26 Jan.
1919; married 31 March 1868 to Sarah Ann
Dicks, born 12 Sept. 1848.

3. **Joshua Wert**, born 15 Feb. 1846, died 15
August 1850.

4. **James Arthur A. Wert**, born 12 June 1849.

5. **Charles Haun or Hahn Wert**, born 2 Oct.
1851, Crawford Co., Ohio; died 16 Oct. 1929;
married 21 Sept. 1873 to Elizabeth Ann
Edwards. Their children were born in Butler
County, Kansas.

6. **Samuel Kaylor Wert**, born 8 August 1855.

7. **William Lincoln Wert**, born 13 Dec. 1862;
died 29 July 1879, age 19 years. Died of
blood poisoning.

JOSEPH WIRT, b. 1775, and BARBARA

Joseph Wirt, baptized at Killinger 9 May 1775,
son of Adam and Elizabeth Wirt. Engle says he
"resided at Carlisle, then removed to Crawford
County, Ohio." (J)   There appear to be two
families of Joseph and Barbara Wirt/Wirth's.
The first has three children baptized at
Killinger, and one child baptized at Carlisle.
This is probably the Joseph baptized 1775.
The second family is in the 1850 and 1860
Census of Dauphin County.

1. **David Wirth**, baptized 7 Sept. 1800 at
Killinger.

2. A. Margaret Wirth, baptized 17 May 1802, at Killinger.

3. Joseph Werth, baptized 20 Oct. 1804, at Killinger.

4. Adam Wert, baptized 17 August 1817, at First Evangelical Lutheran Church, Carlisle, Cumberland Co., Penn.

Another JOSEPH and BARBARA WIRT

This Joseph and Barbara Wirt, are in the 1850 and 1860 Census, Lower Paxton twp., Dauphin Co., Penn., with nine children:
1. Elizabeth Wirt, born a. 1846
2. Fanny Wirt, born a. 1847
3. Mary Wirt, born a. 1848 *
4. Elmira Wirt, born a. 1849
5. Prasilla Wirt, born a. 1851
6. Catharine Wirt, born a. 1852
6. John Wirt, born a. 1852
8. Jacob Wirt, born a. 1857
8. William Wirt, born a. 1857

Note: * a Mary Wirt married 2 Jan. 1868 at the Union Salem Church, Berrysburg, Dauphin Co., Penn. to Benneville W. Holtzman.

JOSEPH WERT and PHEBE

Records of the First Evangelical Lutheran Church, Carlisle, Cumberland Co., Penn. show four children baptized there to a Joseph and Phebe Wert: Could this be the Joseph Wirt, born 1804? (above).
1. Margaret Wert, baptized 24 Dec. 1835 *
2. Anna Barbara Wert, baptized 16 August 1837
3. Elis. Wert, baptized 27 Jan. 1840
4. Emmanuel Wert, baptized 5 March 1842

Note: * a Margaret Wert was married 17 Dec. 1863 at this same church in Carlisle, to Ephraim Wetzel.

JOHN WIRT and ANNA MARIA ELIZABETH MILLER

John Wirt, born 25 Jan. 1788, died 8 Feb. 1858, at the Wirt settlement, Lykens Valley, Dauphin Co., Penn., and is buried at Killinger; son of John Adam and Eva Elizabeth Wirt. John married probably about 1809 to Anna Maria Elizabeth Miller. Eleven children are named by Engle (J), and all eleven were baptized at the Salem Evangelical Lutheran Church near Killinger, Dauphin County, and are recorded in the IGI. (E)

1. Simon Wirt/Werth, born 4 June 1810, baptized 8 July 1810; married Sarah Mark, and they had five children: Linda, Sarah, Mary, Emma, and John Adam. This family is outlined on the next page.

2. Elias Wirt/Werth, baptized 8 Dec. 1811; married Sarah Weaver, had six children and moved to Northumberland Co., Penn. Outline of this family begins on the next page.

3. Maria Anna "Mary" Wirt/Werth, baptized 4 May 1813.

4. Jonathan Wirt/Wert, baptized 13 Nov. 1814.

5. Joseph Wirt, baptized 15 Sept. 1816; died at Indianapolis, Indiana.

6. Josiah Wirt or Jesias Werth, baptized 16 August 1818; "resides at Georgetown, Penn."

7. Amos Wirt/Werth, baptized 25 Feb. 1821; "resides in Philadelphia."

8. Elizabeth Wirt/Wert, baptized 23 March 1823; married Jacob Ginter.

9. Susan Wirt or Susanna Werth, baptized 15 May 1825; married George Shaffer; "resides at Georgetown."

10. John B. Wirt or Johann Benjamin Werth, baptized 2 Sept. 1827; "resides in Massillon, Ohio."

11. Rebecca Wirt, baptized 9 May 1830; married Joshua Martin; "resided at Georgetown."

SIMON WIRT and SARAH MARK

Simon Wirt, born 4 June 1810, baptized 8 July 1810 at Killinger, son of John and Elizabeth Wirt; married Sarah Mark. They had five children, all baptized at Killinger. Simon was a tanner, and burgess of Millersburg in 1850, 1865, and 1870.

1. Melinda Eva Elizabeth "Linda" Werth, baptized 14 Dec. 1840, Killinger.

2. Sarah Amelia Wert, baptized 6 Nov. 1842; married 1st to Harry Mosser, three children; and married 2nd to Jonas Garman, two children. They resided at Lykens Valley.

3. Mary Catharina Wert, baptized 2 June 1844; "married F.S.Bowman, editor of the Millersburg Sentinel, and had issue." (J)

4. John Adam Wirt/Wert, baptized 2 Oct. 1846; married Martha Buchler. They had four boys. "John Adam is a graduate of the Lutheran schools at Gettysburg, Penn., and a minister of the same denomination, residing at Hughesville, Penn." (J)

5. Emma Jane Wert, baptized 14 May 1848; "married Rev. D.S. Lentz, a minister of the Lutheran Church, residing at Chambersburg, Penn. and had issue, four children." (J)

ELIAS WIRT and SARAH WEAVER

Elias Wirt/Werth, baptized 8 Dec. 1811, at Killinger, son of Johannes and Elizabeth Werth (John and Anna Maria Elizabeth Miller Wirt); married Sarah Weaver, whose name is also given as Sally and Salome in the Killinger records. Six children were baptized to Elias Werth at the Salem Evangelical Lutheran Church near Killinger, Dauphin Co., Penn. The mother of the first is given as Sally, and the mother of the other five is given as Salome. This family later resided in Northumberland Co.

1. Carlina Louisa Wert, baptized 21 Feb. 1847.

2. Benjamin Franklin Wert, 10 November 1849.

3. Wm. Bigler Wert, baptized 29 Nov. 1851.

4. Margaret Wert, baptized 29 Oct. 1853.

5. George Hiram Wert, baptized 8 July 1855.

OTHER DAUPHIN COUNTY WERT, WERTH, WIRTH

From records of the Salem Evangelical Lutheran Church near Killinger, Dauphin Co., Penn., a Johannes and Anna Maria Wirth had seven children baptized there. However the dates would preclude them from being grandchildren of John Adam and Eva Elizabeth Wirt. Perhaps they are descendants of his brothers.

Children of Johannes and Anna Maria Wirth:
1. Eva Catharina Wirth, baptized 31 Oct. 1784.
2. Johannes Wirth, baptized 19 Feb. 1786.
3. Anna Margaretha Wirth, 24 March 1788.
4. Anna Christina Wirth, 24 May 1790.
5. Johann Adam Wirth, 18 January 1795.
6. a daughter, baptized 1 April 1798.
7. Elizabeth Wirth, baptized 26 Sept. 1800.

The following also baptized at Killinger, may be grandchildren of the above, or great grand children of John Adam and Eva Elizabeth Wirt.

children of WILLIAM and CATHARINA WERT
1. Amanda Jane Wirt, baptized 4 Sept. 1847
2. Aaron Benjamin Wert, baptized 1 March 1849.

child of **ADAM** and **SARAH ELIZABETH WERT**
Aaron Solomon Wert, baptized 31 Jan. 1868.

children of **JOHN** and **MAGDALENA WERTH**
1. Daniel Werth, baptized 20 July 1817.
2. Catharina Werth, baptized 23 May 1819.
3. Lythia Wirth, baptized 7 Oct. 1821.

child of **JOHANN** and **CATHARINA WERTH**
Johann Daniel Werth, baptized 3 May 1835.

child of **JOHANN** and **SALOME WERTH**
Johann Henrich Werth, baptized 2 June 1833.

child of **JOSIAH** and **SALOME WERT**
John Thomas Wert, baptized 14 Dec. 1845.

child of **ANDREW** and **CATHERINE WERT**
Moses Wert, baptized 28 March 1855.

child of **HENRICH WERTH**
Susanna Werth, baptized 26 March 1807.

Other Dauphin County records: which may also
be for descendants of these families.

child of **H. WERTH** and **EL. HERRMAN**
Sara Elisabeth Werth, baptized 8 Sept. 1853,
at St. Johns Lutheran Church near Berrysburg,
Mifflin twp., Dauphin Co.

child of **JONAS** and **SUSANA WERT**
Charles W. Wert, baptized 31 July 1859, at
Union Salem Church, Berrysburg, Dauphin Co.

child of **JOHN** and **CATHAERINE WERT**
Charles Edwin Wert, baptized 6 May 1865, at
St. Johns Lutheran Church, near Berrysburg,
Mifflin twp., Dauphin Co., Penn.

child of **DANIEL F. WERT** and **EMMA MATTER**
Earl Adam Wert, born 27 Oct. 1895, at
Wiconisco, Dauphin Co.

child of **JEREMIAH FRANKLIN WERT** and
   ANNA REBECCA RIEGEL
Mabel Wert, born 21 Oct. 1913, at Oberlin,
Dauphin County.

children of **EARL ADAM WERT** and
   MARGARET JANE ORR
1. Annie Laraine Wert, born 18 Nov. 1926,
Wiconisco, Dauphin Co.; died in infancy.
2. John Austin Wert, born 3 Jan. 1929, at
Wiconisco, Dauphin Co.; died in infancy.

Dauphin County Marriages

- At the Middletown Monthly Meeting,
Middletown, Dauphin County: Mary Worth married
16 Sept. 1715 to Joseph Chapman.

- At the Zion Evangelical Lutheran Church,
Hummelstown, Dauphin County: Catharine Wert
married 17 January 1829 to David Kiehner.
And Susan R. Wert married 26 Oct. 1876 to S.
C. Reed.

- At St. Johns Lutheran Church near
Berrysburg, Mifflin twp., Dauphin County:
(1) Peter Wert married 6 Jan. 1857 to Sara
Emerich.
(2) Moses Wert married 1 March 1857 to Mary
Ann Spatz.
(3) Mary Ann Wert married 3 Feb. 1857 to
Joseph Zartman.
(4) Elizabeth Wert married 8 Sept. 1861 to
Imanuel Spatz.

- At the Union Salem Church, Berrysburg,
Dauphin County: Samuel Wert married 26 Dec.
1867 to Allice Witmer.

A Cumberland Co. Family:

Dewalt & Madelena Wertz

In the Biographical Encyclopedia of Juniata Valley, published in 1897, on page 1260, it is recorded that "the grandfather of Peter Wertz of Landisburg was Daniel Wertz who came probably from Germany to England and then to Pennsylvania, and settled near Landisburg. He was a farmer and became well known in his community. His son settled with his parents at Landisburg, was a carpenter, and died at the age of eighty-six, his wife surviving him a few years."

Mrs. Laura Theresa Willhide Johnston, in her book, Descendants of my Great Grandparents, discussed at great length (pages 31-38) all the records, reasons, and proofs that led her to conclude that the name of this son of Daniel Wertz, and father of Peter Wertz of Landisburg was Dewalt Wertz, whose wife was Madelena. Dewalt and Madelena Wertz had at least five children, one son, Peter, and four or five daughters: Mary, Rachel, Leah, Ellen, and perhaps another, who probably died young.

1. Mary Wertz, born 1793/4, died 19 Dec. 1856, married 1813/15 to Solomon Shively, and they were the grandparents of Mrs. Johnston.

2. Rachel Wertz, died between 1880 and 1890, married about 1828/9 to a Mr. Shearer.

3. Leah Wertz, married 16 Dec. 1830 to Thomas Humes, They had five children and lived at New Germantown and later at Carlisle, Penn.

4. Ellen Wertz married George Yocum, and they had at least five children and also lived at Carlisle.

5. "Peter Wertz, of Landisburg", born 1 April 1792; died 1 Oct. 1873; married Mary Foose, and they had 14 children. See next page.

PETER WERTZ, of Landisburg

Peter Wertz, born 1 April 1792, Adams County, Penn.; died 1 Oct. 1873, Little Germany, Spring twp., Perry County; son of Dewalt and Madelena Wertz; married Mary Foose, born 1797, died 21 Jan. 1882; fourteen children:

1. Elizabeth Wertz, died unmarried.

2. Mollie Wertz, died unmarried.

3. Sarah Wertz, died unmarried.

4. Margaret Wertz, married Abraham Baer, and they had eight children: (1) Sarah married John Cless; (2) Margaret married George Titzel; (3) Martha married Thomas Gray; (4) Jane married Mr. Foose; (5) John Baer; (6) Washington Baer; (7) Samuel Baer; and (8) Daniel Baer.

5. Catherine Wertz, married Peter Haas, and had four children: (1) Mary Ann married John Rebert; (2) Sarah Jane, died unmarried; (3) Peter Haas; and (4) Henry Haas.

6. John Wertz, born 24 April 1819; died 19 Feb. 1904; married first 22 Dec. 1842 to Mary Fry, born 20 May 1820; died 23 July 1886, daughter of Abraham Fry of Tyrone, Penn.; they had eleven children: William, Eliza Jane, Catharine, Emma Rebecca, Mary E., Martha Eve, John, Margaretta, Peter, Chas. Clinton, and James Ellsworth Wertz. John married 2nd, Mrs. Catharine Zimmerman; no children. This family is outlined beginning on page 241.

7. Henry Wertz, born 15 Oct. 1819; died 2 Feb. 1903; married Catharine Elizabeth Snyder, born 26 July 1821; died 21 Jan. 1902; twelve children: James, David, John, Mary, Peter, Sarah, Susanna, Frances, Annie, Henry, Caroline, and Benjamin Wertz. Outline of this family begins on page 244.

8. Mary Polly Wertz, born 24 Nov. 1823; died 2 March 1896; married William Shover, born 4 Jan. 1821; died 21 Oct. 1882; eleven children: Mary A.; Elizabeth m. Mr. Howard; Susan J.; Wm. P.; Sarah E. m. Mr. Thompson; Peter W.; James H.; John T.; Chancey M.; Alice C., and Eldora B. Shover.

9. Peter Wertz, born 10 July 1832; died 7 Nov. 1913; married 15 Oct. 1859 to Sarah Varntz, born 24 Oct. 1837; died 8 Sept. 1917. This family lived in Newport, Penn. were Peter had a restaurant and confectionery store. They had eight children: Jeremiah N., Ida May, Ellie, Annie E., Carrie, Nellie, George V., and Florence Wertz. This family is outlined on pages 245 and 246.

10. David Wertz, was married and lived in Iowa. They had several children; one daughter lived in Long Beach, Calif. and some of the other children lived in Nebraska.

11. Daniel Wertz, born 18 Jan. 1836; died 14 Feb. 1920; married 10 April 1861 to Elizabeth Foose, born 10 Sept. 1840; died 31 August 1900; six children: Mary Jane, Sarah Malinda, Laura Annie, Maggie Adora, Minnie E., and Mervin P. Daniel Wertz. Daniel married 2nd to Hannah Haas, no children. Outline of this family begins on page 246.

12. Abraham Wertz, born 6 July 1837; died 2 August 1908; married Mary Catharine Garman, born 18 Feb. 1846; they had eleven children: Wm. Henry, Clara Isabella, David Washington, Sarah Jane, Emma Florence, Amelia Annie, Mary Ellen, Ada Elizabeth, Charles Ross, Albert Milton, and Edward Scott Wertz. Outline of this family begins on page 247.

13. Lydia Ann Wertz, born 28 Dec. 1839; died 12 Nov. 1885; married John S. Kistler, born 30 Oct. 1836; died 29 Sept. 1893; son of Abraham and Christina Kistler; lived in Spring twp., where John was a butcher. They had eleven

children: (1) Ida J., born 4 Jan. 1863; (2) Milton O., m. Carrie Hess; (3) Margaret m. Daniel Clouser; (4) Walter; (5) Harry P., married, two sons; (6) Mollie, 1871-1886; (7) Eldora, born 26 July 1873; (8) Reuben, married, four children; (9) Florence, married Frank McGinnes; (10) Oliver C., 1875-1879; and (11) John C. Kistler, 1885-1886.

14. Isabel Wertz, m. Henry Babble, and they lived in Cumberland County. They had nine children: (1) a daughter who m. A. Bierbower, lived near Carlisle; (2) Margaret Jane, m. Daniel Hoy, lived Mechanicsburg, Penn.; (3) Mary m. Wilson Armstrong; (4) Catharine m. Isaac Brenizer; (5) Emma m. Daniel Kunkel; (6) Clara m. Daniel Whitmore; (7) William Babble; (8) Samuel Babble; and (9) Tolbert Babble.

JOHN WERTZ and Mary Fry

John Wertz, born 24 April 1819; died 19 Feb. 1904; son of Peter Wertz and Mary Foose; married first 22 Dec. 1842 to Mary Fry, born 20 May 1820; died 23 July 1886; daughter of Abraham Fry of Tyrone. This family lived in Newport and Lewistown. Eleven children:

1. William Wertz, born 31 Oct. 1843; died 15 May 1914; married 12 July 1863 to Catharine Glaze, born 19 Dec. 1843; died 27 Sept. 1918; daughter of Rev. Samuel Glaze; eight children: (1) M. Margaret, m. Silas E. Clark; (2) Wm. Henry Wertz, married Cora A. Noll, born 7 Aug. 1868; three children; (3) Carrie Letitia married Harry B. Miller, four children; (4) Laura Myrtle married Herman E. Snyder, four children; (5) an infant; (6) J. Price Wertz, married Ada Barrett, eight children; (7) Victor H. Wertz, born 15 Oct. 1877; and (8) Fannie Eleanor Wertz.

2. Eliza Jane Wertz, born 31 March 1845; died 27 Dec. 1907; married O. H. Perry Rider; lived Newport, where he was a butcher. No children.

3. Catherine Wertz, born 11 Dec. 1846; died 23 Dec. 1907; married 28 April 1867 to John M. Barrick, born 27 March 1845; four children: (1) Dennis L. Barrick, born 14 April 1870; married 16 July 1901 to Catharine M. Refroth, two children; (2) Samuel W. Barrick, born 20 Dec. 1871; died 22 Feb. 1920; married 4 Oct. 1901; (3) William H. Barrick, born 2 Nov. 1873; married 18 July 1908 to Carrie M. Pee, born 4 June 1875; lived at Newport, three children; and (4) Charles Melvin Barrick, born 21 Jan. 1876, married Minnie M. Turnbaugh, four children.

4. Emma Rebecca Wertz, born 9 Sept. 1849; died 21 Jan. 1917; married July 1868 to Joseph T. Murphy, born 25 Oct. 1846; died 6 April 1910; eight children: (1) James Franklin; (2) Harry Ervin; (3) John A. Murphy married Sadie C. Wright, two children; (4) Mary M. married J. Harvey Campbell; ten children; (5) Emma F.; (6) Charles C. Murphy married Emma Hoffman, four children; (7) William T. Murphy married Malinda M. Book, no children; and (8) Ivan B. Murphy.

5. Mary E. Wertz, born 29 Sept. 1851; died 5 Nov. 1874; married John Carr; lived at Newport; no children.

6. Martha Eve Wertz, born 15 June 1853; died 22 Jan. 1873, unmarried.

7. John Wertz, born 17 June 1856, twin; married 23 Dec. 1879 to Lydia A. Beard, born 18 Oct. 1862; six children: (1) Harvey F. Wertz, married Bessie Baker, two children: Owen P. and Beatrice; (2) Angeline M. Wertz, 1881-1882; (3) Emory I. Wertz, 1885-1890; (4) Morris B. Wertz married Philomena Lefils, two children: Alfred M. and Harvey L.; (5) Pearl E. Wertz married Chas. H. Barbour, one son: Paul E. Barbour; and (6) Hannah R. Wertz married Warren E. Bell, one daughter, Sarah J. Bell.

8. Margaretta Wertz, born 17 June 1856, twin; died 17 December 1896; married John H. Haines; lived Altoona, Penn.; three children.

9. Peter Wertz, born 13 Nov. 1858; married 25 Dec. 1879 to Jennie Sunday, born 27 June 1860; lived Newport and Harrisburg; nine children:
(1) Roy S. Wertz, born 1 Feb. 1881; married 17 June 1903 to Zora Hemperly, born 28 March 1882; one daughter: Virginia Viola Wertz.
(2) Charles H. Wertz, born 21 Feb. 1883; married 26 Jan. 1903 to Priscilla Bowman, born 14 Sept. 1882; lived at Harrisburg; one son: Charles Wertz.
(3) Marvin G. C. Wertz, born 5 Sept. 1884; not married; lived Harrisburg.
(4) Minnie V.J. Wertz, born 23 June 1886; married 28 June 1906 to George G. Dolbin, born 22 Nov. 1883; lived Harrisburg; one daughter: Catharine I. Dolbin.
(5) Earl G. Wertz, born 9 July 1888; married 23 June 1910 to Clara V. Curry, born 8 Dec. 1891; lived Harrisburg; two children: Donald E. Wertz, and Dorothy J. Wertz.
(6) Emory H. Wertz, born 9 Feb. 1890; married; children; lived Fairview, Cumberland Co.,Penn.
(7) Daisy R. Wertz, born 7 Sept. 1892; married 20 August 1914 to Chas. H. Sorge, born 8 Aug. 1890; one son: Robert E. Sorge.
(8) Alice F. Wertz, born 14 Sept. 1894; married 24 June 1916 to Prentice H. Hartzell, born 23 Jan. 1892; lived Harrisburg; two children: Ray P. and Charlotte E. Hartzell.
(9) Lillie E. Wertz, born 12 June 1896, married Wm. A. McCarthy, born 21 June 1894; one daughter: Dorothy L. McCarthy.

10. Charles Clinton Wertz, born 4 June 1860; married; two children; lived at Mt. Union.

11. James Ellsworth Wertz, born 25 Dec. 1863; not married; a farmer at Mason City, Iowa.

HENRY WERTZ and Catharine E. Snyder

Henry Wertz, born 15 Oct. 1819; died 2 Feb. 1903; son of Peter Wertz and Mary Foose; married Catharine Elizabeth Snyder, born 26 July 1821; died 21 Jan. 1902; twelve children:

1. James Wertz, born 8 April 1845; married; several children; lived in Minnesota.

2. David Wertz, born 3 Oct. 1846; unmarried; lived in Del Norte, Colorado.

3. John Wertz, born 5 Nov. 1848; married Ida Garland, daughter of Daniel Garland of Center, Perry Co.; lived Maniteau, Colorado; one daughter: Ida Wertz, married Paul Barnum.

4. Mary Wertz, born 29 Nov. 1850; married 18 Feb. 1869 to Albert Boger, who died 12 June 1894; no children.

5. Peter Wertz, born 22 July 1852; died 14 April 1910, unmarried.

6. Sarah Wertz, born 10 March 1854; married 6 July 1872.

7. Susanna Wertz, born 9 Feb. 1856; married 2 May 1879 to C.C. Carl; lived Landisburg, Penn.; five children: Dr. Lenus A. Carl married Alice Florence Stewart; (2) Mrs. John Kennedy, no children; (3) Catharine Carl m. Winfield Scott Grey, lived Elliottsburg, Penn., no children; (4) Harry Carl, married, one son; and (5) William Carl, married, no children, lived in Colorado.

8. Frances Wertz, born 10 May 1857; married 1 Jan. 1881 to James Calvin Preisler, born 24 July 1857; five children: (1) Eva Preisler, born 18 Jan. 1882, married 5 March 1906 to C.R.Buckwalter, five children; (2) Emma Preisler, born 25 Nov. 1883, unmarried; (3) John Henry Preisler, born 7 Jan. 1886, married Elizabeth Knecht, one child died young; lived

Philadelphia; (4) Bruce Wertz Preisler, born 7 June 1893; died 10 March 1894; and (5) Kenneth Leroy Preisler, born 12 Nov. 1897, married 17 August 1920 to Olive J. Garber, born 7 Jan. 1899, one daughter, Janet Garber Preisler, born 27 July 1921.

9. Annie Wertz, born 6 April 1859; married 20 April 1879 to Robert Hock Shuman, born 20 Jan. 1859; son of Major George A. Shuman of Landisburg; four children: (1) George Albert Shuman, born 12 June 1884; (2) Robert Henry Shuman, born 6 August 1886, a Dentist at Quarryville, Lancaster Co., unmarried; (3) John William Shuman, born 8 Sept. 1889, a Dentist at Quarryville, unmarried; and (4) Frances Christina Shuman, born 6 July 1895, unmarried.

10. Henry Wertz, born 12 Jan. 1861; died 9 Jan. 1864.

11. Caroline Wertz, born 29 April 1862; died 19 Dec. 1863.

12. Benjamin Wertz, born 13 June 1865; died 25 Nov. 1866.

PETER WERTZ and Sarah Varntz

Peter Wertz, born 10 July 1832; died 7 Nov. 1913; son of Peter Wertz and Mary Foose; married 15 Oct. 1859 to Sarah Varntz, born 24 Oct. 1837; died 8 Sept. 1917; eight children:

1. Jeremiah N. Wertz, born 26 Dec. 1860; died 16 April 1900, unmarried.

2. Ida May Wertz, born 26 June 1862; married 30 June 1907 to Harvey M. Hunter, born 2 May 1864; lived Marysville, Penn.; no children.

3. Ellie Wertz, born 26 June 1864; died 12 May 1920; married 3 Oct. 1903 to John W. Gray, born 5 Sept. 1852; lived Duncannon, Penn.; no children.

4. Annie E. Wertz, born 15 Nov. 1866; died 15 Feb. 1886, unmarried.

5. Carrie Wertz, born 22 Feb. 1869; unmarried.

6. Nellie Wertz, born 1 March 1872; m. 24 Aug. 1896 to William G. Frank, born 24 June 1865; lived Harrisburg; three children: (1) Delos E. Frank married 30 Oct. 1921 to Elmira M. Rudy; (2) Paul K. Frank; and (3) Carrie V. Frank.

7. George V. Wertz, born 29 Feb. 1875; unmarried; lived Marysville, Penn.

8. Florence Wertz, born 21 April 1879; married 12 Nov. 1900 to Walter Albright, born 29 Aug. 1876; lived Harrisburg; one daughter, Mary B.

DANIEL WERTZ and Elizabeth Foose

Daniel Wertz, born 18 Jan. 1836; died 14 Feb. 1920; son of Peter Wertz and Mary Foose; m. 10 April 1861 to Elizabeth Foose, born 10 Sept. 1840; died 31 August 1900; six children:

1. Mary Jane Wertz, born 19 Jan. 1862; died 1 Sept. 1862.

2. Sarah Malinda Wertz, born 18 June 1863; died 28 May 1917, Clark, So. Dakota; married 1878 to John C. Shenk, ten children: (1) David Shenk married Zella Wilkie, lived Hopkins, Minnesota; (2) John A. Shenk married Mary Elva Foss, a farmer at Clark, So. Dakota; (3) Daniel Shenk, married, farmer in So. Dakota; (4) Daisy Shenk married Elmer A. Tompkins; (5) George Fulmore Shenk married Hazel Pearl Ackerman, three children; (6) Clarence A. Shenk married Myrtle Holmes, lived Olanda, Montana; (7) Roy Shenk, married, lived Clark, So. Dakota and Minneapolis, Minn.; (8) Lizzie Shenk m. J. C. Carlson; lived Minneapolis, Minn.; (9) Jacob Shenk married Lottie Cloud, lived Garden City, So. Dakota; and (10) Emma Shenk, unmarried, lived Minneapolis, Minn.

3. Laura Annie Wertz, born 12 July 1866; married John Witmer; eight children: (1) Lloyd Witmer, born 13 Jan. 1884; married 23 July 1903 to Hattie White; lived Mechanicsburg, Penn. (2) Herbert L. Witmer, born 17 May 1890; married 30 July 1914 to Emily Heggen; lived Harrisburg; three children; (3) Esther Witmer, born 20 April 1892, unmarried; (4) Mary Mabel Witmer, born 14 July 1894; married 26 Nov. 1914 to Floyd C. Merris, born 5 April 1891, four children; (5) Harry Witmer, born 2 Sept. 1896, m. 28 April 1920 to Esther Waggoner, lived Bode, Iowa; (6) Viola Witmer, born 18 April 1901; (7) Preston Witmer, born 9 Nov. 1903; and (8) Grace Witmer, born 25 Feb. 1907.

4. Maggie Adora Wertz, born 13 August 1868; died 12 Sept. 1871.

5. Minnie E. Wertz, born 13 June 1871.

6. Mervin P. Daniel Wertz, born 23 March 1879; died 17 Oct. 1903.

ABRAHAM WERTZ and Mary C. Garman

Abraham Wertz, born 6 July 1837; died 2 August 1908; son of Peter Wertz and Mary Foose; married Mary Catharine Garman, born 18 Feb. 1846; eleven children:

1. William Henry Wertz, born 18 August 1865.

2. Clara Isabella Wertz, born 18 Nov. 1866; m. 1 April 1892 to Smiley T. Dunkelberger, born 13 Sept. 1853; one son: Gordon Clay Payne Dunkelberger, born 22 August 1896.

3. David Washington Wertz, born 29 Oct. 1868.

4. Sarah Jane Wertz, born 31 Dec. 1870; married George Stambaugh, born 12 Oct. 1868; three children: (1) Seibert Arthur Stambaugh, born 29 Jan. 1895; married 9 Oct. 1916 to Mary Reisinger, born 14 Jan. 1893; one daughter: Sarah Louise Stambaugh; (2) Clinton Milfred

Stambaugh, born 6 Sept. 1896, m. 7 June 1918 Hattie May Kitner, no children; (3) Catharine Margarette Stambaugh, born 23 July 1905.

5. Emma Florence Wertz, born 26 April 1872; married Milton Reeder, born 7 Oct. 1867; seven children: (1) Solomon Brooks Reeder, born 4 May 1896; (2) Mary Bernice Reeder, born 5 June 1898, married 7 Dec. 1920; (3) Milton Raymond Reeder, born 22 Oct. 1901, lived Greenpark, Perry Co., Penn.; (4) Foster Wertz Reeder, born 30 Dec. 1903; (5) Beatrice Myrhl Reeder, born 24 August 1906; (6) Boyd Lesley Reeder, born 19 August 1910; and (7) Thelma Kathryn Reeder, born 21 Nov. 1913.

6. Amelia Annie Wertz, born 1 June 1874; married Thomas H. Garber; lived Falling Springs, Perry Co. and New Bloomfield; two children: (1) John Abraham Garber, born 28 Feb. 1895; married 24 Dec. 1917 to Laura Isabella Rice, born 3 June 1896; two children: Donald Thomas and Virginia Rice Garber; and (2) Mary Wertz Garber, born 16 Oct. 1904.

7. Mary Ellen Wertz, born 29 July 1876.

8. Ada Elizabeth Wertz, born 22 Oct. 1878; m. Charles Armstrong, lived Mechanicsburg, Penn.; one daughter: Mary Armstrong married Blaine Shuggert, lived Carlisle, Penn., and have one child: Gladys Shuggert.

9. Charles Ross Wertz, born 7 Feb. 1881.

10. Albert Milton Wertz, born 22 Jan. 1884; unmarried; lived with his sister, Mary Lightner.

11. Edward Scott Wertz, born 6 March 1886; married Rose Morrison; lived East Waterford, Juniata Co., Penn.; no children.

OTHER CUMBERLAND COUNTY WERT(Z)

Carlisle

Baptisms and marriages at the First
Evangelical Lutheran Church, in Carlisle,
Cumberland County, Pennsylvania: (E)

Children of **MARTIN WERT** and **ANNA SALOME**
1. Elizabeth Wert, baptized 25 June 1826.
2. Samuel Wert, baptized 19 Jan. 1828.
3. Peter Wirth, baptized 10 July 1829.
4. Catharine Wert, baptized 18 June 1831
5. Martin Wert, baptized 20 Feb. 1833.
6. Jacob Wert, baptized 27 Jan. 1834.
7. Solma Ann Wert, baptized 30 May 1835.
8. Anna Maria Wert, baptized 2 May 1837.
9. Joseph Wert, baptized 10 Dec. 1838.
10. Susanna Wert, baptized 21 Nov. 1840.

A child of **JOHN WERT** and **MARIA MAGDALENE**;
John Peter Wert, baptized 10 Nov. 1831.

Children of **JOHN WERT** and Mary; William Wert,
baptized 8 Dec. 1836; and Mary Ann Elisabeth
Wert, baptized 9 May 1840.   (Note: a Mary E.
Wert married 9 March 1875 at this same church,
to Jacob N. Brubaker.

Children of **WILLIAM WERT** and **MARY ANN**;
1. Henry Peter Wert, baptized 30 Dec. 1838.
2. William David Wert, 2 January 1842.
3. Margaret Elizabeth Wirt, 3 Sept. 1843.
4. George Oliver Wirt, 19 October 1845.
5. Chas. Edwin Wirt, 31 Jan. 1847.
6. Joseph Edom Wirt, 14 Nov. 1848.
7. Abner Rhoads Wirt, 7 Jan. 1853.

A PERRY COUNTY WERTZ FAMILY

Nicholas Wertz of Greenwood township

Daniel Fahnstock Wertz came to America about 1770 from Switzerland and settled first near Boston, Massachusetts and later in Northumberland County, Penn.; and finally in Perry Co., Penn. Daniel is known to have had at least two sons: Paul Wertz, who married Catherine Stiffler and settled in Bedford County (see Chapter 7 - page 177); and a Nicholas Wertz who married 1st to Margaret Sidel; and 2nd to Mrs. Anna Thompson. They lived in Greenwood township of Perry County, and Nicholas' will, which was proved in Perry County 2 August 1824, names eleven children.

1. Nicholas Wertz, married Sofia Winghart.

2. Daniel Wertz, married Maria Miller.

3. Elizabeth Wertz married Mr. Wolf.

4. Susanna Wertz married Mr. Hetrick.

5. Sally Wertz also married a Mr. Hetrick.

6. Hanna Wertz married W. L. Kipp.

7. Jeremiah Wertz married Mary Kauffman. A daughter, Mrs. Sarah E. Rapp, lived at Thompsontown, Juniata County, Penn.

8. Juliana Wertz married Mr. Humes.

9. Eliza Wertz married Mr. Tibbens.

10. John Wertz.

11. Peter Wertz. In the Nicholas Wertz estate settlement in 1828, the court appointed a guardian for "Nicholas Wertz's minor son, Peter, under 14 years of age."

MONTGOMERY COUNTY Records

Records from the New Hanover Lutheran Church, at Falckner Swamp, Montgomery County, Penn. show the following families... which may or may not be related to these of Dauphin Co.

PHILIP WIRTH and MARGRETHA HUBERIN

Philip Wirth and Margretha Huberin, a widow were married 21 Feb. 1749; and had two sons baptized there:
1. Johannes Wirth, born 21 Jan. 1750, baptized 11 Feb. 1750.
2. Johann Conrad Wirth, born 9 March 1752, baptized 21 Nov. 1752.

child of PHILIP HENRY WIRTH and MARIA EVA
Bernhard Wirth, born 14 Dec. 1750, baptized 25 Dec. 1750.

JOHANNES WERTZ and CATHARINE BARBARA

Johannes Wertz and Catharine Barbara had four children baptized at New Hanover, and another son baptized at Tulpehocken. We have no proof that these are the same parents in both locations, but the dates would make that seem probable.
1. Maria Catharine Wertz, born 27 Nov. 1764, baptized 19 March 1765.
2. Johannes Wurtz, born 7 Nov. 1767, baptized 8 May 1768.
3. Anna Maria Wirz, born 22 Dec. 1771, baptized 19 April 1772.
4. Johann Friederich Wirz, born 2 March 1774, baptized 4 Sept. 1774.

Baptized at the Little Tulpehocken Church, Jefferson twp., Berks County, Penn.:
5. Benjamin Wertz, born 30 Aug. 1787, baptized 4 Nov. 1787, son of John Wertz and wife Catharine.

George Werts, married 11 Sept. 1812 Muskingum County to Willmina Swank.

Michael Wirts, married 6 August 1815 Columbiana County to Christena Borman.

Israel Wertz, married 24 May 1820 Darke County to Jane Dugan.

Henry Wertz, married 1 April 1824 Preble County to Anna Neity.

John Werts, married 3 January 1825 Preble County to Susannah Smith.

Abraham Wertz, married 13 Sept. 1825, Fairfield County to Anna Brederstone.

George Denny Wertz, married 2 Feb. 1826 Muskingum County to Eliza Caroline Lindza.

William Wertz or Werts, married 7 August 1827 Muskingum Co. to Catherine Bigham or Bingham.

George Werts, married 13 Nov. 1827 Guernsey County to Margaret Maple.

John Wertz, married 28 May 1829 Montgomery County to Catherine Bartmass.

Charles Wertz, married 11 Oct. 1829, Preble County to Catharine Simonton.

Jacob Werts, married 16 Sept. 1830 Holmes County, to Catharine Werts.

Baltzer Wertz, married 12 Feb. 1832, Preble County to Nancy Piles.

Christian Wertz, married 3 May 1832, Pickaway County, to Jemima Jordan.

Christian Wertz, married 5 August 1832, Preble County to Polly Neightly or Neighly.

John Wertz, married 4 Nov. 1832 Preble County to Jane Weaver.

Benjamin Wertz, married 18 April 1833, Montgomery County to Margaret Hoobler.

Henry Wertz, married 7 April 1834 Darke County to Ann Deeter or Teeter.

George Wertz, married 24 April 1834 Preble County to Mary Piles.

John Wertz, married 27 July 1834 Darke County to Elizabeth Faler.

John Werz, married 1 August 1835 Cuyahoga County to Catherine Girley.

John Wertz, married 12 Nov. 1835 Fairfield County to Mary Anderick.

John Werts, married 7 Jan. 1836 Preble County to Sarah Judy.

John Wertz, married 26 May 1836 Montgomery County to Elizabeth Strove.

Orliff Wertz, married 18 June 1836 Scioto County to Permelia Corothers.

Jacob Wertz, married 8 August 1836 Clark County to Catharine Kisling.

John Werts, married 27 April 1837 Wayne County to Sarah Morris.

John Wertz, married 4 Nov. 1838 Muskingum County to Eliza Williams.

Albright Wertz, married 17 Jan. 1839, Fairfield County to Elizabeth Oly.

Jacob Werts, married 28 Nov. 1839 Muskingum County to Elizabeth Ann Harris.

John Wirts, married 28 Nov. 1839 Columbiana County to Polly Sheffner.

Peter Wirts, married 19 Sept. 1841 Columbiana County to Elizabeth Crowl.

Adam Wertz, married 6 Oct. 1842, Montgomery County to Sarah Strouse.

David Wertz, married 7 Sept. 1844 Preble County to Elizabeth Cyler.

David Werts, married 30 March 1845 Darke County to Elizabeth Miller.

Daniel Wertz, married 26 March 1846 Stark County to Sophia Cook.

William Wertz, married 24 July 1847 Preble County to Lydia Wilson.

Daniel Wertz, married 30 Nov. 1847 Preble County to Sarah Burk.

Solomon Werts, married 26 March 1848 Muskingum County to Malinda Gaumer.

John Wertz, married 25 January 1849 Darke County to Reebl Jane Dye.

George Wertz, married 10 Feb. 1849 Preble County to Margaret Fleagle.

George Wertz or Werts, married 1 or 23 April 1849 Muskingum Co. to Naomi Tilden.

Peter Werts, married 22 Nov. 1849 Montgomery County to Esther Rarick.

Christian S. Wertz, married 1 Jan. 1857 Wayne County to Sue S. Slater.

John W. Wirtz, married 16 Nov. 1871 Crawford County to Caroline Beach.

Chapter 10

EARLY PENNSYLVANIA WERTZ RECORDS

Most of the following records were obtained in the search for records of our Wertz family, but we have been unable to attach them to our family, or any of the other Wertz families outlined in the preceding chapters. They are reported here for the benefit of future researchers, in hopes they may benefit from our searchings, avoid duplication of effort, and move on toward making the ties we were unable to clearly establish.

1700 to 1800 WERTZ EMIGRANTS to PENN.

1739 - Barnet Waerth, ship "Loyal Judith" (R)
1741 - Carl Philip Wirtz, ship "St.Andrew"(B)
1740 - Caspar Wert or Wirth, age 32, ship "Lydia" (A)
1735 - Conrad Wurtz or Wuertz, age 26, Swiss, ship "Mercury" (A) (B) (R)
1743 - Conrad Wird, ship "Robert & Alice" (A)
1743 - Conradt or Konrudt Weit or Wirdt, age 31, "Lydia" (A)
1753 - Ferdinand or Ferdinandt Wurtz or Wetz, age 35, ship "Patience" (A) (B) (R)
1772 - Frantz Wertz, ship "Catherine" (A) (R)
1747 - Friederich Wirtz, ship "Vernon" (A) (B) (R)
1751 - Friederich Wurth, ship "Duke of Bedford" (A) (R)
1754 - Georg Wirst, ship "Bannister" (R)
1767 - Georg Keller Werth, ship "Sally" (R)
1743 - Gottlieb Werth, ship "Charlotte" (R)
1732 - Hance or Hans Jacob Wurth or Wartt, age 56, ship "Mary" (R)
1732 - Hance Jacob Wartt or Wurth, age 17, ship "Mary" (A) (R)
1743 - Hans Jacob Wurst, ship "Francis & Elizabeth" (R)
1750 - Hans Martin Wurtz or Weertz, ship "Royal Union" (B) (R) or "Royal S" (A)
1752 - Hans Conrad Wird, ship "Halifax" (A)

1739 - Hendrich or Henry Wert or Wirth, ship "Jamaica Galley" (A) or ship "Jamaica" (R)
1749 - Henry Wirdt, ship "Jacob" (A)
1750 - Henry Wurtz, ship "Royal Union" (B) (R) or ship "Royal S" (A)
1731 - Jacob Wirtz or Wurts, age 26, ship "Britannia" (A) (B) (R)
1744 - Jacob Wurtz, ship "Carterel" (A)
1749 - Jacob Wirth, ship "Edinburgh" (A)
1749 - Jacob Wurtz, ship "Crown" (B) ^R
1750 - Jacob Wurtz (A) or Wurth (R), ship "Nancy" (A) (R)
1755 - Jacob Wurtz or Wertz, ship "Neptune"(A)
1749 - Jeorge Jacob Wird (A), or Jerrig Werth (R) ship "Two Brothers" (A) (R)
1744 - Johan Christ Wirt, ship "Aurora" (A)
1749 - Johan Jacob Wurth, ship "Dragon" (R)
1767 - Johan Georg Wutzer, ship "Sally" (R)
1768 - Johan George Wurtz, ship "Pennsylvania Packet" (B) (R)
1752 - Johanes Wurtz, ship "Phoenix" (A)
1742 - Johann Wilhelm Werth, ship "Francis & Elizabeth" (R)
1749 - Johann Jacob Wurth, ship "Dragon" (A)
1752 - Johann Wurtz, ship "Phoenix" (R)
1752 - Johann Henrich Wirth, ship "Two Brothers" (A)
1753 - Johann Adam Wirth, ship "Two Brothers"
1754 - Johann Peters Werth, or Johann Tiel Wertz, ship "Brothers" (R)
1768 - Johann Georg Wurts, ship "Pennsylvania Packet" (A)
1772 - Johann Werth, ship "Crawford" (R)
1732 - Johannes Werth, ship "Mary" (R)
1753 - Johannes Wirtz, ship "Two Brothers" (B)
1732 - Kathrina Wertzin, age 9, "Samuel" (R)
1743 - Konradt Wirdt, ship "Rosannah" (A)
1740 - Lenard Werts, ship "Friendship" (R)
1748 - Lorentz Werthes, ship "Edinburgh" (R)
1753 - Ludwig or Lodwick or Lutwigh Wirtz, Wurtz or Vertz or Virtz, age 25, ship "Halifax" (A) (B) (R)
1754 - Ludwig or Lodewick Wert, Wird or Whart, "Phoenix" (A)
1752 - Michael Wuth, ship "Ann Galley" (R)

1754 - Michael Wirt or Wirth, ship "Mary &
       Sarah" (A)
1754 - Michael Werther, ship "Barclay" (R)
1753 - Peter Wertz, ship "Neptune" (A)
1754 - Peter Wertz, ship "Neptune" (R)
1753 - Philip Friedrich Warth, "Louisa" (R)
1753 - Samuel Wertz, ship "Edinburgh" (B)
1748 - Ulrich Wirth or Wirt, ship "Two
       Brothers" (A)
1753 - Wilhelm or Wilholm Wertz or Wurtz Jr.
       and Sr., ship "Neptune" (A) (B)
1754 - Wilhelm Wurtz or Wertz Jr. and Sr.,
       ship "Neptune" (R)

EARLY GERMANTOWN WERTZ FAMILIES

Among the first settlers at Germantown, 1683
to 1710 was a Cornelius Werts, who was
naturalized in 1708/9. (B)

Inscriptions in the Upper Germantown Burying
Ground include: Eve Mary Wert, wife of P. Wert
Sr. (Vertz), born 15 Feb. 1731.   (I)

A Johannes van der Wert was in Germantown
before 1710. (B) (S) page 413.
Also a Richard van der Werff was in Germantown
before 1710. (B)

EARLY PENN. WERTZ MARRIAGES

1742, Rebecca Worth married at First Reformed
Church, Lancaster twp., Lancaster Co. to
Jonathan Farnon, both single and from Chester
Co. at the large Brandywine. (K)

1750, April 17th, Barbara Wurtz from Canton
Basel, Switzerland, married at First Reformed
Church, Philadelphia to Jacob Pantley from
Murr, Canton Zurich, Switzerland. (K)

1754, Feb. 5th, Anna Wirth married at Germantown Reformed Church to Jacob Maurer. (K)

1759, April 17th, **Anna Maria Worth** married at New Goshenhopen Reformed Church, Upper Hanover Montgomery County to Jacob Beyer. (K)

1772, May 19th, Catharina Wirt, single, Lutheran, married at Seltenreich Reformed Church, New Holland, Lancaster Co. to John Penter, elder, Reformed, widower. (K)

1775, Nov. 14th, Geo. Henry Werty married at Lutheran Church, New Hanover, Montgomery Co. to Anna Barbara Herbst.

1776, July 9th, **Elizabeth Wirtz** married at First Reformed Church, lancaster twp. & Co. by Rev. Charles L. Boehme, to Jacob Boatz. (K)

1777, Sept. 15th, Jacob Wert married at St. Paul's Church, Philadelphia to Mary Miller.

1778, Oct. 25, **Dorothea Wirt**, married at First (Trinity) Reformed Church, York, York County to Jose Gray. (K)

1779, January 6th, Catharina born, daughter of Balser Wirth and wife Anna. Catharina married Johann George Rex. Catharina Wirth Rex died 12 May 1832, leaving two children, eight grand children, and having been a widow for 24 years. From Helffrich Pastoral Record, Berks and Lehigh Counties. (K)

1780, March 27th, **Mary Wirt** married at First (Trinity) Reformed Church, York, York County to Arthur M'Cann. (K)

1782, April 7th, Elizabeth **Wertz** of Millerstown, married at First Reformed Church, Lancaster twp. and Co. by Rev. Charles L. Boehme, to Killian Boos. (K)

1790, March 14th, **Susanna Wurtz** of Manor, married at First Reformed Church, Lancaster twp. and Co. by Rev. Charles L. Boehme, to Jacob Pottsfield. (K)

1791, Jan. 16th, Elizabeth Werz married at St. Michael's & Zion Church, Philadelphia to Johann Andreas Uhler.

1792, May 8th, Jacob Werth married Robeson twp., Berks Co. to Catharina Weidner. (K)

1793, January 29th, Magdalena Werth, married Heidelberg twp., Berks Co. to Johannes Rity.

1795, April 30th, Barbary Wert married at 2nd Pres. Church, Philadelphia to William Durnell.

1795, Oct. 12th, Philip Wert married at Swedes Church, Philadelphia to Mary White.

1796, Nov. 6th, Anna Werth married at Amity, Berks County to George Benner. (K)

1796, February 24th, Elizabeth Wirth married at Christ Union Church, Lower Saucon twp., Northampton County to Rudolph Reutner. (K)

1797, August 1st, Matthias Wirtz, widower, married at St. Michael's & Zion Church, Philadelphia to Rebecca Denny.

1798, January 21st, Christian Wurth married at the Minister's home to Maria Margaretha Rex. From Helffrich Pastoral Records, Berks and Lehigh Counties. (K)

1799, Nov. 17, Thomas Worth married at the West Bradford Monthly Meeting (Quaker) to Lydia Wiliamson. (E)

1801, August 30th, Joh. Wertz married at Schwartzwald Reformed Church, Exeter twp., Berks County to Anna Maria Meinder of Ruscomb Manor. (K)

1802, February 16th, Samuel Wertz married at Schwartzwald Reformed Church, Exeter twp., Berks County to Susanna Kremer of Maidencreek.

1805, November 19th, **Margaret Wert** married at Trinity Tulpehocken Ref. Church, Jackson twp., Lebanon County to John Domen.   (K)

1806, November 9th, **Peter Wurtz** married at Longswamp, Berks County to Catharina Gaumer. From Helffrich Pastoral Records.   (K)

1807, Nov. 8th, **John Wirt** married at Tohickon Reformed Church, Bedminster twp., Bucks Co. to Eva Shellenberg.   (K)

1807, Dec. 15th, **Jacob Wertz** married at Schwartzwald Reformed Church, Oley, Berks Co. to Elisabetha Kelchner. (K)

1809, Oct. 12th, **Peter Wert** married at Tabor First Reformed Church, Lebanon twp. & Co. to Magdalena Riess.   (K)

1813, Daniel Geiger and wife, **Catharina Wirth** were sponsors to a Jost baptism at Catawissa Congregation, Columbia, Northumberland Co.

1813, May 9th, **Johannes Wirth** married at Tabor First Reformed Church, Lebanon twp. & Co. to Anna Maria Fassnacht.   (K)

1821, August 5th, **Elizabeth Worth** m. at First Reformed Church, Phila. to Jacob Rusk. (K)

1828, June 5th, **Elizabeth Wurtz** married at First Reformed Church, Philadelphia to George McDonald. (K)

1833, June 4th, **David Wirt** married at Tabor First Reformed Church, Lebanon twp. & Co. to Sarah Miller. (K)

1846, Jan. 13th, **Hannah Wirth** married at Tohickon Reformed Church, Bedminster twp., Bucks County to Henry Shellenberger. (K)

WERTZ IN THE 1790 CENSUS RECORDS

Including the surnames spelled Wirt, Wert, Werts, Wertz, Wirts, Wirtz, and Wurtz... there were 45 families with 211 family members in the United States in 1790: Seven in New York; one in Massachusetts; one in South Carolina; two in Maryland; and 34 in Pennsylvania.

1790 Wert/Wirtz in New York

Hillsdale town, Columbia Co.: John Wirtz,2-0-2

Caughnawaga town, Montgomery Co.: Nicholas Wert, 3-0-4; and Michael Wert, 1-0-1.

Mohawk Town, Montgomery Co.: Morris Wert, 1-2-5... next door to a Richard Hoff Jun.!,1-2-2.

New York City, West Ward: James Wert, 1-0-1; and Joshua Werts, 2-0-3.

South Hempstead Town, Queens Co., James Wirt, 1-0-3.

1790 Massachusetts

Gloucester Town, Essex Co., Benj. Wert, 1-2-1

1790 South Carolina

Newberry County, 96th District, John Wirts, age 78, 1-1-6.

1790 Maryland

Back Creek Hundred, Cecil County, Thomas Wirt, 5-3-4.

Dorchester County, E. Wirt, 0-1-1.

1790 Pennsylvania

Bedford County, Peter Wart, 1-2-4; Hendrey Wart, 3-5-2 plus 2 slaves; Powel Wart, 1-1-2; and Eve Werts, 0-1-0.

Berks County: Cumru twp., George Wert, 1-2-2; Heidelberg twp. Jn. Wurtz, 1-3-3 (probably the Johannes Wertz in Jefferson twp., Berks Co. in 1787. See Chapter 9 - page 251); Robeson twp., Philip Wirtz, 1-1-3; Jacob Wirt, 3-0-3 (see Ch. 7 - page 196); Tulpehocken twp., Geo. Wm. Wirt, 2-2-6 (see Ch. 7 - page 196 or Ch. 8-page 216); and Jacob Wirtz, 2-2-3, (see Ch. 7 - page 196); Union twp., Bernard Wirt, 1-3-3.

Bucks County: Christian Wirtz, 2-1-2; John Wert, 1-2-5; and John Warts, 1-1-2.

Cumberland County: Hopewell, Newton, Tyborn, or West Pensboro township; Adam Wirt, 2-1-3, (see chapter 9 - page 221).

Dauphin County, Lebanon Town, Christopher Wartz, 3-4-5.

Fayette County, Springhill twp., Jonathan Wert, 1-2-2.

Franklin County, Conrad Warts, 4-3-2 (see Chapter 3); John Warts, 1-2-3 (see Chapter 5); and George Warts, 1-2-4 (see Chapter 6).

Huntingdon County, Henery Wirts, 1-2-5; and John Wirtz, 1-1-1.

Lancaster County, Caernarvon twp., Jacob Wertz, 1-2-2; and Peter Wertz, 1-2-3; and Cocalico twp., Fred(k) Wertz, 2-2-1 (see Chapter 7 - page 199).

Montgomery County, Cheltenham township, Christian Wertz, 2-1-5; 1-1.

Northampton County, Heidelberg twp., Balser Wert, 1-3-2; and Nicholas Wirt, 1-1-4 (see Chapter 9 - page 250); Upper Milford twp., Elizabeth Werts, 2-0-2; and Elizabeth Werts, 0-2-2; Weisenberg twp., Daniel Wirt, 1-2-5.

Northumberland County, Jacob Wert, 1-1-3; and John Wertz, 1-3-3.

Philadelphia County, Northern Liberties twp.,
Philip Wirt, 1-0-5; Phila. City, Middle
district, South Third Street from Market to
Chestnut Street, Westside, Joseph Wert,
Painter, 2-1-2; Phila. City, Middle District,
Arch Street,South, Henry Wurtz, Barber, 3-0-3.

Washington County, Martin Wirt, 1-3-5.

York County, Berwick, Cumberland, Franklin,
Germany, Hamiltonban, Heidelberg, Mount Joy or
Straban townships: Jacob Werts, 2-3-4; Jacob
Werts, 1-0-1; Ulmick Werts, 1-0-1; and
Christian Wirt, 3-3-0.

REVOLUTIONARY WAR PENSIONERS

Daniel Wertz, Pennsylvania, wife = Catherine,
application #R11328.

George Wertz, Maryland and Pennsylvania,
application #S11329.

Jacob Werts/Wertz, Pennsylvania, wife =
Catherine, application #W2980.

John Wirtz, Pennsylvania, appl. #S22590.

Philip Wirt/Wirtz/Wurtz, Pennsylvania, wife =
Dorothy, application #R11735,

William Wirtz/Wuertz, Pennsylvania, #R11736.

Chapter 11

SOUTHERN WERTZ FAMILIES

In Chapter 9, mention was made of the eldest son of John Adam and Eve Elizabeth Wirt, Adam Wirt who went to Virginia, married there and raised a "large family". (see page 221) It is not known what date he went to Virginia, but probably about 1780 to 1790. It is also not known what part of Virginia he settled in, or if any of the families outlined below are descended from him.

Also, in Chapter 8 is mention of a William Wirt who was admitted to the bar in 1792, had a law office at Culpepper Court House, in Virginia; and then in Richmond in 1799. (L) (see page 220) Perhaps some of these Virginia families are his descendants.

LOUDOUN COUNTY VIRGINIA WERTZ FAMILIES

Conrad Wirtz and Barbara, had a daughter, Christina, born 25 Feb. 1786, Lovettsville; baptized 29 March 1787 at New Jerusalem Evangelical Lutheran Church, Lovettsville, Loudoun County, Virginia. (E)

Johannes Wirtz/Wurtz married 25 Sept. 1788 at Lovettsville, to Elizabeth Stedlerin. They had at least two daughters born there:
1. Elizabeth Wirtz/Wurts, born 13 Sept. 1790.
2. Catharina Wirtz, born 8 July 1792. (E)

Wilhelm Wirtz and wife, Christina Beber, had a daughter, Christina, born 2 March 1791 at Lovettsville. (E) A Christina Wertz married 25 Dec. 1814 at the New Jerusalem Evangelical Lutheran Church, Lovettsville to George Adams.

Peter Wirtz and Christina had nine children, all born at Lovettsville, Loudoun County. (E)

1. Conrad Wirtz, born 6 June 1791. Note: a Conrad and Elisabeth Wertz had a son, George Wilhelm Wertz, born 27 Jan. 1820, Lovettsville, baptized 25 Feb. 1821 at New Jerusalem Evangelical Lutheran Church, Lovettsville.

2. Jacob Wirtz/Wertz, born 5 July 1793. A Jacob Wertz married 7 April 1818 at Lovettsville to Elisabetha Slacks. They had at least three children born there:
(1) Catharina Wertz, born 4 Jan. 1820.
(2) George Wirtz, born 22 Dec. 1821.
(3) Elisabetha Wertz, born 20 August 1854 (this date must be incorrect), baptized 26 April 1825, New Jerusalem Evang. Luth. Ch.

3. Sibylla Wirtz, born 13 June 1795.

4. Anna Elisabetha Wirtz, born 2 August 1799. Possibly the Anna Wertz married 23 Jan. 1816 at New Jerusalem Evangelical Lutheran Church, Lovettsville, to Georg Boecker.

5. Margaretha Wirtz, born 18 Dec. 1801.

6. Adam Wirtz/Wertz, born 28 Feb. 1804. An Adam Wertz married 28 Nov. 1826 at New Jerusalem Evang. Luth. Church, Lovettsville to Sussana Lilly, and they had five children, all born at Lovettsville and/or baptized at the New Jerusalem Evang. Lutheran Church there:
(1) Johannes William Wirtz, born 21 Jan. 1827.
(2) Christina Sarah Wirtz, born 7 Dec. 1828.
(3) Lisa Ann Wirtz, born 3 Dec. 1830.
(4) Peter Tilgman Wertz, baptized 10 March 1834
(5) Susannah Wertz, baptized 16 March 1834.

7. George Wirtz, born 20 Oct. 1806.

8. Catherina Wirtz, born 20 Jan. 1809.

9. Sarah Philibina Wirtz, born 17 Jan. 1813.

Michael Wirtz/Werz and Catherina or Catharine, had at least two children, both born at Lovettsville and baptized at the New Jerusalem Evangelical Lutheran Church there.

1. **Wilhelm Wirtz/Werz,** born 23 Dec. 1792; baptized 28 June 1795. Note: a William Willhelm Wertz and wife, Phillibina, had six children all born at Lovettsville and/or baptized at this same Church:
(1) Junity Wertz, born 7 March 1812.
(2) Maria Wertz, born 23 June 1814, baptized 7 August 1814.
(3) Henrich Wertz, born 30 July 1817.
(4) Joseph Ludwig Wertz, born 18 July 1821.
(5) Carolus Phenton Wertz, born 12 July 1823.
(6) Mandy Catharine Wertz, born 22 Jan. 1827.

2. **Elizabeth Werz/Wirtz,** born 6 April 1794, baptized 28 June 1795.

Wilhelm Wirtz/Wurth and Barbara had two children born at Lovettsville:
1. **Jacob Wirtz,** born 24 Sept. 1795. (This could also be the Jacob m. Elizabeth Slacks, see children of Peter and Christina, above.)
2. **Sarah Wirth/Wurth,** born 6 Nov. 1801.

Adam Wertz and Catharina had seven children born at Lovettsville and/or baptized at the New Jerusalem Evangelical Lutheran Church.

1. **Samuel Wertz,** born 15 Dec. 1801; baptized 24 Feb. 1811.
2. **Johannas Wertz,** born 25 May 1806.
3. **Isaac Wertz,** born 14 Nov. 1808; baptized 10 Nov. 1808. (Note, these dates may be confused)
4. **Maria Wertz,** born 14 Jan. 1813.
5. **Henrich Wertz,** born 12 August 1815.
6. **Elisabeth Wertz,** born 14 Nov. 1817.
7. **Peter Wertz,** born 23 July 1820.

Henrick Wurtz and Sibilla, had a son, Wilyam Wurtz, born 4 August 1805 at Lovettsville.

Peter Wertz and Susanna or Susan, had four children, all born at Lovettsville.
1. Rosina Catharine Wertz, born 28 May 1806.
2. Malinda Wertz, born 24 Nov. 1809.
3. Johannes Wertz, born 12 April 1812.
4. Salomon Wertz, born 20 Jan. 1815.

Johannes Wertz/Wentz and Christina, had three children born at Lovettsville.
1. Phillip Wertz, born 25 May 1807.
2. Elizabetha Wertz, born 26 July 1809.
3. William Wertz, born 22 April 1813.

Jacob Wertz and Louisa/Lousia/Lowisa, had seven children born at Lovettsville, or baptized at the New Jerusalem Evangelical Lutheran Church at Lovettsville.
1. Johannes Wertz, born 10 Dec. 1808.
2. Jacob Wertz, born 30 March 1811.
3. Susanna Wertz, born 30 March 1815.
4. Maria Anna Wertz, baptized 3 Sept. 1815.
5. Lusinda Wertz, born 17 May 1816.
6. Benjamin William Wertz, born 11 Feb. 1819
7. Henrich Wertz, baptized 23 May 1824.

Jacob Wertz and Catherine Ann had two daughters, born at Lovettsville.
1. Minerva Susan Wertz, born 15 Oct. 1830, baptized 27 Oct. 1832 at New Jerusalem Evangelical Lutheran Church, Lovettsville.
2. Lucy Augusta Wertz, born 28 April 1834.

CHRISTIAN WERTZ and NANCY BRUBAKER
of ROANOKE COUNTY, VIRGINIA

John Wertz, born 23 August 1767, possibly in Fairfax of Loudoun County, Virginia; died 12 April 1862, Roanoke Co., Virginia; son of Conrad Wertz, will proved 1822; married 26 March 1812 to Anna Frantz. John and Anna were the parents of Christian Wertz, born 19 Nov. 1815 at Cave Spring, Roanoke Co., Virginia; died 3 April 1880 at Cave Spring; married 13 or 18 March 1837, Botetourt Co., Virginia to Nancy Brubaker, born 12 Dec. 1812, Middlebrook, Virginia; died 1 Jan. 1894, Roanoke Co., Virginia; daughter of Henry Brubaker (1775-1848) and Sarah Eller.
Christian Wertz and Nancy Brubaker had at least four children born in Roanoke County.

1. Abraham J. Wertz, born 16 August 1852, Salem, Roanoke County; died 31 Jan. 1939 at Las Vegas, New Mexico; married 25 Feb. 1874. One son, Joseph Karl Wertz, was born 20 Nov. 1853 at Adamsboro, Indiana. Information on this family was received by correspondence in 1988 from a grand son of Joseph Karl Wertz, Bruce Wertz of Las Vegas, New Mexico.

2. Eliza Worts, born 16 April 1854, Cave Spring, Roanoke County, Virginia.

3. Lucy Wortz/Wertz, born 3 August 1856, Roanoke, Roanoke County; died in infancy.

4. Benjamin Wertz, born August 1859, Roenoke County; died in infancy.

There are many other Roanoke County births and marriages listed in the IGI, but they have not been copied here.

WERTZ FAMILIES in the CAROLINIAS

George Henry Werts, born 1765 in Newberry County, South Carolina; served as a private in the South Carolina militia; died 1840, Newberry County, South Carolina; married Mollie Singley, born 1762; died 1847. One son known:

1. Michael Werts, born 1790; died 1853; married in 1815 to Susan Summer, born 1793; died 1833. A daughter...

(1) Caroline Werts, born 1818; died 1889; married William D. Reagin, born 1811; died 1886. (D.A.R. Lineage Book, page 181; #125555)

From pedigree chart #1481, in the Jacksonville, Florida Family History Library:

"Miss Wertz or Werts, born about 1776, died in 1833 in South Carolina; married about 1800 to Adam Bedenbaugh, born about 1760 in Newberry County, South Carolina. They had a son: John Bedenbaugh, who was born about 1803 in Newberry County, South Carolina."

Chapter 12

THE 1915 WERTZ FAMILY ASSOCIATION

Apparently our Franklin County, Penn. Wertz families established a Family association in the early 1900's. The letter heading shown on the next page, indicates a rather active and extensive group. The letter on this heading reads: "Dear Friend: If you wish to become a member of the Wertz Family Association you have but to send $1.00 money order to W.J. Snyder, Sec'y-Treas., 1305 Ashland Block, Chicago, for life membership, and in return you will receive a handsomely engraved membership certificate.
"Any one bearing the name of Wertz, or related thereto, is eligible for membership. Our Association now numbers 689 members and is steadily increasing.
"If you desire further information regarding the Wertz history, Paul Wirtz's fabulous estate - in fact, everything in detail that we are cognizant of, send $1.00 extra to W.J. Snyder and get a printed booklet containing the family history as far as known.
"You are cordially invited to join our Association at once. Members only will be kept informed as new developments occur. Always enclose stamped self-addressed envelope for your reply. We are trying to save our funds as much as possible and our heavy mail is a serious drain upon our finances. Yours in the work, Estelle Ryan Snyder, President"

It is not known by the present generation how many years this Wertz Association existed. It is certain that they were the authors of the Wertz charts upon which the first six chapters of this book are largely based. The "printed booklet containing the family history"

Wertz Family Association

1ST VICE-PRES. WILLARD W. WERTZ
PRES. WERTZ AUTO. CO.
LINCOLN, NEB.

2D VICE-PRES. LEE POTTERFIELD
VALLEY PARK, MO.

3D VICE-PRES. C. H. WORTZ
PRES. FT. SMITH BISCUIT CO.
FT. SMITH, ARK.

SEC'Y-TREAS. WILLIAM J. SNYDER
1305 ASHLAND BLOCK
CHICAGO, ILL.

COR. SEC'Y GEO. W. WERTZ, JR.
ATTORNEY AT LAW
ALEDO, ILL.

ASST. COR. SEC'Y CORA HOSELTON
MILLERSBURG, IOWA

ESTELLE RYAN SNYDER, PRESIDENT
1305 ASHLAND BLOCK
CHICAGO, ILL.

ADVISORY BOARD
WILLARD W. WERTZ—CHAIRMAN—LINCOLN, NEB.
PAUL D. WERTZ, ZANESVILLE, OHIO
B. F. WERTZ, BROKEN ARROW, OKL.
JAMES M. WERTZ, GRAND JUNCTION, IA.
JOHN W. WERTZ, STUART, NEB.

Dear Friend:

I am sending this to you it might
help you. My grand parents did not
join the association to many
information. They felt this would aid placement
information of Wertz family

mentioned in the letter above, has never come into the possession of any of the current generation, as far as we now know. Thus we cannot say if it contains records not on the charts that were preserved for our benefit.

There is a record available at the Newberry Library in Chicago, and the L.D.S. Library in Salt Lake City, that is indexed under Wurtz, Wirtz, and Wertz by William J. Snyder, titled "Stenographic report of proceeding had at the second reunion of the Wertz family held at Harrisburg, Pennsylvania. October 25, 26, 27, 1912", Chicago, Illinois, 1912. The 102 pages include a history of "Jacob Wuertz born 1705 in the Palatinate of Germany, and immigrated via Rotterdam in 1731 to Chester Co. Penn.; married Anna Barbara Hoff in 1734, and later moved to Cumberland (now Franklin) Co., Penn." This record also included names and addresses of the members of the Wertz Family association in 1912; and a four page publication by Estelle Ryan Snyder titled "Logical reasons why the Wirtz inheritance case should be re-opened and properly adjudicated." The gist of this material is recorded below.

Both of these libraries also have copies of Estelle Ryan Snyder's charts as we have them.

THE PAUL WIRTZ INHERITANCE CASE

Paul Wirtz was born 28 September 1612 in Husum, Germany. He served in the Imperial, Swedish and Dutch service during his lifetime. He became Field Marshall of Holland. In recognition of brilliant military service Sweden conferred upon him the title of Baron of Ornholm. In 1673 he retired from active service in Hamburg, Germany. On March 21st or 23rd, 1676 he died unmarried.

Paul Wirtz' father, Nicholaus Wirtz, was married twice. His first marriage was to a woman by the name of Catrina Orth. Their three children were Peter, Anna, and Heinrich

273

Wirtz. After the death of his first wife, Nicholaus married Anna Bauschen. They also had three children: Paul, Herman, and Benedict.

Paul, the eldest son of Nicholaus' second marriage, became the great Field Marshal Paul Wirtz, one of the greatest military men of his generation.

Paul Wirtz' brothers, Herman, born in 1622; and Benedict, born in 1625; were both killed in the "War of Thirty Years". Both brothers were killed in battle, unmarried, and without heirs. Field Marshal Paul Wirts also died unmarried. Thus, Paul Wirts' two half brothers, Peter and Heinrich, and half sister, Anna, became his natural heirs.

However, a will dated December 28th, 1672 at Gorcum, Holland, gives all his moveable goods and 12,000 gulden to his housekeeper Johanna von der Planken and her daughter Berta.

Paul Wirtz retired to private life in Hamburg, Germany in 1673, and died there in 1676. Soon after his death his housekeeper, Johanna von der Planken, produced another will, acknowledged by a Notary Public, in which she was constituted as Paul Wirtz "exclusive heir" and charged with numerous legacies. This will was not signed by Paul Wirtz himself, but by one of the witnesses. This will was opened, read and confirmed and Johanna von der Planken took charge of the Wirtz inheritance.

Then in the latter part of the year 1676 the president of the Court of Chancery received notice that the Wirtz inheritance had been wrongfully obtained by a forged will. And on January 28, 1677 by issue of an Imperial decree at the Court of Windischgratz, the Bremen Ambassador, was commissioned to investigate the case and if it was found as alleged, to confiscate the inheritance.

274

On February 13th and 25th, 1677 Windisengratz
reported, among other things, that the Mayor
Schulz and the Imperial Counselor von Rondeck,
had been bribed by Johanna von der Planken so
there would be no contest of the Wirtz will.
For this von Rondeck had received 1000
Reichsthaler. The bribery of von Rondeck is
proven by documentary evidence contained in
the Archives of the City of Amsterdam under an
"Original Act" of May 4, 1676, in which von
Rondeck acknowledged receipts for 3000
Reichsthaler in order to uphold the testament.
The 34th Register of the Orphan Court of the
City of Amsterdam, folio 318, shows that von
Rondeck received on May 4th, 1676, a loan of
107,500 florin from Wirtz' housekeeper,
Johanna von den Planken.

This documentary evidence proves that as a
result of this collusion the von der Planken
woman assumed control of the Wirtz inheritance
until March 20th, 1677, when, by the direction
of Count Windischgratz the inheritance was
confiscated and the Notary Public, Johanna von
der Planken, and the steward Sievert Kerk, who
had also been remembered in the forged Wirtz
will with a legacy, were arrested and all
persons present at the drawing up of the will
had to testify under oath.
Soon after, by the direction of Johanna von
der Planken, who had been set free through the
activities of a Dutch resident, by name
Kuysten, the Hamburg Courts issued a summons
to all who thought they had a claim to the
inheritance to come forward. Many who thought
themselves heirs, came forward to be present
at the hearing of the witnesses, this hearing
having been demanded by Johanna von der
Planken.

Among the "pretender heirs" that came forward
were Mrs. Ingeborg Kirutz of Helsinger,
Denmark, and Mrs. Herlige Teets of Amsterdam;
also the Attorney General and the Hamburg
Attorney General took part in this lawsuit. On
November 6th, 1678 the court concluded not to

275

turn over the inheritance to Johanna von der Planken, but to allow her a yearly sum of 500 Reichsthaler for maintenance until the case was settled.

Early in the year 1679 Johanna von der Planken died. Her will is in the archives of Amsterdam. The guardian of her daughter, Berta, obtained an agreement on 7 March 1679 from Mrs. Kirutz, that Mrs. Kirutz would surrender all her claims on the Wirtz estate in favor of the daughter, Berta, for the sum of 15,000 Reichsthaler and one half of a Holstein bond for 16,000 Reichsthaler.

On Sept. 26th, 1679 the Hamburg Court decided that this agreement between the Planken guardians and Mrs. Kirutz should stand. There are also reasons mentioned in Vienna Acts 39 which would indicate that the question of the legality of the Wirtz will was at that time still unsettled. This judgment was confirmed by the Imperial Counselor July 27th, 1691.

Great changes had meantime taken place with the inheritance. The city of Hamburg had, in the beginning of April 1677, seen to it that all and everything which had been confiscated by the imperial Court was released and brought to the house of Mayor Meurer.

Immediately upon the seizure of the Wirtz inheritance by the Imperial Court, the woman, Johanna von der Planken asked her friends, gentlemen of Amsterdam to act on her behalf and to protect her. Knysten, a dutch resident at Hamburg, had most energetically protested against the imprisonment of his country woman, and it was through his efforts that the woman secured her release.

It is evident that by this Knysten's direction the General States took an active part in the matter by a direct request made by the city of Amsterdam, for resolutions to this effect were made by the General States August 10, 1678;

the Mayor and officials of the city of Amsterdam worked on the woman's behalf and interceded for her frequently. On the foregoing date, the General States threatened Hamburg with reprisals, demanded the handing over of the Wirtz inheritance, and stated under affidavit that the Wirtz will lacked very essential points regarding validity. Their protests were to no avail, however, and the protection of the Emperor was also powerless. The handing over of the Wirtz inheritance was finally accomplished on November 6th, 1678. The Mayor and counsellors could not do otherwise than seize some of the Wirtz inheritance, more of which had come to light, and to confiscate a part of it.

Final reprisals were threatened again on April 28th, 1679, and so much influence brought to bear that the city of Hamburg fearing a devastating war, agreed to turn over the inheritance to the city of Amsterdam. The confiscated goods were transferred in 28 trunks. Among the court documents there is a legally acknowledged inventory which was made June 11th and 12th, 1679 in Amsterdam.

Not only was the Wirtz inheritance seized, but the body of the deceased Paul Wirtz was also demanded and taken from Hamburg to Amsterdam where it was buried in the Old Kirke with great military honors.

In the second will, said to have been made by the Field Marshal, Paul Wirtz, but which it is contended was forged by Johanna von der Planken, this will particularly specifies: "After my death my lifeless body shall be buried with Christian ceremonial in the Church of St. Michael's, situated in Hamburg, and it shall rest there until that great day on which God designated to reunite body and soul".

Not content with obtaining the inheritance by threat of reprisal, the General States desecrated the grave of the native born German, disinterred the body, two years after burial and conveyed it to foreign shores in utter defiance to the wishes of the deceased wherein he specified his burial place at St. Michael's Church at Hamburg, Germany.

In the Archives of the city of Amsterdam there is a second inventory dated 1679. The total amount of this one inventory alone reaches the sum of 545,439 gulden. This includes a number of notes for interest, which were in arrears from three to four years in each instance. Many of these notes were for 5,000 gulden, and were amounts loaned to the General States; a bond of 10,000 florin issued by the Holstein Government in the year 1633 had interest years in arrears. 17 buildings situated in the city of Lubeck, Germany were a part of the Wirtz inheritance, and contents of two of the trunks said to contain very valuable tapestries were not sold, but placed in the vault at Amsterdam.

At the time the city of Amsterdam took possession of the Wirtz inheritance by threats of reprisals against the officials of Hamburg, the Commissioners of the Exchange of the city of Amsterdam, and the Mayor and Administration Board of Hamburg, made an agreement in regard to the Wirtz inheritance. The agreement was that the inheritance should be brought under seal to Amsterdam, an inventory, and appraisal of goods made and then same was to be sold under the condition that it should then be handed over to the Exchange to be kept in trust for those to whom it belonged by right.

Enclosed with this account, which was presumably written in 1912 to 1915 by Estelle Ryan Snyder, is a chart, titled "Genealogy of the Wurtz Family — stepbrothers and stepsister of the Field Marshall Paul Wurtz — Peter, Anna, Heinrich, Time 1612 — 1772" under this title is written "Hans Escher, retired Police kommissioner, Essen — Ruhr".

The chart outlines the following families:

Conrad Wurz, wife Gertrude; five sons:
1. Johannes Wurz, of Birgden County of Julich.
2. Mathias Wurz, of Birgden County of Julich.
3. Nicholaus Wurz, first wife = Catrina Orth, three children: Petrus, Anna, and Henricus; second wife = Anna Bauschen, three sons: Paulus, Hermann, and Benedict. (see below)
4. Engelmann Wurz of Birgden, County of Julich
5. Arth Wurz of Birgden, County of Julich.

Nicholaus Wurz, and 1st wife Catrina Orth:
1. Petrus Wurz and wife Anna of Neudorff. Eight children: Jacobus, Theodorus, Christina, Joannes, Henricus, Agnes, Anna Sophia, and Engelbertus. (see below)
2. Anna Wurz, married --?-- Bucher; one son: Laurentius Bucher; who had three children: Catrina, married Michael --?-- of Niederberg; Dorothea, married Jacob Saal of Simmerns; and Antonius Bucher of Niederberg.
3. Henricus Wurz, and wife Catharina of Neuzdorff. He moved to Embs, Oranien. Six children: Petrus, Philippina, Odilia, Joannes, Jacobus, and Philippus. (see below)
Nicholaus Wurz and 2nd wife Anna Bauschen:
4. Paul Wurz, born 30 Oct. 1612 in Husum (Germany); died 21 March 1676 in Hamburg.
5. Hermann Wurz, died single.
6. Benedict Wurz, died single.

Petrus Wurz, and wife Anna of Neudoff:
1. Jacobus Wurz and wife Margaretha of Bendorff; seven children:
(1) Joannnes Wurz, disappeared in Bendorff
(2) Henricus Wurz of Bendorff.
(3) Elisabeth Wurz of Bendorff.
(4) Anna Maria Wurz, disappeared.
(5) Anna Christina Wurz, disappeared.
(6) Georgius Wurz of Bendorff.
(7) Maria Margaretha Wurz of Pfaffenberg.
2. Theodorus Wurz and wife Magdalena of Bendorff; two children:
(1) Anna Maria Wurz, disappeared in Bendorff
(2) Nicolaus Wurz of Bendorff.

3. Christina Wurz and husband Petus Wolff, of Niederberg; two children:
(1) Dorothea Wolff of Niederberg.
(2) Mathias Wolff of Niederberg.

4. Joannes Wurz and wife Agnete, of Oberlahnstein, Maguntini territory; two children:
(1) Josephus Wurz of Oberlahnstein.
(2) Barbara Wurz of Oberlahnstein.

5. Henricus Wurz and wife Agnete, of Buchholz, Maguntini territory; two children:
(1) Christine Wurz of Buchholz, Maguntini territory.
(2) Catharina Wurz of Durstheck, Maguntini territory.

6. Agnes Wurz and husband Laurentius Langeroth of Bendorff; four children:
(1) Joannes Lanzeroth.
(2) Mathias Lanzeroth.
(3) Anna Maria Lanzeroth.
(4) Peter Lanzeroth.

7. Anna Sophia Wurz and husband Antonius Eysenbarth of Arzheim; two children:
(1) Elisabeth Eysenbarth of Arzheim.
(2) Catharina Eysenbrth of Arzheim.

8. Engelbertus Wurz and wife Anna Maria, of Niederberg; five children:
(1) Catharina Wurz.
(2) Petrus Wurz of Niederberg.
(3) Magdalena Wurz of Niederberg.
(4) Henricus Wurz of Niederberg.
(5) Laurentius ? Wurz of Niederberg.

Henricus Wurz, and Catharina of Neuzdorff, and Embs, Oranien; six children:
1. Petrus Wurz and wife Maria Margareta of Embs; thirteen children:
(1) Joann Jacob Heinrich Wurz of Embs.
(2) Hedwig Margaretha Wurz and husband Joann Seck of Embs.
(3) Joann Egnelmann Wurz, died single, in Embs.

280

(4) Joann David Wurz of Adolfsfurth.
(5) Joann Georg Wurz of Adolfsfurth.
(6) Johann Anton Wurz of Neuhoff Ysenburg.
(7) Margaretha and husband Jos. Bachen of Offenbach.
(8) Joannes Matheis Wurz arrived in Hungary.
(9) Maria Philippina Wurz of Embs.
(10) Joann Peter Wurz, in the imperial service
(11) Johannes Jacobus Wurz, disappeared.
(12) Joann Heinrich Wurz, of Embs.
(13) Anna Sophia Wurz, married to Anton Beuber, in Silesia.

2. Philippina Wurz, and husband Martinus Castarff, of Embs; three children:
(1) Maria Loisa Castarff, of Embs.
(2) Joann Barthel Castarff, in Obershausen.
(3) Rosina Catharina and husband, Wilhelm Kannes of Kamensus.

3. Odilia Wurz, and husband, Servatius Hell of Bendorff; two children & two grandchildren:
(1) Veronica Hell and husband, Petrus Eisenbarth, of Arzheim; one son: Antonius Hell, of Bendorff.
(2) Margaretha Hell, married to Theodor Wirges, of Bendorff; one son: Joannes Wurges of Urbar.

4. Joannes Wurz and wife, Catharina, of Niederberg; three children:
(1) Joannes Wurz of Niederberg.
(2) Maria Magdalena Wurz of Niederberg.
(3) Anna Wurz of Niederberg.

5. Jacobus Wurz, twin, died single.
6. Philippus Wurz, twin, died single.

At the bottom of this chart is the following: "That this is the signature of Sebastiani, notary and court secretary of the Electoral government of Trier, and that the seal is the Thal Ehrenbreitstein court seal, and is hereby attested and confirmed." signed Johann Jacob Spitz, Government registrar of the Electorate of Trier.

"This is to certify that the above draft is correct according to the baptismal records and original documents of the Court Archives, and that the persons named thereon, should be recognized as the true relatives and the real heirs of the Hoillandisch Field Marshal Paul Wurz, who died in 1676, and that this draft was drawn by our court secretary. We the magistrate and judicial deputies of the court of the Electorate of Trier, seated in Thal Ehrenbreitstein and parish Niederberg, attest herewith with signature and common court seal. Executed in Ehrenbreitstein at an extra session of the Court August 28, 1772. By judicial order." (signed) F.H. Sebastiani, court secretary.

"The above draft of Genealogy has been compared with the original and has been found to conform in every detail. In testimony whereof I affix my signature and my seal. October 2, 1772. signed Joannes Josephus Christophorus Scholz, apostolic imperial notary public, duly authorized and under oath. In faith."

Now it is obvious that since the copy we have of this chart is written in English, it is not the original written in 1772 in Germany or Holland. Perhaps Estelle Ryan Snyder made this copy also, perhaps from records she received from Germany or Holland. Record as to just how this chart came to be in its current form is missing. But the genealogical and historical data on it is none the less of interest, and no doubt accurate.

References

(A) Pennsylvania German Pioneers, by R. B. Strassburger, 1934. Volume I, pages 106, 110, and 111.

(B) 30,000 Names of Immigrants in Pennsylvania, by Daniel Rupp; page 70.

(C) Historical Sketch of Franklin County, by I. H. M'Cauley, 1878. Page 138.

(D) Old Ties and New Links to our Wertz Chain, by Mrs. Robert N. Ungerer, 1978;p.8.

(E) International Genealogical Index (IGI), March 1984 edition.

(F) Biographical Annals of Franklin County Pennsylvania, published 1905, reproduced 1978.

(G) Records of the Kittochtinny Historical Society Library, Chambersburg, Franklin County, Penn., including their magazine: Franklin County Footnotes, Volumes 1-4, 1980 to 1988.

(H) Records of the Fisher Family Reunion Association, from "Fisher History" compiled in 1980 by John M. Fisher of Franklin Co., Pennsylvania.

(I) Penn. German Immigrants, 1709-1786; and Penn. German Church Records, Volumes I-III; and Penn. Vital Records, Volumes I-III; all edited by Don Yoder.

(J) Notes and Queries, Historical and Genealogical, Chiefly Relating to Interior Pennsylvania, by William Henry Engle, 12 volumes, 1970.

(K) Pennsylvania German Marriages, compiled by Donna R. Irish, 1984.

(L) The German Element in the United States, by Albert Bernhardt Faust, Volumes I and II, 1909.

(M) The National Cyclopeadia of American Biography, Volume 6.

(N) Genealogies of Pennsylvania Families, Volume I, compiled from the Pennsylvania Genealogical Magazine, by Don Yoder, 1982.

(O) The Early Germans of New Jersey, by Theodore Frelinghuysen Chambers, 1969.

(P) A Brief History of one Branch of the Hoover Family, by Fox.

(Q) Indian Eve and her Descendants...of Bedford County, Pennsylvania, by Emma A.M. Replogle, 1911.

(R) Penn. Oaths of Allegiance, by Egle

(S) William Penn and the Dutch Quaker Migration to Pennsylvania, by William I. Hull, 1935.

(T) The Historical Register, edited by Edwin Charles Hill, 1921.

(U) Levering Family, History and Genealogy, by Col.John Levering of LaFayette, Indiana.

(V) Emigrants to Pennsylvania, 1641-1819, by Tepper.

(W) Pennsylvania Mennonite Heritage, January 1988, "An Essay on the Stoner/Steiner Families of Pennsylvania", by Samuel S. Wenger.

(X) Knepper Families in Pennsylvania, 1950, by Laura Knepper, of Franklin County, Penn.

(Y) Bedford County, Penn. Cemeteries, Volumes 1-8, compiled by Robertta and Thomas C. Imler.

(Z) American Revolutionary Soldiers of Franklin County, Pennsylvania, page 280; and Fifth Series Penn. Archives, Volume 5, p.120.

(AA) Antietam Ancestors, Volume 2, Number 4, Fall 1987; pages 88 and 89.

(BB) National Genealogical Society Quarterly, Volume 73, Number 2, June 1985; article by Cathy D. Knepper of Kensington, Maryland, titled "Wilhelm Knepper (1691-1766) and His Descendants in Franklin County, Pennsylvania"

(CC) Baker and Hoover Records, from Wanda C. Smith, of Auburn, Indiana, by correspondence in 1989; including Franklin Co., Penn. deeds, Baker family records compiled by Mary C. Bennett and Agnes Hoover Wells; and excerpts from the following Hoover Histories: A Genealogical History of the Descendants of Johannes or John (Huber) Hoover and his wife Mary Watson, who settled in Lancaster Co., Penn., by Mary Ruthrauff Hoover; Matthias and Mary (Hoover) Hoffman of "Necessity" and their Descendants, by Jacob A. Hoffman of Hagerstown, Maryland. A History of Henry Isaiah Hoover, His Ancestors and Descendants, by Ernest Hoover, Evansville, Indiana and Mrs. Ernest Field, Bourbon, Indiana, 1975.

(DD) The David Wertz Family, by Willard Wertz and Mary C. Bennett. This work includes a journal by David Wertz, written by him in 1896, covering his own life up to 1864. Additions were made by his son, Willard W. Wertz in 1911.

(EE) Records of the Simom Peter Wertz family, obtained from Kathy Wertz Zerbe of Santa Rosa, California by correspondence in 1984.

(FF) Records of Kathryn S. Huber, descendant of Joshua Knepper and Mary Short (see pages 83 and 96).

Collateral Surname Index

```
Baer, James Edward                              140
Baer, Jane (Mrs. Foose)                         239
Baer, John                                      239
Baer, Judith Ann                                139
Baer, Karen Elizabeth                           139
Baer, Larry Elmer                           139,140
Baer, Lester Raymond                        139,140
Baer, Linda Sue                                 140
Baer, Margaret (Mrs.George Titzel)              239
Baer, Margaret Lucille Spencer(Mrs.R.W.)140
Baer, Margaret Wertz (Mrs.Abraham)              239
Baer, Martha (Mrs. Thomas Gray)                 239
Baer, Mary Graber (Mrs. Elmer E.)               139
Baer, Maud Eva Wertz (Mrs. Raymond) 133,139
Baer, Nettie Elizabeth Long (Mrs.W.D.)  139
Baer, Pearl Catharine                           139
Baer, Raymond Andrew                        133,139
Baer, Robert Michael                            139
Baer, Roberta Francis Rutter (Mrs.L.E.) 140
Baer, Robyn Lynn                                140
Baer, Russell Winfield                      139,140
Baer, Ruth Eileen (Mrs.Lewis Beech) 139,140
Baer, Samuel                                    239
Baer, Sarah (Mrs. John Cless)                   239
Baer, Shawn Michael                             140
Baer, Thomas Raymond                            140
Baer, Washington                                239
Baer, Wilmer Dale                               139
Bainter, Sadie Swoveland (Mrs. M.)               68
Baker, Abraham                          89,150,152
Baker, Amanda Gater (Mrs. Abraham)               89
Baker, Amanda Warner                             39
Baker, Anna (Mrs. Jacob Byers)                   45
Baker, Anna Launchbaugh                          59
Baker, Annie (Mrs. John Rowe)                    89
Baker, Bessie (Mrs.Harvey F.Wertz)              242
Baker, Catharine Hoover (Mrs. Daniel)           152
Baker, Christena(Mrs.Jacob Andrews) 150,152
Baker, Cyrus                                     89
Baker, Daniel                            39,150,152
Baker, David                               150,152
Baker, Elizabeth (Mrs.Daniel Fox)      150,152
Baker, Emma (Mrs. Daniel Fortney)                89
Baker, Henrietta Knepper (Mrs.Abraham)           89
Baker, Henry                                     89
Baker, Isaac/Israel                        150,152
```

```
Benedick, Peter                              83,84,90
Benedick, Rebecca (Mrs. Bryan)                     84
Benedick, Rebecca (Mrs.William H.Knepper)96
Benedick, Sarah (Mrs. Snively)                     84
Benedick, Susan (Mrs. Abraham Stoner)              84
Benedick, Susan (Mrs. Bicker)                      84
Benedict, Elizabeth (Mrs.Abe.Knepper) 83,90
Benedict, George                                   92
Benedict, J. Glenn                                 92
Benedict, Marguerite Knepper (Mrs.George)92
Bener, Ann Justina (Mrs.John Peter)       199
Bener, Eve Barbara Wirz                   199
Bener, John Peter                         199
Benetz, Florence Knepper (Mrs. John H.)  62
Benetz, John H.                            62
Benner, Anna Werth (Mrs. George)          259
Benner, George                            259
Bennett, Cora Batlorf                      60
Bennett, Kate Snyder (Mrs.)               160
Bennett, Mary C.                          285
Bennett, Rebecca E. (Mrs. John Wertz)     191
Bennett, Sarah Swoveland (Mrs. M.)         68
Berkey, Alice                              34
Berkey, Andrew                             34
Berkey, David                              34
Berkey, Elizabeth                          34
Berkey, Hiram                              34
Berkey, Magdalena (Mrs. Andrew Wertz)
                        32,40,65,68,70,72
Berkey, Marinda                            34
Berkey, Rachel Wertz                       34
Berkey, Susan                           33,34
Berkley, Mary (Mrs. Jacob F. George)      171
Berlin, Charles Emil                      140
Berlin, Daniel Charles                    140
Berlin, Doris Marie (Mrs.Larry D.Wertz) 134
Berlin, Janet Pearl                       140
Berlin, Jeanne Ann                        140
Berlin, Jeffry Allen                      140
Berlin, John Eric                         140
Berlin, Loyal Delou or Delu            134,140
Berlin, Pearl Catharine Baer (Mrs.C.E.) 140
Berlin, Sabina Bell Oplinger (Mrs.L.D.) 140
Berlin, Savina Bell Oplinger (Mrs.L.D.) 134
Betz, Dollie Wertz (Mrs. Parce)            56
Betz, Grace Wertz                          56
```

Brown, John Daniel   139
Brown, John Raymond   139
Brown, Margaret Vernell Zaugg(Mrs.C.O.) 143
Brown, Mary Helen   139
Brown, Mary Irene (Mrs. David C.Wertz) 143
Brown, Ralph William   139
Brown, Robert William   139
Brown, Rozetta Julia Ott (Mrs. John D.) 139
Brown, Ruth Ann   139
Brown, William   29,30
Brown, William A.   143
Brown, Wilma Almeda(Mrs.Robert C.Wertz) 143
Browning, Charles H.   219
Brubaker, Bruce E.   97
Brubaker, Della Clara(Mrs.Maxwell Long) 139
Brubaker, Esther Knepper (Mrs. Bruce E.) 97
Brubaker, Henry   269
Brubaker, Jacob N.   249
Brubaker, Mary E. Wert (Mrs.Jacob)   249
Brubaker, Nancy (Mrs. Christian Wertz) 269
Brubaker, Sarah Eller (Mrs. Henry)   269
Brumbaugh, Isabelle Stites (Mrs.)   87
Brumbaugh, Nancy (Mrs.Hezakiah Swoveland)68
Bryan, Amanda Knepper (Mrs.)   95
Bryan, Rebecca Benedick (Mrs.)   84
Bryant, Adeline Knepper (Mrs. Harrison) 98
Bryant, Cinthia   98
Bryant, Harrison   98
Bryant, Viva   98
Bucher, Anna Wrtz (Mrs.)   279
Bucher, Antonius   279
Bucher, Catrina (Mrs. Michael --??--)   279
Bucher, Dorothea (Mrs. Jacob Saal)   279
Bucher, Laurentius   279
Buchler, Martha (Mrs. John Adam Wirt)   234
Bucker, Louise (Mrs. Ezariah Wertz)   69
Buckhill, Catharine (Mrs. Jacob)   194
Buckhill, Jacob   194
Buckingham, Charles B.   147
Buckingham, Cora Morret (Mrs.Chas.B.)   148
Buckingham, George P.   147
Buckingham, Grace Verhea Adams(Mrs.Roy) 141
Buckingham, Hazel C. Rich (Mrs. George) 147
Buckingham, Helen Marie Gillespie(Mrs.) 148
Buckingham, Jane Marie (Mrs.H.V.Nelson) 148
Buckingham, Mary Ann   148

Bushman, Samuel Augustus   172
Bushman, Solomon   157,171
Bushman, Solomon   171
Bushman, Solomon Davidson   172
Bushman, Susan (Mrs. Baughman)   172
Butarf, Amanda (Mrs. Austin Wertz)   149
Butterfield, Charles   133
Butterfield, Estella Fernhom (Mrs.Chas.)133
Butterfield, Isabella M.(Imhoff-Wertz)   133
Butzer, Amy May   126
Butzer, Delmar D.   126
Butzer, Dennie Lee   127
Butzer, Faye Elizabeth Musser(Mrs.R.L.) 127
Butzer, Florence Wertz (Mrs.Patrick)   126
Butzer, Kenneth Ray   127
Butzer, Luella F. Geiser (Mrs. Delmar)   126
Butzer, Patrick D.   126
Butzer, Patrick H.   126
Butzer, Raymond Leo   127
Butzer, Rebecca Lynn   127
Byers, Anna Baker   45
Byers, Anna Bunkhold?   45
Byers, Annie E. (Mrs. David Yeager)   45
Byers, Charles C.   45
Byers, Elizabeth Wertz   45
Byers, Frederick   45
Byers, Hiriam   45
Byers, Jacob W.   45
Byers, John   45
Byers, Maggie C. (Mrs. Jacob Meredeth)   45
Byers, Maggie Slatzer   45
Byers, Martha Anderson   45
Byers, Mary Ann Wertz   45
Byers, Mary Richardson   45
Byers, Philip W.   45
Byers, Rachael A. (Mrs. Jacob Dutinler)   45
Byers, Susan (Mrs. Peter Honker)   45
Byers, Susan Stoner   45
Byers, William   45
Byers, William M.   45
Cahoy, Edna Wertz (Mrs. Mert)   76
Cahoy, Mert   76
Campbell, Colin   168
Campbell, J. Harvey   242
Campbell, Mary (Mrs. Benjmain F. Wertz) 163
Campbell, Mary Murphy (Mrs.Harvey)   242

```
Cook, Johann George Adam                    27,43
Cook, J. F.                                    171
Cook, John                                      25
Cook, Mary (Mrs. McFerren)                     101
Cook, Mary Jane (Mrs.Henry Keylor Jr.)         159
Cook, Sophia (Mrs. Daniel Wertz)               254
Cook, Susannah Geesaman (Mrs. Adam)             91
Cook, W. I.                                    169
Cooling, Emma Wertz (Mrs. Fred)                162
Cooling, Fred                                  162
Cooper, Estelle Wertz (Mrs. Vernon)             61
Cooper, Vernon                                  61
Cordell, Anna Hubbert (Mrs. Joseph)            173
Cordell, Blanche                               173
Cordell, David                             157,173
Cordell, Eva (Mrs. Hunter)                     173
Cordell, Eva (Mrs. L. H. Lloyd)                173
Cordell, Grace                                 173
Cordell, Harriet Poper (Mrs. Henry)            174
Cordell, Henry                         157,173,174
Cordell, Henry Jr.                         157,174
Cordell, Jacob                             157,174
Cordell, Jennie (Mrs. Carie/Crew)              173
Cordell, John H.                               110
Cordell, Joseph                            157,173
Cordell, Maria/Mary Wertz(Mrs.Henry)157,173
Cordell, Ralph                                 173
Cordell, Samuel                            157,174
Cordell, Scott                                 173
Cordell, Tell Philippy                         174
Cordray, Ida E. (Mrs. George W. First)         144
Corothers, Permelia (Mrs. Orliff Wert)         253
Cover, Christina Wertz (Mrs.)                  107
Cowan, Ellen Wertz                              72
Cox, Bertha E. (Mrs. Harry Wertz)               79
Coyle, Nellie Wertz                             56
Coyle, Nona                                     56
Crawford, Althea (Mrs. Alex. R. Wertz)         120
Creary or Cleary, Verna (Mrs.W.H.Croft)         52
Cresky, Emma Wertz                              56
Cresky, John                                    56
Creutz, Maria Salomea                           15
Crew, Jennie Cordell (Mrs.)/Carie              173
Crissman, Catharine Wertz                       33
Crissman, Elias (2)                             33
Crissman, George Washington                     33
```

```
Crissman, Lucinda                                    33
Crissman, Mary                                       33
Criswell, Cora Effie Hazlett(Mrs.Sam.S.)130
Criswell, Maude Eliza. (Mrs.K.M.Shafer) 130
Criswell, Samuel Snyder                      130
Croft, Almeda Summer                         53
Croft, Amanda Smucker                        49
Croft, Anna Mary Embich                   49,52
Croft, Carrie Lucretia(Mrs.John Croft)49,52
Croft, Charles Luther                        49
Croft, Charlotte Elizabeth(Mrs.W.J.Clark)55
Croft, Chester A. (2)                        52
Croft, Clara S. Gelwix                       53
Croft, Clarence                              53
Croft, Clayton Howard                        52
Croft, Daniel Calvin                         55
Croft, David (2)                             52
Croft, Don K.                                52
Croft, Eleanor Kinnard (2)                   52
Croft, Elizabeth                             52
Croft, Ella May                              53
Croft, Elva Ruth (2)                         52
Croft, Etta Sellers                          55
Croft, Frank Wesley                          53
Croft, George                                53
Croft, George Albert                         52
Croft, George Wertz                          53
Croft, Harry C.                              52
Croft, Helen                                 52
Croft, Ida Grace (Mrs.J.Ambrose Welsh)    52
Croft, John                      44,49,51,52
Croft, John Clarence                         52
Croft, John David Jr.                     44,49
Croft, John Irvin (2)                        52
Croft, John Walker; Dr.                      53
Croft, Kathryn                               52
Croft, Lydia Strock                          53
Croft, Magdalena "Martha" Wertz     44,49,50
Croft, Martha Blanche (Mrs.Frisby Brake) 52
Croft, Martha Elizabeth                      53
Croft, Martha Myrtle (Mrs. Harry Lesher) 52
Croft, Mary Catherine (Mrs.Stafford Pyne)52
Croft, Mary Ellen (Mrs. John W Cell)      53
Croft, Mary Grace                            53
Croft, Mrs. Emma Brewer                      52
Croft, Nell Prsssman                         52
```

```
Davidson, Harry W.                                      71
Davidson, Herbert B.                                    71
Davidson, John                                          71
Davidson, Lucinda E. Wertz (Mrs. John)                  71
Davidson, Pearl (Mrs. Glen E. Moore)                    71
Davidson, Walter                                        71
Davis, Amanda Wertz                                     39
Davis, Arthur                                           79
Davis, Effa Wertz (Mrs. James)                         162
Davis, Hannah (Mrs. Jonathan Knepper)                   85
Davis, Harriet A. Wertz (Mrs.Arthur)                    79
Davis, James                                           162
Davis, Mary Wertz                                       42
Davis, Sam                                              42
Davy, Edmund                                            39
Davy, Ida Warner                                        39
Deardorff, Elizabeth Benedick (Mrs.)                    84
Decker, Abraham                                         99
Decker, Amanda Funk (Mrs. Jacob)                        88
Decker, Catherine                                       99
Decker, Estella Knepper (Mrs. Jacob)                    99
Decker, Jacob                                        88,99
Decker, John                                            99
Decker, Julia (Mrs. Mentzer)                            99
Decker, Martha (Mrs. Gossart)                           99
Decker, Mary Ann (Mrs. Smetzer)                         99
Decker, Susan (Mrs. Shockey)                            99
DeCoursey, George E.                                   203
DeCoursey, Marian S.Wurts (Mrs.Geo.E.)                 203
Dedy, Elizabeth "Polly" Wertz                           57
Dedy, John                                              57
Deeter, Ann (Mrs. Henry Wertz)                         253
Deetz, Emiline "Emma" Knepper (Mrs.Sam)                 63
Deetz, Samuel A.                                        63
Dehart, Lizzie B. (Mrs.David C.Knoll)                  171
Deibler, Maria Eliz. (Mrs.George Shupp)                224
Dells, Elizabeth Kaufman (Mrs.Morgan)                   66
Dells, Morgan                                           66
Denny, Rebecca (Mrs. Matthias Wirtz)                   259
Detmeir, Susie (Mrs. Jacob Swoveland)                   67
Detrick, Francy/Irene Wertz (Mrs.David)                107
Detrick or Dietrich, David                             107
Detwiler, Phoebe (Mrs.Harvey Swoveland)                 68
Deuchler, Philipp Jacob                                 16
Dibert, Charles                                        183
Dibert, Eve (Mrs. Thomas Wertz)                        183
```

```
Eggman, Thomas                                      78
Eisenbarth, Antonius Hell                          281
Eisenbarth, Petrus                                 281
Eisenbarth, Veronica Hell (Mrs.Petrus)             281
Eisenzimmer, Amanda Wertz                           56
Eisenzimmer, James                                  56
Eisenzimmer, Perry                                  56
Elbel, Regina Renno (Mrs.)                         158
Elden, Addie                                        86
Elden, Clara B.                                 81,86
Elden, Corwin W.                                    86
Elden, Elizabeth Knepper (Mrs.Melchor)             86
Elden, George K.                                    86
Elden, Jennie                                       86
Elden, Mae                                          86
Elden, Melchor                                      86
Ellen, Kathryn Mable Baxter (Mrs.Knox)            125
Eller, Sarah (Mrs. Henry Brubaker)                269
Elliott, Rebecca A. (Mrs.John Wertz)               61
Ely, Warren S.                                     219
Embich, Anna Mary (Mrs. Samuel Croft)              49
Embich, Henry                                       49
Emerich, Sara (Mrs. Peter Wert)                    237
Emerick, Catherine (Mrs. George Wertz)
                    156,160,162,163,165,167
Emerick, Elizabeth (Mrs. David Wertz)
                            157,168,169
Emerson(s), Hannah                              31,37
Emminger, Barbara Elizabeth (Mrs. Smith)
                                    156,158
Emminger, Catherine (Mrs.Zimmerman) 156,158
Emminger, Catherine (Mrs.Luther Garver) 159
Emminger, Elizabeth (Mrs. Miller)          158
Emminger, Elizabeth Wertz (Mrs. Michael)
                                    156,157
Emminger, Ephraim                         156,157
Emminger, Jacob                               159
Emminger, James                               159
Emminger, John                            156,157
Emminger, Lydia Keylor (Mrs. Jacob)       159
Emminger, Margaret (Mrs.John Renno) 156,158
Emminger, Marie (Mrs. Storm)              156,158
Emminger, Michael                         156,157
Emminger, Susan Ann (Mrs. Weisman)  156,158
Emmons, Hannah (Mrs. Jacob Wertz)
                         31,37,38,39,101

                        310
```

Engle, William Henry   283
Enterline, Elizabeth(Mrs.Henry Wirt)222,229
Enterline, John Michael, Rev.   222,229
Escher, Hans   278
Eskey, Nellie Robinson(Mrs.Clyde Wertz) 147
Etter, Amanda (Mrs. Peter Knepper) 103,104
Etter, Jacob   104
Etter, Susan Miller (Mrs. Jacob)   104
Evans, Hattie (Mrs. Earl D. Hunter)   173
Ewing, Mary Jane (Mrs.George Tinsler)   131
Ewinger, Johann Jakob   16
Eysenbarth, Anna Sophia Wurz (Mrs.A.)   280
Eysenbarth, Antonius   280
Eysenbarth, Catharina   280
Eysenbarth, Elisabeth   280
Fahrney, Catharine (Mrs.U.Burkholder)   111
Fahrney, John   103
Fahrney, Lucy A. Knepper (Mrs. John)   103
Fairchild, Mary (Mrs.Christian Wertz) 65,70
Faler, Elizabeth (Mrs. John Wertz)   253
Farhoning, Zelda (Mrs.William Trimproly) 71
Farnon, Jonathan   257
Farnon, Rebecca Worth (Mrs. Jonathan)   257
Fassnacht, Anna Maria (Mrs.Joh.Wirth)   260
Faust, Albert Bernhardt   284
Fauver, Betsy (Mrs. Jacob Wirth)   224
Feedt, Daniel   228
Feedt, George   228
Feedt, Lydia Wirth (Mrs. Daniel)   228
Feedt, Rachel (Mrs. George)   228
Feller, Louise (Mrs. Nicholas Guill)   80
Ferguson, Elizabeth Goshart (Mrs.Richard)86
Ferguson, Jannett (Mrs. Henry Wirt)   208
Ferguson, Richard   86
Ferney, Isabel Magee (Mrs. Peter Wert)   230
Fernhom, Estella (Mrs.Chas.Butterfield) 133
Fetterhoff, Elizabeth (Mrs.P.McFerren)   101
Field, Ernest (Mrs.)   285
Files, Grace B. Rider (Mrs. William)   64
Files, William   64
Finley, Elizabeth Harris (Mrs.John)   207
Finley, John   207
Finley, Margaret   207
First, Daisy Mae (Overholt) (Garn)   144
First, George W.   144
First, Ida E. Cordray (Mrs. George W.)   144

```
Fischer, Anna Maria (Mrs.Peter Kneppern) 81
Fischer, Johannes                          81
Fisher, Amos                    157,168,169
Fisher, Andrew                          111
Fisher, Belinda                 157,168,169
Fisher, Benjamin Samuel                 118
Fisher, Catherine      33,157,167,168,227
Fisher, Catherine (Mrs.John Meily/Mosly)168
Fisher, Catherine Parthemore (Mrs.D.)   227
Fisher, Catherine Wertz (Mrs.Fred.) 157,167
Fisher, Daniel                          227
Fisher, David                            33
Fisher, Elias                       157,168
Fisher, Elisa      157,161,164,165,168,169
Fisher, Elisa (Mrs. Shickard)           169
Fisher, Eliza Elizabeth (Mrs. David Wertz)
                                161,164,165
Fisher, Elizabeth
        31,33,57,58,59,60,62,63,64,87,111
Fisher, Elizabeth (Mrs. Christian Wertz)
                                 57,62,63,64
Fisher, Elizabeth (Mrs. Hiram Gift)      87
Fisher, Elizabeth Wertz (Mrs.Samuel) 33,111
Fisher, Francis                     157.168
Fisher, Francis(Mrs.Jacob Leiter/Lester)168
Fisher, Frederick Jr.& Sr.
                  25,57,155,157,167,168
Fisher, Gertrude Wertz (Mrs. John A.)    79
Fisher, Grace Kent (Mrs.Floyd L.Snyder) 145
Fisher, Ida Margaret (Mrs.S.Seigfried)  146
Fisher, Iva Loy Sellers (Mrs.Ben.Sam.)  118
Fisher, Jacob                            33
Fisher, Jacob Fahrney               111,118
Fisher, John                             33
Fisher, John A.                          79
Fisher, John M.                       8,283
Fisher, John William                    118
Fisher, Jonathan                         33
Fisher, Joseph                          111
Fisher, Lydia (Mrs. Hamilton)       157,168
Fisher, Margaret Wertz                   39
Fisher, Martin                           33
Fisher, Mary                             33
Fisher, Mary Ellen Baker (Mrs.John W.)  118
Fisher, Mary M. Rennecker (Mrs. J.F.)   118
Fisher, Miss (Mrs. Joseph Caven)        117
```

Goshart, Harvey   86
Goshart, Henry   86
Goshart, Jemina (Mrs. Dimmick Linn)   86
Goshart, Jeremiah   86
Goshart, John   86
Goshart, Laural Hankerson (Mrs. Henry)   86
Goshart, Martha Ann Heeffer (Mrs.Will.)   86
Goshart, Martha E.Hoffer (Mrs.Jeremiah)   86
Goshart, Mary Alice Hickman (Mrs.Harvey)   86
Goshart, Rebecca Dunnuck (Mrs.David)   86
Goshart, Saluda Dove (Mrs. George P.)   86
Goshart, Sarah Ellen(Mrs.Jacob Dillsaver)86
Goshart, William   86
Gossart, Martha Decker (Mrs.)   99
Graber, Mary (Mrs. Elmer E. Baer)   139
Grandin, Samuel   215
Grandin, Sarah (Mrs.John Wi(u)rtz)   215,216
Grandin, Susanna Johnston (Mrs.Samuel)   215
Grass, David   98
Grass, Hannah Knepper (Mrs. David)   98
Gray, Dorothea Wirt (Mrs. Jose)   258
Gray, Ellie Wertz (Mrs. John W.)   245
Gray, Jennie   41,42
Gray, John W.   245
Gray, Jose   258
Gray, Martha Baer (Mrs. Thomas)   239
Gray, Thomas   239
Green, Belle (Mrs. Otis D. Trimproly)   70
Grey, Catharine Carl (Mrs. Winfield S.) 244
Grey, Winfield Scott   244
Grollinger, Elizabeth L. (Mrs. Harry)   186
Grollinger, Harry   186
Grollinger, Laanna (Mrs.George E.Wertz) 186
Gross, Charles Lester Wilden   80
Gross, Clara Belle (Mrs.Chauncey Wertz) 80
Grove, Mary Magdalena(Mrs.John M.Baker) 152
Guill, Anna Eva (Mrs. Gerald W.Wertz)   80
Guill, Nicholas   80
Gurgar, Lord George   168
Gurgar, Mary Victoria Leiter/Lester(Mrs)168
Haas, Catherine Wertz (Mrs. Peter)   239
Haas, Hannah (Mrs. Daniel Wertz)   240
Haas, Henry   239
Haas, Mary Ann (Mrs. John Rebert)   239
Haas, Peter   239
Haas, Sarah Jane   239

```
Holsopp, Lucy                                     35
Holsopp, Marion                                   35
Holsopp, Sarah                                    35
Holtzman, Benneville W.                          232
Holtzman, Mary Wirt (Mrs. Benneville)           232
Holzhalb, Ursula (Mrs. Joh.Conrad Wirz)         212
Honker, Peter                                     45
Honker, Susan Byers                               45
Hoobler, Margaret (Mrs.Ben. Wertz)              253
Hood, Anna Margaretha Wertz                       24
Hoover, Andrew                                   208
Hoover, Anna K. (Mrs. Edwin S. Wertz)           176
Hoover, Catharine (Mrs. Daniel Baker)           152
Hoover, Catherine (Mrs. Edwin Wertz)            176
Hoover, Christena (Mrs. John Wertz)             150
Hoover, David                                    208
Hoover, Elizabeth Poffenberger (Mrs.)           152
Hoover, Ernest                                   285
Hoover, Henry m. Elizabeth Poffenberger         152
Hoover, Henry, d.1798, m.Anna Wertz              24
Hoover, John                                     150
Hoover, Joseph S.                                176
Hoover, Lydia (Mrs. Jacob Baker)                152
Hoover, Mabel Chloe Shafer (Mrs.Norman)         131
Hoover, Mary Ruthrauff                           285
Hoover, Mary Small (Mrs. Joseph S.)             176
Hoover, Mary Watson (Mrs. John)                 150
Hoover, Norman Leroy                             131
Hoover, Rachael Wertz (Mrs. Andrew)             208
Horn, Catherine Knepper (Mrs. Johann)            99
Horn, Henry                                      193
Horn, Johann                                      99
Horner, Constance Jo                             127
Horner, Deborah Lynn                             127
Horner, Edward                                    63
Horner, Larry James                             127
Horner, Margaretha (Mrs. Franz Wirz)            212
Horner, Mary E. Knepper (Mrs. Edward)            63
Horner, Russell Dwight                          127
Horner, Thelma Maxine Frase(Mrs.Russell)127
Horner, Thomas Keith                            127
Hosfman, Miss (Mrs. Samuel Bushman)             172
Hoskins, Ila                                       8
Hostleton, Bessie (Mrs. H. Allen)                73
Hostleton, Catherine Annie                        73
Hostleton, Chris                                  73
```

```
Hostleton, Cintha (Mrs. John L. Gay)       72
Hostleton, Cora Mary                       73
Hostleton, Edna (Mrs. H. Gilbert)          72
Hostleton, Everett                         73
Hostleton, Garrett                         73
Hostleton, George Sylvester                73
Hostleton, Hazel                           73
Hostleton, Hulda E. (Mrs.William Snyder) 73
Hostleton, Jacob                        66,72
Hostleton, James Monroe                    73
Hostleton, Jewel Downing (Mrs.James M.)    73
Hostleton, John Henry                      72
Hostleton, Laura Francis (Mrs.W.Wilson)    73
Hostleton, Lela                            73
Hostleton, Lillie Belle                    73
Hostleton, Magdalena Wertz (Mrs.Jacob)66,72
Hostleton, Merridith                       73
Hostleton, Minerva (Mrs.O.VanVolkenburg)  73
Hostleton, Morilla Ophilia (Mrs.J.Stepp)  73
Hostleton, Purdy or Birdy                  73
Hostleton, Roy                             72
Hostleton, Sara Margaret                   73
Hostleton, William Allen                   73
Houck or Houcker,Mary(Mrs.Marks Brindle)  46
Hougham, Naomi (Mrs.)                      74
Houk, Catherine                         43,44
Howard, Elizabeth Shover (Mrs.)           240
Hoy, Daniel                               241
Hoy, Kathryn (Mrs. William Raubenolt)    130
Hoy, Margaret Jane Babble (Mrs. Dan.)    241
Hubbert, Anna (Mrs. Joseph Cordell)      173
Huber, John                          155,156
Huberin, Margretha (Mrs. Philip Wirth)   251
Huegie, Ursula                            17
Huff, Anna Barabara                       23
Huffman, Leathea (Mrs. Abraham Baker)    152
Hull, William I.                         284
Humes, Juliana Wertz (Mrs.)              250
Humes, Leah Wertz (Mrs. Thomas)          238
Humes, Thomas                            238
Hummell, Fannie                        40,41
Hungerford, Cora Wertz (Mrs. Herman)      61
Hungerford, Herman                        61
Hungerford, Mary Wertz (Mrs. Herman)      61
Hunker, Mary (Mrs. Cyrus Knepper)         95
Hunt, Charles                            166
```

```
Knepper, Alex                                    90,92
Knepper, Alexander                          85,88,89
Knepper, Alfred                                     94
Knepper, Alice                             95,99,105
Knepper, Alice (Mrs. Blobaugh)                   95
Knepper, Alice Harris (Mrs. Henry)               99
Knepper, Amanda     62,89,91,93,94,95,97,102
Knepper, Amanda (Mrs. Bryan)                     95
Knepper, Amanda (Mrs. Dunmore)                   93
Knepper, Amanda (Mrs. John Bonner)       91,95
Knepper, Amanda (Mrs. King)                      94
Knepper, Amanda Elberta Jones (Mrs.B.F.) 95
Knepper, Amanda McFerren (Mrs. James) 89,97
Knepper, Amos                              63,102,103
Knepper, Andrew                     83,84,85,88,90
Knepper, Andrew Jackson                          90
Knepper, Anita                                  104
Knepper, Ann                             92,93,96,105
Knepper, Ann Elizabeth                        92,96
Knepper, Ann Lucinda (Mrs. Edward Rice)  63
Knepper, Ann (Mrs. L. Anderson)              105
Knepper, Anna Elizabeth (Mrs.JohnKeller) 96
Knepper, Annie                                89,93
Knepper, Anthony                           83,98,99
Knepper, Arletta (Mrs.Charles Pomeroy)   95
Knepper, Benjamin D.                          91,95
Knepper, Benjamin Franklin                       95
Knepper, "Bob" (baseball player)                 88
Knepper, Caroline (Mrs. George McCleary) 96
Knepper, Catharine        26,82,83,84,87,89,
              96,97,98,99,100,101,102,103,105
Knepper, Catharine Smetzer (Mrs.E.K.)97,103
Knepper, Catherine (Mrs. David)              101
Knepper, Catherine (Mrs. George Walk)        96
Knepper, Catherine (Mrs. Johann Horn)        99
Knepper, Catherine (Mrs. M.A. Hill)          105
Knepper, Catherine (Mrs. Samuel)             102
Knepper, Catherine (Mrs.John Benedick)82,83
Knepper, Catherine Small (Mrs. Adam)         98
Knepper, Catherine Smetzer (Mrs.Ephraim) 89
Knepper, Catherine Sollenberger (Mrs.A.) 99
Knepper, Catherine Thompson (Mrs.Sol.)   103
Knepper, Cathy D.                            285
Knepper, Charles (baseball player)           88
Knepper, Charles             94,99,102,104
Knepper, Charlotte                        93,102
```

```
Knepper, Chester                               62
Knepper, Christina Stump (Mrs. William)  98
Knepper, Clara                         86,95,98
Knepper, Clara (Mrs. Ervin Zeis)         95
Knepper, Clara K. (Mrs. Wilson Reynolds) 86
Knepper, Clara Smith (Mrs. Benjamin D.)  95
Knepper, Clarabell                       93
Knepper, Conrad                        83,96
Knepper, Cora (Mrs. A.R.Helmas)          62
Knepper, Cyrus            63,85,88,90,91,95
Knepper, Cyrus Eugene                    90
Knepper, Dan                             92
Knepper, Daniel                 90,91,92,93
Knepper, David                      81-106
Knepper, David II                        87
Knepper, David III                       87
Knepper, David W.                        63
Knepper, Dekel, Theckla, or Zekiel 83,84,86
Knepper, Delia                           98
Knepper, Don                            104
Knepper, Dorothy or Dolly             83,98
Knepper, Edith                          104
Knepper, Edith May (Mrs. R.M.Linton)     62
Knepper, Edward                        88,94
Knepper, Eleanor Reems (Mrs. Benjamin)   95
Knepper, Eliz. Foreman (Mrs.Solomon)100,104
Knepper, Eliz. Geesaman (Mrs. Peter)  91,94
Knepper, Eliz.Cath.Reed (Mrs.Daniel)  90,92
Knepper, Eliza                           93
Knepper, Eliza Wagoman (Mrs. Jeremiah)   94
Knepper, Elizabeth                  82-106
Knepper, Elizabeth (Mrs. Joshua)         97
Knepper, Elizabeth (Mrs. McFerron)  102,103
Knepper, Elizabeth (Mrs. Melchor Elden)  86
Knepper, Elizabeth (Mrs. Mentzer)     91,95
Knepper, Elizabeth (Mrs. Peter Knepper) 100
Knepper, Elizabeth (Mrs.David Moun) 100,102
Knepper, Elizabeth (Mrs.George Smetzer) 100
Knepper, Elizabeth (Mrs.J. Westerhouse) 105
Knepper, Elizabeth (Mrs.Samuel Burgess) 105
Knepper, Elizabeth (Mrs.Samuel Reed)  90,91
Knepper, Elizabeth Benedick (Mrs. Abe.)  90
Knepper, Elizabeth Lowry (Mrs.George) 90,92
Knepper, Elizabeth or Lizzy              93
Knepper, Elizabeth Smith (Mrs. Joseph)   94
Knepper, Elizabeth Stahl (Mrs. John)    106
```

```
Knepper, Ella                                          98
Knepper, Emiline (Mrs. Sam.A.Deetz)           63
Knepper, Emma             88,93,94,95,96,103
Knepper, Emma (Mrs. Curtis Edwards)           95
Knepper, Emma (Mrs. Swartzmiller)             94
Knepper, Emma George (Mrs. Obadiah)           88
Knepper, Emma or Erma Benedick                96
Knepper, Emma Small (Mrs. Jeremiah)          103
Knepper, Ephraim                           83,93,96
Knepper, Ephraim K.                        89,97,103
Knepper, Ephraim S.                          89,97
Knepper, Estella                                99
Knepper, Esther            83,84,87,97,102
Knepper, Esther (Mrs. Bruce E. Brubaker) 97
Knepper, Esther (Mrs. Jacob Stites)           87
Knepper, Esther Foreman (Mrs. David)     83,84
Knepper, Esther Foreman (Mrs.David)           84
Knepper, Esther Youkey (Mrs. Solomon)87,102
Knepper, Eva (Mrs. Frank Beck)                95
Knepper, Eva VanFleet (Mrs. George A.)        90
Knepper, Fanny                                  98
Knepper, Feronica or Veronica (Secrist) 100
Knepper, Florence (Mrs. John H.Benetz)        62
Knepper, Frances or Frany              83,98,99
Knepper, Frank                             93,98
Knepper, Fred                            102,104
Knepper, Frederick                         83,84
Knepper, Fredrica Stull (Mrs. Hiram)          88
Knepper, George 83,84,85,86,87,90,91,92,93
Knepper, George A.                              90
Knepper, George 6.                              87
Knepper, George L.                         91,93
Knepper, Grover C.                              90
Knepper, Hannah            83,85,91,93,98
Knepper, Hannah (Mrs. David Grass)            98
Knepper, Hannah (Mrs. Wingert)                85
Knepper, Hannah Davis (Mrs. Jonathan)         85
Knepper, Harriet              94,96,97,104
Knepper, Harriet (Mrs. Levi C. Row)           97
Knepper, Harriet K. (Mrs. Levi Row)           96
Knepper, Harriet Sechrist (Mrs.Jeremiah) 94
Knepper, Harvey or Harry                   93,94
Knepper, Helen                                 104
Knepper, Helen Todhunter (Mrs. Chester)       62
Knepper, Henrietta            85,88,89,105
Knepper, Henrietta (Mrs. Abraham Baker)       89
```

```
Knepper, Henrietta Rosan Houer (Mrs.W.) 105
Knepper, Henry                     85-103
Knepper, Henry Franklin                62
Knepper, Henry Roscoe                  90
Knepper, Hiram                   85,87,88
Knepper, Howard                        94
Knepper, Ida                           92
Knepper, Ida B. (Mrs. J. C. Dundor)    90
Knepper, J. H.                    103,104
Knepper, Jack                          92
Knepper, Jacob     83,85,87,88,96,100,105
Knepper, James    85,88,89,90,92,94,96,97
Knepper, James A.                      92
Knepper, James H.                      89
Knepper, James Peter                   94
Knepper, James S.               85,88,90
Knepper, Jennetta "Nettie"(Mrs.W.G.Smith)96
Knepper, Jeremiah "Jerry"         102,103
Knepper, Jeremiah                91,94,98
Knepper, Jerome                        93
Knepper, Jerre                    102,104
Knepper, Jessie                        99
Knepper, Joel                         104
Knepper, John & Elizabeth Stahl       106
Knepper, John                     85-102
Knepper, John A.                 91,93,94
Knepper, John Albert             85,88,90
Knepper, Jonathan                83,84,85
Knepper, Joseph                  91,94,95
Knepper, Joshua                   81-102
Knepper, Joshua Jr.                 83,96
Knepper, Josiah                        98
Knepper, Judith                  85,87,88
Knepper, Judy (Mrs. Samuel)            84
Knepper, Kate E. Loury (Mrs. Amos)    103
Knepper, Kathy                          8
Knepper, Katie                         95
Knepper, Katie K. (Mrs.George Nickley)89,98
Knepper, Kevin                   85,87,88
Knepper, Kitty May                     90
Knepper, Konrod or Conrad              97
Knepper, Laura (Mrs. Peter Baush)      62
Knepper, Laura                    84,284
Knepper, Lavina (Mrs. David Small)     85
Knepper, Leah (Mrs.Joseph Geesaman) 85,106
Knepper, Leah                       83,84
```

```
Knepper, Lettie                                        98
Knepper, Levi                                       91,94
Knepper, Lewis                                        105
Knepper, Lidy or "Pet"                                 93
Knepper, Loren                                         94
Knepper, Lucy A.(Mrs.John Fahrney)    102,103
Knepper, Luella                                        98
Knepper, Lydia (Mrs. Frederick Dull)         97
Knepper, Lydia                                      83,96
Knepper, Lydia May or Mary            103,104
Knepper, Lydia Walk (Mrs. Jacob)             96
Knepper, Mabel (Mrs. William Irvin)          95
Knepper, Mae Hand (Mrs. Grover C.)           90
Knepper, Maggie (Mrs. Mullen)                92
Knepper, Maggie K. (Mrs. George Peters)      98
Knepper, Malinda K. (Mrs. Henry Knepper)
                                             89,97,103
Knepper, Mamie Cune (Mrs. Russell M.)        95
Knepper, Margaret (Mrs. John)                93
Knepper, Margaret (Mrs. Prentice)            99
Knepper, Margaret                      89,102,105
Knepper, Margaret K. (Mrs.George Peters) 89
Knepper, Margaret Spangler (Mrs. H.F.)       63
Knepper, Marguerite (Mrs.Geo.Benedict)90,92
Knepper, Maria (Mrs. Levi)                   94
Knepper, Maria Catharine Wertz(Mrs.Abraham)
                         24,81,82,84,90,96,98,99
Knepper, Martha (Mrs. James)                 92
Knepper, Martha McFerron (Mrs.Jonathan)      85
Knepper, Mary (Mrs. George Adam Martin)      99
Knepper, Mary               82,83,96,97,98,100
Knepper, Mary Alice                          96
Knepper, Mary Ann (Mrs. George Reed)         89
Knepper, Mary Ann Reed (Mrs. Andrew)         88
Knepper, Mary Catherine (Mrs.Geo.Gift)       87
Knepper, Mary Catherine                   85,87
Knepper, Mary Catherine Geesaman          85,87
Knepper, Mary E. Dickson or Jackson          90
Knepper, Mary Elizabeth (Mrs.E.Horner)       63
Knepper, Mary Ellen Reems (Mrs.Benjamin) 95
Knepper, Mary Harris (Mrs. Josiah)           98
Knepper, Mary Harris (Mrs. Joshua)           88
Knepper, Mary Hunker (Mrs. Cyrus)            95
Knepper, Mary Jane (Mrs. John Funk)          88
Knepper, Mary Jane                        85,88
Knepper, Mary McFerran (Mrs.George G.)86,87
```

McCann, Blanche Naomi Garn (Mrs.B.F.)   144
McCann, Franklin   144
McCarthy, Dorothy L.   243
McCarthy, Lillie E. Wertz (Mrs. Wm. A.) 243
McCarthy, Wm. A.   243
McClain, Catharine Jane(Mrs.Paul Wertz) 137
McClain, Howard Franklin   137
McClain, Lydia Kathryn Moss (Mrs.H.F.)   137
McClanahan, Earl   105
McClasky, Lydia (Mrs. Peter Wert)   230
McCleary, Caroline Knepper (Mrs.George)   96
McCleary, George W.   96
McClintock, Alice Mullendore (Mrs.W.O.)   77
McClintock, John W.   77
McClintock, Lawrence O.   77
McClintock, Lloyd A.   77
McClintock, William O.   77
McCoy, Bill   61
McCoy, Caroline Wertz (Mrs. Bill)   61
McCoy, Ella May (Mrs. Jay Picksal)   61
McCoy, Emma Heefner (Mrs.)   89
McCoy, Frank   61
McCoy, Miss Heefner   89
McCoy, Ralph   61
McCullough, Marcella (Nolan)(Wertz)   142
McCullough, Sarah Gey (Mrs. Warren)   142
McCullough, Warren   142
McDonald, Elizabeth Wurtz (Mrs. George) 260
McDonald, George   260
McDowell, Addie (Mrs. George Rider)   64
McEvers, Edna Cordella Alexander (Mrs.) 149
McEvers, Flossie Ellen(Townsbell)(Bell) 149
McEvers, William Albert   149
McFarlin, Iris Lillian(Mrs.W.G.Clapper) 136
McFern, Elizabeth "Lizzie" Knepper   103
McFerran, Martha Wertz   181
McFerran, Mary (Mrs. George G.Knepper)   87
McFerren, Amanda (Mrs. James Knepper) 89,97
McFerren, Eliza.Fetterhoff (Mrs.Peter)   101
McFerren, Elizabeth Wertz (Mrs.John) 37,101
McFerren, George   43,100,101
McFerren, Henry   100,101
McFerren, Jacob   100,101
McFerren, John   37,100,101
McFerren, Martha (Mrs. Jonathan Knepper) 85
McFerren, Mary (Mrs.George Knepper)   86

343

346

Mussar, Jacob R.   125,127
Musser, Abram   62
Musser, Amanda Knepper Pritts   62
Musser, Daniel   127
Musser, Fannie Ellen(Mrs.Cloid C.Wertz) 127
Musser, Fannie Liechty (Mrs. Daniel)   127
Musser, Faye Elizabeth (Mrs.R.L.Butzer) 127
Musser, Fayetta Mae   127
Musser, Flossie Wertz (Mrs. Jacob R.)   127
Musser, Jacob R.   127
Musson, Mary Florence (Mrs. John F.Cell) 53
Mutz, Dorothea Catharina   17
Myers, Adella (Mrs.Cyrus E.Knepper)   90
Myers, Amanda (Mrs. Geroge Wertz)   68,69
Myers, Amanda   65
Myers, Eliza (Mrs. John Wertz)   76
Myers, Ethel Croft   55
Myers, Flora Ann (Mrs.Harley D.Hinton) 136
Myers, George W.   55
Myers, Homer Wertz   55
Myers, Janet   8,55
Myers, John Croft   55
Myers, Josephine Croswell   55
Myers, Martha (Mrs. John W. Miller)   55
Myers, Rachel C. Croft   55
Myers, Sarah Kenpper (Mrs. Henry M.)   87
Nafzger, Carroll Wayne   80
Nafzger, Patricia Ann Wertz (Mrs.Carroll)80
Neff, Catherine/Margaret Wertz   45
Neff, David (or Neaof/Nerof/Nuof/Neiof) 173
Neff, Solomon   45
Neff, Susanna Wertz (Mrs. David)   173
Neightly, Polly (Mrs. Christian Wertz) 252
Neity, Anna (Mrs. Henry Wertz)   252
Nelson, Charles M.   148
Nelson, Hazel Charlotte Rich (Mrs.H.V.) 148
Nelson, Horace Vinton   148
Nelson, Lorelda Wertman (Mrs. Charles) 148
Newbery, Miss (Mrs. Jeremiah Brecker)   43
Newbold, Katharine (Mrs.R.K.Wurts)   203
Newman, Susanna (Mrs. John Austen)   120
Newton, Eliza E. (Mrs. Joseph W.Wertz)   78
Nichols, Elaine Dian(Mrs.Terry W.Wertz) 136
Nicodemus, Mary Susan (Mrs. Samuel Knepper)
                                                87,103
Nirode, Blanche Ferne Shafer (Mrs.C.W.) 131

```
Preisler, Bruce Wertz                          245
Preisler, Elizabeth Knecht (Mrs.J.H.)          244
Preisler, Emma                                 244
Preisler, Eva (Mrs.C.R. Buckwalter)            244
Preisler, Frances Wertz (Mrs.James C.)         244
Preisler, James Calvin                         244
Preisler, Janet Garber                         245
Preisler, John Henry                           244
Preisler, Kenneth Leroy                        245
Preisler, Olive J. Garber (Mrs.Ken.L.)         245
Prentice, Margaret Knepper (Mrs.)               99
Pressel, Adam                                  191
Pressel, Evalina Wertz (Mrs. Adam)             191
Pressman, Nell (Mrs. George A. Croft)           52
Pringle, Mary Wertz (Mrs. William)             198
Pringle, Susan (Mrs. John Garn)                198
Pringle, William                               198
Pritts, Amanda Knepper (Mrs. Joseph)            62
Pritts, Ella (Mrs. Walter Heffby)               62
Pritts, Irvin                                   62
Pritts, Joseph                                  62
Pritts, Milton J.                               62
Profit, Amanda Wertz                            41
Profit, David                                   41
Pugh, Mary (Mrs. Oliver Knepper)                62
Pyne or Pine, Mary Catherine Croft              52
Pyne or Pine, Stafford                          52
Radel, David                                   222
Radel, Jacob                                   222
Radel, Joseph                                  222
Radel, Michael                             222,223
Radel, Philip                                  222
Radel, William                                 222
Raer, Russell Winfield                         140
Rafflespanger, Anna Maria Wertz                 43
Rapp, Sarah E. Wertz (Mrs.)                    250
Rarick, Esther (Mrs. Peter Werts)              254
Raubenolt, Fae Vera                            130
Raubenolt, Helen Margaret                      130
Raubenolt, Iona Emma                           130
Raubenolt, John Clyde                          130
Raubenolt, Kathryn Hoy (Mrs. William)          130
Raubenolt, Roxie Cathryn                       130
Raubenolt, William                             130
Ray, Alice Belle (Mrs. Archie Kurtz)           142
```

Reagin, Caroline Werts (Mrs.William D.) 270
Reagin, William D.   270
Rebert, John   239
Rebert, Mary Ann Haas (Mrs. John)   239
Redding, Margaret E. (Mrs. James L. Wertz)
                                 162,166,167
Reddy, Mary(Mrs.James Luther Wertz) 162,167
Reed, Amy A.L. (Mrs. Walter C. Wertz)   79
Reed, Anne Bronson (Mrs. W.B. Robins)   203
Reed, Benjamin   91
Reed, Betty Louise Wertz Boydanoff   128
Reed, Christiania Burger (Mrs. Henry)   91
Reed, Edward Harry   128
Reed, Eliz.Catherine (Mrs.D.Knepper)   90,92
Reed, Elizabeth (Mrs. Levi Heefner)   91
Reed, Elizabeth Knepper (Mrs. Samuel)   91
Reed, Emily (Mrs. William Burger)   91
Reed, George   89
Reed, Henry   91
Reed, Jack Edward   128
Reed, James   85,88
Reed, Mary Ann (Mrs. Andrew Knepper)   88
Reed, Mary Ann   91
Reed, Mary Ann Knepper (Mrs. George)   89
Reed, Maviern or Mary Ann (Mrs.Knepper) 85
Reed, Nancy Oma   128
Reed, Rebecca (Mrs. John Wertz)
                         111,113,115,116
Reed, S. C.   237
Reed, Samuel   91
Reed, Samuel Jr.   91
Reed, Susan R. Wert (Mrs. S. C.)   237
Reeder, Beatrice Myrhl   248
Reeder, Boyd Lesley   248
Reeder, Emma Florence Wertz(Mrs.Milton) 248
Reeder, Foster Wertz   248
Reeder, Mary Bernice   248
Reeder, Milton   248
Reeder, Milton Raymond   248
Reeder, Solomon Brooks   248
Reeder, Thelma Kathryn   248
Reems, Mary Ellen or Eleanor (Knepper)   95
Refroth, Catharine M. (Mrs.D. Barrick) 242
Reichard, Maud Edith (Mrs. W.C. Wertz) 176
Reichert, Kathryn May (Mrs.Ray.S.Wertz) 138

```
Riess, Magdalena (Mrs. Peter Wert)         260
Riggle, Lydia Mary (Mrs. Isaac Baker)      152
Riggs, Benjamin R.                         203
Riggs, Rosamund Wurts (Mrs.Benjamin R.)    203
Rity, Johannes                             259
Rity, Magdalena Werth (Mrs. Johannes)      259
Robbins, Elizabeth W. (Mrs.E.V. Wurts)     203
Roberts, Cora (Mrs. Charles W. Wertz)      186
Robertson, Lulu M. Wertz (Mrs.)            163
Robins, Anne Bronson Reed (Mrs. W.B.)      203
Robinson, Charles D.                       147
Robinson, Mary Catherine Rogers(Mrs.C.)    147
Robinson, Nellie (Eskey)(Mrs.C. Wertz)     147
Rock, A. F.                                 59
Rock, Alverda                               59
Rock, Anna Marie (Mrs. Peck)                59
Rock, David                                 59
Rock, David Andrew                         129
Rock, Elizabeth (Mrs. Lewis Launchbaugh)    59
Rock, Ella Alexander                        59
Rock, Ella M. (Mrs. Clarence R. Wertz)     129
Rock, Essie (Mrs. Shaskston & Mrs. Dale)    59
Rock, George A.                             59
Rock, Harriet Lone                          59
Rock, Henry C.                              59
Rock, Ida                                   59
Rock, Ira W.                                98
Rock, Iva Myrtelle Barnes(Mrs.David A.)    129
Rock, Jacob                                 96
Rock, Jesse F.                              59
Rock, John                          57,58,59,89
Rock, Josiah                                58
Rock, Katherine                             59
Rock, Louise (Mrs. David Rock)              59
Rock, Maggie Vance                          59
Rock, Maria Walk (Mrs. Jacob)               96
Rock, Mary Baker (Mrs. John)                89
Rock, Mary Elizabeth                        98
Rock, Melissa (Mrs. Richer)                 59
Rock, Mrs.David(Nancy)(Mrs.Amos Wertz)58,61
Rock, Olive                                 59
Rock, Oneida Belle                          59
Rock, Perry                                 59
Rock, Rosie Mickley (Mrs. Ira W.)           98
Rock, Roxina                                59
Rock, Susan                                 59
```

```
Rock, Susanna Wertz (Mrs. John)        57,58
Roddy, Alice                              35
Roddy, Amanda                             35
Roddy, Elizabeth Wertz                    35
Roddy, Elsie                              35
Roddy, Mary Jane                          35
Roddy, Nelson W.                          35
Roddy, Samuel                             35
Roddy, Sydney E.                          35
Roddy, Wilson L.                          35
Rodegers, Elizabeth                    66,68
Rogers, Mary Catherine (Mrs.C.Robinson) 147
Rohrer, Gladys Jane (Mrs.N.E.Burger)     136
Rollwagen, Maria Juliana                  17
Rondeck, Imperial Counselor              275
Rood, Madero                              69
Rood, Noah                                69
Rood, Rolla                               69
Rood, Sarah Ann Wertz (Mrs. Madero)       69
Rood, Sarah B. (Mrs. Jacob Wertz)         69
Rood, Thomas J.                           69
Rook, Ella Madelaine (Mrs.C.R.Wertz)126,129
Roosevelt, Theodore, President       217,219
RosanHouer, Henrietta (Mrs.Will.Knepper)105
Rosenburg, George                        169
Rosenburg, Henry (Dr.)                   169
Rosenburg, Kate                          169
Rosenburg, Lucuis                        169
Rosenburg, Matilda Wertz (Mrs.Henry)     169
Ross, Catherine (Mrs.George Seilhamer)   112
Ross, Margaret (Mrs. Jacob Wert)         206
Rothengatter, Maria Elizabetha            18
Rothengatter, Maria Susanna               17
Rottengatter, Anna Christina              17
Roung, Lena Weisman (Mrs.)               158
Roush, Barbara (Mrs. Simon)              204
Roush, Catherine (Mrs.Christian Rich)    147
Roush, Jacob                             204
Roush, Margaret (Mrs. Jacob)             204
Roush, Simon                             204
Row, Harriet K.Knepper (Mrs. Levi C.)  96,97
Row, Ida (Mrs. George Shaffer)            97
Row, Levi                                 96
Row, Levi C.                              97
Row, Mary (Mrs. George Heefner)           97
Row, Rachael Wirth (Mrs. Wendel)         227
```

```
Sackman, Annie                                49
Sackman, Cora                                 49
Sackman, Edward                               49
Sackman, Jerome                               49
Sackman, John                                 49
Sackman, Katie                                49
Sackman, Lucretia Coble                       49
Sackman, Mary                                 49
Safton, George                                63
Safton, Mary Sullivan (Mrs. George)           63
Sanborn, Anna Eliza Keyler/Keylor (Mrs.)159
Sanborn, Emmett F.                           159
Sand, Ellen Mullendore (Mrs. Jacob)           77
Sand, Jacob                                   77
Saum, Anna Margaret George (Mrs.John)        113
Saum, Catherine                              113
Saum, Catherine Burkholder (Mrs.Chas.)       113
Saum, Charles W.                             113
Saum, John                                   113
Saum, Margaret                               113
Sayers, Hiram                                 38
Sayers, Nancy Wertz                           38
Sayers, Spencer                               38
Scarbrough, Mary                              66
Schaffer, Annie                               39
Schanook, Sarah A. (Mrs. Jerome Wertz)        76
Schleg, Minnie Wertz (Mrs. S.)                70
Schlessman, Elizabeth Worth (Mrs. Wm.)       196
Schlessman, William                          196
Schmid, Rosina                                17
Schmidt, Elizabeth Catharina                  16
Schmidt, Elizabeth (Mrs. George Wirtz)       215
Schmidt, Juliana Clara                        17
Schnug, Eva Elizabeth (Mrs. J.A. Wirt)       221
Scholz, Joannes Josephus Christoph.          282
Schulz, Mayor                                275
Schuman, Emily Wertz                          42
Schuman, George                               42
Schunk, Franklin                              35
Schunk, Hattie Wertz                          35
Schunk, John                                  35
Schunk, Lucy                                  35
Schunk, Mary                                  35
Schunk, Seth                                  35
Schunk, William (2)                           35
Schwarz, Maria Elisabeth                      17
```

```
Shenk, John A.                                    246
Shenk, John C.                                    246
Shenk, Lizzie (Mrs. J.C. Carlson)                 246
Shenk, Lottie Cloud (Mrs. Jacob)                  246
Shenk, Mary Elva Foss (Mrs. John A.)              246
Shenk, Myrtle Holmes (Mrs. Clarence)              246
Shenk, Roy                                        246
Shenk, Sarah Malinda Wertz (Mrs. John)            246
Shenk, Zella Wilkie (Mrs. David)                  246
Sherman, Esther Ann (Mrs. P. S. Wertz)            209
Sherman, Mary Lowe (Mrs. Walter)                  162
Sherman, Walter                                   162
Sherwin, Louise (Mrs. John Brindle)                48
Shetterly, Andrew                                 204
Shetterly, Anna Maria (Mrs. Andrew)               204
Shickard, Elisa Fisher (Mrs.)                     169
Shive, John                                       227
Shive, Sarah/Salome Wirt(h) (Mrs. John)           227
Shively, Mary Wertz (Mrs. Solomon)                238
Shively, Solomon                                  238
Shockey, Susan Decker (Mrs.)                       99
Short, Mary (Mrs. Joshua Knepper)              83,96
Shoup, Mary Ann Cell                               55
Shoup, Sherman                                     55
Shover, Alice C.                                  240
Shover, Chancey M.                                240
Shover, Eldora B.                                 240
Shover, Elizabeth (Mrs. Howard)                   240
Shover, James H.                                  240
Shover, John T.                                   240
Shover, Mary A.                                   240
Shover, Mary Polly Wertz (Mrs.William)            240
Shover, Peter W.                                  240
Shover, Sarah E. (Mrs. Thompson)                  240
Shover, Susan J.                                  240
Shover, William                                   240
Shover, Wm. P.                                    240
Shrock, Dolores Ann Wertz (Mrs.Paul D.)           134
Shrock, Paul Dean                                 134
Shuggert, Blaine                                  248
Shuggert, Gladys                                  248
Shuggert, Mary Armstrong (Mrs. Blaine)            248
Shuman, Annie Wertz (Mrs. Robert H.)              245
Shuman, Frances Christina                         245
Shuman, George A., Major                          245
Shuman, George Albert                             245
```

Snowberger, Andrew   108
Snowberger, Barbara Karper (Mrs.Andrew) 108
Snowberger, John   25
Snowberger, Maria/Martha (Mrs.Jacob Wertz)
              107,108,110,113,117,118
Snowberger, Widow   25
Snyder, Alexine (Mrs. Stewart)   160
Snyder, Catharine E.(Mrs.Hen.Wertz) 239,244
Snyder, Cynthia Lee   145
Snyder, David   41
Snyder, Elizabeth Keyler/Keylor (Mrs.)   159
Snyder, Emily Wertz   41
Snyder, Emma   160
Snyder, Estelle Ryan (Mrs. William J.)
      7,8,11,32,65,71,81,110,271-273,278,282
Snyder, Ethel Estelle   72
Snyder, Floyd Lozene   145
Snyder, Grace Kent Fisher (Mrs.Floyd)   145
Snyder, Henry   145
Snyder, Herman E.   241
Snyder, Hulda E.Hostleton (Mrs.William)   73
Snyder, Jacob Leroy   41
Snyder, James   160
Snyder, James B.   123,145
Snyder, John B.   160
Snyder, John Edwin   160
Snyder, Joyce Beverly   145
Snyder, Kate (Mrs. Bennett)   160
Snyder, Laura Myrtle Wertz (Mrs. H.E.)   241
Snyder, Lee Roy   159
Snyder, Martha Lana Wertz (Mrs.John B.)   160
Snyder, Mary Belle (Mrs.Jonas J.Weaver)   141
Snyder, Millard   160
Snyder, Miss (Mrs. John Light Jr.)   107
Snyder, Mural   159
Snyder, Roy Wilbert   145
Snyder, Ryan Lowman   72
Snyder, Samuel   159
Snyder, Sarah Ann Black (Mrs.Henry)   145
Snyder, Sarah Ellen Wertz (Mrs.James B.)
                                      123,145
Snyder, Sprankle(?)   159
Snyder, William J.   71,73,160,271-273
Snyder, Zack   160
Sollenberger, Catherine (Mrs.A.Knepper)   99
Someftzer, Sofia (Mrs. Jacob Swoveland)   67

Stiffler, Catherine (Mrs. Paul Wertz)
177,179,180,181,250
Stiltner, Bonita Kay Wertz (Mrs.D.C.)   134
Stiltner, Danny Charles   134
Stiltner, Herbert Jack   128
Stiltner, Sylvia Merideth Wertz (Mrs.H.)128
Stites, Elizabeth (Mrs. Barnhart)   87
Stites, Esther Knepper (Mrs. Jacob)   87
Stites, Isabelle (Mrs. Brumbaugh)   87
Stites or Sites, Jacob   87
Stites, Susan   87
Stitt, John; Lieut.   84
Stoever, Johann Caspar; Rev.   22
Stone or Stine, Elizabeth Wertz   75
Stone or Stine, Frederick   75
Stonebraker, Bessie Werts(Mrs.Harry C.) 209
Stonebraker, Eugene   209
Stonebraker, Harry C.   209
Stonebraker, Herold   209
Stonebraker, Samuel Asbury   209
Stonebraker, Susan D.Strunck (Mrs.Sam.) 209
Stonebraker, Vernon   209
Stoner, Abraham   84
Stoner, Barbara (Mrs. John Wertz)   204
Stoner, Barbara Shank (Mrs. Christian) 204
Stoner, Catherina or Catherine (Mrs. George
    Wertz)   24,153-173
Stoner, Christian   204
Stoner, Celia Martin (Mrs. Jacob)   84
Stoner, David or Daniel   84
Stoner, Elizabeth (Mrs.Louis Bonebrake) 84
Stoner, Elizabeth Herr (Mrs. John)   204
Stoner, John   204
Strassburger, R. B.   283
Strouse, Sarah (Mrs. Adam Wertz)   254
Strove, Elizabeth (Mrs. John Wertz)   253
Strunck, Susan D. (Mrs.Sam.Stonebraker) 209
Stuby, Charles   183
Stuby, Elizabeth Earnest   183
Stuby, Frederick   183
Stuby, Henry Heckerman   183
Stuby, Jane Wertz (Mrs. Frederick)   183
Stuby, Maggie   183
Stuby, Minerva   183
Sullivan, Susan   63
Sullivan, William   63

```
Summer, Almeda (Mrs. Clarence Croft)          53
Summer, Susan (Mrs. Michael Werts)           270
Summers, Belle Wertz (Mrs.)                  162
Summers, Daniel Jacob                         89
Summers, Mary Ann Heefner (Mrs. Daniel)       89
Sunday, Jennie (Mrs. Peter Wertz)            243
Suters, Kate (Mrs. William Earnest)          183
Swab, Catharine Metz (Mrs. John Jacob)       228
Swab, Eli                                    228
Swab, John Jacob                             228
Swain, Lillie Mae (Mrs. Thomas G. Wertz)
                                         123,145
Swain, Matthew Elder                         145
Swain, Susanna Kiser (Mrs.Matthew E.)        145
Swank, Willmina (Mrs. George Werts)          252
Swartzmiller, Emma Knepper (Mrs.)             94
Sweigert, Eva Metz (Mrs.)                    228
Swinford, Addie B. Wertz (Mrs. James A.)      79
Swinford, James A.                            79
Swoveland, Andrew                          66,68
Swoveland, Anthony                            66
Swoveland, Barbara Miller (Mrs.Henry)         68
Swoveland, Charlie                            68
Swoveland, Dess Posta (Mrs. Joel)             67
Swoveland, Earl                               68
Swoveland, Elizabeth                          67
Swoveland, Elizabeth Rodegers              66,68
Swoveland, Elizabeth Wertz                 65,66
Swoveland, Emma (Mrs. James Whitehead)        68
Swoveland, Eva                                66
Swoveland, George                             67
Swoveland, Harvey                             68
Swoveland, Henry                              68
Swoveland, Hezakiah                           68
Swoveland, Jacob M.                           67
Swoveland, Joel                               67
Swoveland, Julia (Mrs. William Penrod)        68
Swoveland, Lewis                              68
Swoveland, Lidy (Mrs. John Ebby)              67
Swoveland, Michael                      65,66,67
Swoveland, Nancy Brumbaugh(Mrs.Hezakiah) 68
Swoveland, Norman                             68
Swoveland, Phoebe Detwiler (Mrs.Harvey)       68
Swoveland, Sadie (Mrs. M. Bainter)            68
Swoveland, Sarah                           67,68
Swoveland, Sarah Plough (Mrs. Andrew) 66,68
```

```
Weimer, Frederick Jr.                         32,74
Weimer, Sarah (Mrs. Daniel Wertz)    32,74-80
Weisgarber, Clarissa Grace Keller(Mrs.) 138
Weisgarber, Margaret Mae(Mrs.V.F.Wertz) 138
Weisgarber, Raymond Ralph                 138
Weisman, Catherine (Mrs. Haslet(?)       158
Weisman, Christina                        158
Weisman, Henry                            158
Weisman, Lena (Mrs. Roung)               158
Weisman, Mary (Mrs. Hamelton)            158
Weisman, Susan                            158
Weisman, Susan Ann Emminger (Mrs.)       158
Wells, Agnes Hoover                       285
Welsh, Harold                              52
Welsh, Ida Grace Croft                     52
Welsh, J. Ambrose                          52
Welsh, Jacob                               52
Welsh, Mary Ellen                          52
Wendel, Rosina                             17
Wenger, Samuel S.                         284
Werner, Elizabeth Metz (Mrs. Peter)       228
Werner, Peter                             228
Wertman, Lorelda (Mrs.Charles M.Nelson) 148
Wesinger, Barbara                          15
West, Effie Luella(Mrs.George W.Foutty) 134
Westerhouse, Elizabeth Knepper (Mrs.J.) 105
Westerhouse, John                         105
Weston, Alice Replogle (Mrs. James)       108
Weston, James                             108
Wetzel, Ephraim                           232
Wetzel, Margaret Wert (Mrs. Ephraim)      232
Whistler, Rebecca Wertz                    43
White, Hattie (Mrs. Lloyd Witmer)         247
White, Mary (Mrs. Philip Wert)            259
Whitehead, Anna (Mrs. M. Muhler)           68
Whitehead, Dorothy                         68
Whitehead, Emma Swoveland (Mrs.James)      68
Whitehead, Everett Earl                    68
Whitehead, Glen                            68
Whitehead, Hulda                           68
Whitehead, James                           68
Whitehead, Violet                          68
Whitehead, Walter                          68
```

Alexander Wurtz, m. 1585   11,19
Alfred B. Wertz, son of Jerome   76
Alfred M. Wertz, son of Morris B.   242
Alice/Allie Elizabeth Wertz, b.1903   166
Alice C. Wertz, dau. of Peter   160,163
Alice F. Wertz Hartzell, dau. of Peter   243
Alice Gertrude Haymond Wertz, b.1866   209
Alley Wertz, b.a.1854, dau. of Zacheus   186
Allice Witmer Wert, m.1867 to Samuel   237
Almedes/Almira S. Wertz, dau. of William   184
Alonzo/Alanza Wertz, son of Conrad Jr.   56
Alonzo/Elonzo Wertz, b. 1872   79
Alphonso Wertz, 1867-1879   78
Amanda Butarf Wertz, m.1884 to Austin   149
Amanda Jane Wirt,chr.1847, dau./William   235
Amanda Myers Wertz, 1817-1904, wife of George
                                          65,68,69
Amanda Wertz, b.1847/8, dau. of William   184
Amanda Wertz, dau. of David B.,b.1838   35
Amanda Wertz, wife of Valentine, b.a.1828   192
Amanda Wertz-Davis, b. 1845   39
Amanda Wertz-Eisenzimmer, dau.of Conrad Jr.56
Amanda Wertz-Pierce, b. 1863   42
Amanda Wertz-Profit, 1835-1908   41
Amber Ganade Wertz, wife of Frank   70
Ambrose Wertz, b.1865, son of Josiah   149
Amelia Annie Wertz Garber, dau. of Abraham
                                          240,248
Amos Wertz, 1810-1893,son of Christian   58,61
Amos Wirt/Werth, chr.1821, son of John   233
Amy A.L.Reed Wertz, m. 1904 to Walter C.   79
Andreas Wertz, b.1807-died in infancy   65
Andrew Wert, a. 1830   236
Andrew Wertz, b.1774   30,32,40,65,66,68,70,72
Andrew Wertz, 1813-1848, son of Andrew   34
Andrew Wertz, 1841-1901, son of George   69
Andrew Wirth, a. 1765   201
Andrew Wirth, chr.1767, son of Valentine   197
Angeline M. Wertz, dau. of John   242
Ann C. Wertz, b.a.1850, dau. of William   184
Ann Deeter/Teeter Wertz, m.1834, Henry   253
Ann Elizabeth Wurtz, chr.1757, dau./Lewis   199
Ann Maria Worth, chr.1823, dau.of William   196
Ann Maria Wortz, chr.1836, dau. of Jacob   206
Ann Wertz, b. 1832, dau. of Henry   180
Ann Wertz, dau. of Paul   178

Ann Wurts Bissell, wife of Ellison P.   203
Anna Barbara Hoff Wertz, m.1734, wife of Hans
   Jacob   13,22,23,25,27,29,81,107,153,196,273
Anna Barbara May Wurtz, m. 1725   17
Anna Barbara Wert, chr.1837, dau./Joseph   232
Anna Barbara Werth, chr.1809, dau./Henry   229
Anna Barbara Wirth, wife of Jacob by 1755 201
Anna Barbara Wurtz, b. 1662   13
Anna Barbara Wurtz, b. 1664   11
Anna Barbara Wurtz, b. 1672   13
Anna Bauschen Wirtz, wife/ Nicholaus   274,279
Anna Bell Wertz, wife of George   42
Anna Brederstone Wertz, m.1825 to Abraham 252
Anna Catarina Wirth, chr.1799, /Christian 199
Anna Catharina Hoffmann Wurtz, m. 1759   16
Anna Catharina Wirth Hocker, dau.of Geo.   228
Anna Catharine Miller Wirt, wife of Johann
      George   222,228
Anna Catharine Wirt Metz, dau. of John Adam
                                        222,227
Anna Catherina Wurtz, b. 1660   13
Anna Christina Rottengatter Wurtz, m.1688 17
Anna Christina Werth,chr.1778,dau./Conrad 199
Anna Christina Wertz, wife of Johannes   205
Anna Christina Wirth, chr.1790,/Christian 199
Anna Christina Wirth, chr.1790, dau./Joh. 235
Anna Christina Wirth, chr.1795,of Jacob   224
Anna Christina Wurz, dau. of Jacobus   279
Anna Elisabeth Catharina Wurtz, chr.1769   205
Anna Elisabetha Wirtz, b.1799, dau./Peter 266
Anna Eliza Taylor Wertz, wife of John   75,80
Anna Elizabeth Wurtz, b. 1669   11
Anna Elizabeth Wurtz, b. 1681   13
Anna Elizabeth Wurtz, b. 1709   13
Anna Eva Guill Wertz, b.1912   80
Anna Eve Wirt Shaffner, dau.of Christian   227
Anna Ferndah(?) Wertz, b. 1909   170
Anna Frantz Wertz, wife of John   269
Anna Goetschi Wirtz/Wurtz, wife of Hans/Joh.
      Conrad   213,214,215
Anna K. Hoover Wertz, wife of Edwin S.   176
Anna K. Wurtz, b.1872, dau.of John K.   202
Anna Kleiner Wirz, wife of Casper   212
Anna Louisa Wertz, b.1866,of William   161,167
Anna Margarehta Wurster Wurtz, m. 1766   17

Anna Margaretha Wertz-Flood/Hood/Hoover 24,26
Anna Margaretha Wirth, chr.1788,dau./Joh. 235
Anna Margaretha Wuertz, chr.1740,of Jacob 196
Anna Margaretha Wurtz, b. 1665   11
Anna Maria Bittmann Wurtz, m. 1838   17
Anna Maria Cook Wertz, 1775-1867, wife of
      Conrad Wertz   31,43,101
Anna Maria Elizabeth Miller Wirt, wife of
      John   223,233,234
Anna Maria Fassnacht Wirth, wife/Johannes 260
Anna Maria Magdalena Wurtz, b. 1735   213,214
Anna Maria/Mary Wertz, b.1796   57
Anna Maria Meinder Wertz, m.1801 to Joh. 259
Anna Maria Sophia Miller Wirt, wife of Jacob
                                            221,223
Anna Maria Ursula Wurtz, m. a.1699 13,14,19
Anna Maria Wert, chr.1837, dau.of Martin   249
Anna Maria Werth, b.1787, dau. of John   204
Anna Maria Werth, chr.1805, dau.of Henry   229
Anna Maria Werth, chr.1841, dau.of Isaac   225
Anna Maria Werth, chr.1843, dau.of Daniel 200
Anna Maria Werth Heckart, m.1824   229
Anna Maria Wertz-Rafflespanger, b. 1798   43
Anna Maria Wirth Miller,b.1788,/Christian 226
Anna Maria Wirth, wife of Johannes   235
Anna Maria Wirth/Wirt Paul, dau./Jacob   224
Anna Maria Wirz, b.1771, dau./Johannes   251
Anna Maria Worth Beyer, m.1759 to Jacob   258
Anna Maria Wuertz, chr.1771, dau.of Peter 207
Anna Maria Wurtz, b. 1660   11
Anna Maria Wurtz, b. 1670   13
Anna Maria Wurtz, b. 1677   13
Anna Maria Wurtz, b. 1716   13
Anna Maria Wurtz, chr. 1620   15
Anna Maria Wurtz, m. 1768   16
Anna Maria Wurz, dau. of Theodorus   279
Anna Maria Wurz, dau.of Jacobus   279
Anna Maria Wurz, wife of Engelbertus   280
Anna Maria Zeltmann Wurtz, m. 1773   17
Anna Mary Cook Wertz, 1775-1867, wife of
      Conrad   31,43,44,46,48.49.56
Anna Mullons Wertz, m.1875 to George H.   70
Anna Neity Wertz, m.1824 to Henry   252
Anna Rebecca Riegel Wert, wife of Jer.F.   237
Anna Rosina Frey Wurtz, m. 1756   18
Anna Rosina Wurtz, m. 1783   16

```
Catherine --??-- Wertz, m. by 1793          29,30
Catherine --??-- Wertz, wife of George      37,38
Catherine "Katie" Wertz-Rinehart               107
Catherine Ann Wertz, m.by 1830 to Jacob     268
Catherine Bartmass Wertz, m.1829 to John    252
Catherine Bigham/Bingham Wertz, w/William   252
Catherine Bretz Wirt, wife of Christian     222
Catherine/Catrina Wertz-Wertz,1811-1879 40,65
Catherine Colby Wertz, w.of Augustus L.     173
Catherine Emerick Wertz, a.1790-1858
                    156,160,162,163,165,167
Catherine Girley Werz, m.1835 to John       253
Catherine Hoover Wertz, wife of Edwin S.    176
Catherine Houk Wertz, 1806-1892             43,44
Catherine Margaret Wertz-Neff, b.1839         45
Catherine Starr Wertz,m.by 1796    31,32,34,36
Catherine Sterret Wertz, wife of Charles    161
Catherine Stiffler Wertz, wife of Paul
                    177,179,180,181,250
Catherine Stoner Wertz, 1758-132
                    153-160,167,169,170,172,173
Catherine Viet Wertz, m.1881 to Ambrose     149
Catherine Wert, wife of Andrew by 1855      236
Catherine Werth, chr.1802, dau./Christian 196
Catherine Werth, wife of Daniel by 1812     200
Catherine Wertz, 1840-1864, never married    41
Catherine Wertz, b.a.1826 (see Fletcher)    191
Catherine Wertz, b.a.1827, wife of George 193
Catherine Wertz, dau. of Paul               177
Catherine Wertz, dau.of George,1818-1881     34
Catherine Wertz Haas, dau. of Peter         239
Catherine Wertz, wife of John          179,198
Catherine Wertz-Crissman, 1798-1885          33
Catherine Wertz-Fisher, b.a.1788  153,157,167
Catherine Wertz-Holsopp, b.a.1843            35
Catherine Wertz-Lauber, b.1840,m.1869        36
Catherine Wertz-Warner, b. 1837              39
Catherine Wertz-Wertz, 1811-1879  40,41,42,65
Catherine Wertz-Wertz, b.a.1826        157,170
Catherine Wertz-Willis, b. 1803/5            58
Catherine Wertz-Williston-Anderson,b.1796   43
Catherine Wirt, b. 1750, dau.of Henry       205
Catherine Wirt, b.a.1729, wife of Jasper    207
Catherine Worth/Wertz, b.1783, dau. J.G.    195
Catherine Worth/Wertz, wife of John Geo.    195
```

Catrina Orth Wirtz, wife of Nicholaus
                                273,274,279
Cecelia Litrell Wert, b.1818, wife/Peter   230
Ceila Adell Ryan Wertz, wife of Charles W.186
Charles Augustus Wortz,chr.1848,son/David 206
Charles C. Wertz, b.1864, son of Augustus;173
Charles Clinton Wertz,b.1860,son/John 239,243
Charles Edwin Wert, chr.1865, son/John   236
Charles Fay Wertz, 1883-1899,son of Andrew 69
Charles H. Wert, 1851-1929,son/Peter   230,231
Charles H. Wertz, b.1883, son of Peter   243
Charles M. Wertz, son of Henry   161,163
Charles Ross Wertz, b.1881, son of Abraham
                                    240,248
Charles Stewart Wurts, son of John   215
Charles W. Wert, chr.1859, son of Jonas   236
Charles Werts, b.a.1826   192
Charles Wertz, 1857-1860, son of Jerome   41
Charles Wertz, b.1863, m.1888   209
Charles Wertz, b.1892, son of Charles   209
Charles Wertz Jr., d.1888   161
Charles Wertz, m.1829, Catharine Simonton 252
Charles Wertz, son of Charles H.   243
Charles Wertz, son of George Jr.   156,161
Charles Wertz, son of John 1829-1885   80
Charles Wertz, son of Thomas   183
Charles Wesley Wertz, b.1875, son of George
                                    186,188
Charles Wesley Wertz Jr., 1902-1942   189
Charles Wort, b. 1828, son of Israel   201
Charlotte --??-- Wertz, wife of Frank E.   61
Charlotte Austen Wertz, wife of Jacob
            119-121,125,130,131,143,145,147,148
Charlotte/Sharlott Wertz-Batlorf,1838-1905 60
Charlotte Werts, b.1845/6, dau.of Josiah   185
Charlotte Wertz, b.a.1854, dau.of Michael 185
Charlotte Wertz-Younker, b.1870   150
Chas. Edwin Wirt, chr.1847, son/William   249
Chauncey Frost Wertz, 1889-1935,m.1912   79,80
Christena Borman Wirts, m.1815, Michael   252
Christena/Christiana Hoover Wertz   150
Christian S. Wertz, m.1857, Sue S.Slater   254
Christian Werth, a. 1780   196
Christian Wertz, 1772-1851   30-32,57-59,61-64
Christian Wertz, 1790 Census, MontgomeryC.262
Christian Wertz, 1813-1854   65,70

Daniel Werth, chr.1817, son of John   236
Daniel Werts, b.a.1800.   192
Daniel Wertz, 1781-1873/8   30,32,65,74,76,80
Daniel Wertz, 1820-1883, son of Andrew 66,72
Daniel Wertz, 1827-1910   75,77,78.79.80
Daniel Wertz, 1836-1920, son of Peter 240,246
Daniel Wertz, a. 1740   238
Daniel Wertz, b. 1849, son of Paul Jr.   181
Daniel Wertz, b.1827, son of George   38
Daniel Wertz, m.1846 to Sophia Cook   254
Daniel Wertz, m.1847 to Sarah Burk   254
Daniel Wertz, Rev. War Pensioner   263
Daniel Wertz, son of George   182
Daniel Wertz, son of Jacob 1812-1876   76
Daniel Wertz, son of Nicholas   250
Daniel Wilden Wertz, b.1941, m.1970   80
Daniel Wirt, 1790 Census, Northampton Co. 262
Daniel Wirth/Wirt, 1796-1858,son of Jacob 224
Daniel Wirtz, a. 1760   205
David A. Lincoln Wertz, b.1863;David; 161,166
David Aaron Wertz, 1826-1896,of David;157,169
David B. Wertz, b.a.1838   35
David Clair Wertz, b.1940   142,143
David K. Wurtz, b.1880, son of John K.   202
David Kevin Wertz, b.1964   129
David Maurice Wertz, b.1863, s.of Hiram   170
David Maurice Wertz Jr., 1905-1907   170
David Robert Wertz, b.1958   143
David Washington Wertz, b.1868, son of
     Abraham   240,247
David Werth, chr. 1810, son of Peter   200
David Werth, chr. 1821, son of Daniel   200
David Werts, m. 1845 to Elizabeth Miller 254
David Wertz, 1 in 1850, son of George   175
David Wertz, exec. for Jacob Wertz   110
David Wertz, 1789-1866   153-157,169
David Wertz, 1807-1890,son of Christian 58-60
David Wertz, 1819-1900; son of George Jr.
                  22,23,156,161,164,465,285
David Wertz, a.1834, son of Peter   240
David Wertz, b. 1834, son of Henry   180
David Wertz, b.1846, son of Henry   239,244
David Wertz, b.a.1841/4, son of Paul Jr. 180
David Wertz, b.a.1845, son of Fable   193
David Wertz, m.1844 to Elizabeth Cyler   254
David Wertz, son of Andrew, 1813-1848   34

                    391

H. Werth, a. 1825   236
Hallene Wertz, b.1910, dau. of Ora E.   42
Hance Jacob Wartt/Wurth, b.1715,1732 emi.   255
Hance Jacob Wurth/Wartt, b.1676,1732 emi.   255
Hanna Wertz Kipp, dau. of Nicholas   250
Hannah Emmons/Emerson Wertz, b.1765, wife of
        Jacob   31,37-39,101
Hannah Haas Wertz, wife of Daniel   240
Hannah R. Wertz Bell, dau. of John   242
Hannah Werth, wife of Johann George   228
Hannah Wertz, 8 in 1860, dau. of William   183
Hannah Wertz, b.a.1842, dau. of Henry   192
Hannah Wertz-Reid, b. 1838   36
Hannah Wirth Shellenberger, m.1846/Henry   260
Hans Bunkardt Wurtz, b.a.1630, m.1653   11
Hans Bunkardt Wurtz II, b. 1674   11
Hans Conrad Wird, 1752 emigrant   255
Hans Conrad Wirtz,1706-1763,1735 emigrant   213
Hans Conrad Wurtz, b.1665, m.a.1699
                                11,12,13,14,19
Hans Jacob Wertz/Worts/Wuertz, 1705-1775
        13,14,19,21,22,29,81,107,153,196,273
Hans Jacob Wurst, 1743 emigrant   255
Hans Jorg Wurtz, chr. 1581   15
Hans Martin Wurtz, a. 1745   205
Hans Martin Wurtz, chr. 1616   15
Hans Martin Wurtz/Weertz, 1750 emigrant   255
Hans Michael Wurtz, chr. 1623   15
Hans Wurtz Jr., chr. 1567   15
Hans Wurtz, m. a. 1566   15
Hariet Wertz, wife of Joseph H.   163
Harieth Clyde Wertz, b.1920   136
Harold Scott Wertz, b.1896   133,138
Harold Wertz, son of John b. 1831   38
Harriet A. Wertz-Davis, b. 1869   79
Harriet Wertz, b. 1832, dau. of Henry   39
Harriet Wertz, b.a.1843, dau.of Paul Jr.   181
Harriet Wertz-Hartzel, b.1824, m.1844   75
Harriet Wertz-Stutz, b. 1833   38
Harrison Wertz, 1855-1861, son of Josiah   149
Harry E. Wertz, 1868-1900   162,167
Harry J. Wertz, m. 1891   176
Harry James Werts, m. 1932   176
Harry Wertz, b. 1871, m.1892   79
Harry Wertz, son of Jacob Augustus   162
Harry Wertz, son of John   175

```
Mabel Wert, b.1913, dau. of Jeremiah F.      237
Mabel Wertz, b.1891, dau. of Charles         209
Mable Caroline Wertz, b.1909, dau.of John     42
Mable Thompson Wertz, wife of Leroy           69
Mable Wertz, dau.of James Luther         162,167
Madelena Wertz, wife/Dewalt by 1793      238,239
Magdalena Berkey Wertz, b.1779,wife of Andrew
                         32,40,65,66,68,70,72
Magdalena Klinger Wirz, wife of Johannes     212
Magdalena/Martha Wertz-Croft, 1816-1903 44,49
Magdalena Riess Wert, m.1809 to Peter        260
Magdalena Shupp Wirth, wife of Johannes      224
Magdalena Werth Rity, m.1793 to Johannes     259
Magdalena Werth, wife of John, by 1817       236
Magdalena Wertz, wife of Jacob               205
Magdalena Wertz-Hostleton, 1822-1909      66,72
Magdalena Wirt, wife of Theobald             195
Magdalena Wurt, wife of Michael              195
Magdalena Wurtz, chr. 1626                    15
Magdalena Wurz, dau. of Engelbertus          280
Magdalena Wurz, wife of Theodorus            279
Maggie --??-- Wertz, wife of Lemuel           62
Maggie Adora Wertz, 1868-1871,/Daniel 240,247
Maggie B. Stewart Wertz, wife of John A.     176
Malinda Gaumer Werts, m.1848 to Solomon      254
Malinda Wertz, 5 in 1850, dau. of George     175
Malinda Wertz, b.1809, dau. of Peter         268
Malinda Wertz, dau.of William,b.1836          35
Malvina Wertz Oster, 1843-1916               194
Manda E. Wertz-Burdick, dau. of John          80
Mandy Catharine Wertz, b.1827, dau./Wilh.    267
Marcella McCullough Nolan Wertz              142
Marcie Lee Wertz, b.1955                     129
Marcus Wortz, a. 1815                        195
Margarehta Wurtz, chr. 1603                   15
Margaret "Polly" Labe/Loeb/Lorb Wertz 157,172
Margaret Catherine Wertz-Neff, b. 1839        45
Margaret Elizabeth Wirt,chr.1843,/William 249
Margaret F. Wertz, b.1870,dau.Augustus;      173
Margaret Fleagle Wertz, m.1849 to George     254
Margaret Hoobler Wertz, m.1833, Benjamin     253
Margaret J. Wertz, b.a.1827 (see Horn)       193
Margaret Jane Orr Wert, wife of Earl Adam 237
Margaret Jane Wortz, chr.1849, dau./Jacob 206
Margaret Kolcun Wertz, b.1925                129
Margaret Maple Werts, m.1827 to George       252
```

S. John Wertz, b.1825   157,173
S. Witner Wertz, b.1798, m.1823 to Henry
                                38,39,40,175
Sadie Dugan Wertz, wife of Orra H.   120
Sally McKinnon Wertz, wife of Daniel   75,78
Sally Wertz Hetrick, dau. of Nicholas   250
Salome Weaver Wirt/Werth, wife/Elias 234,235
Salome Wert, wife of Josiah by 1845   236
Salome Werth, wife of Johann by 1833   236
Salome Wirth Shive, c.1801,dau./Christian 227
Salomon Wertz, b.1815, son of Peter   268
Samuel Adam Wertz, chr.1844, son of Jacob 206
Samuel Grandin Wurtz, b.a.1774/5,son/John 215
Samuel Kaylor Wert, b.1855, son/Peter 230,231
Samuel R. Wertz, b.1860, son of William   184
Samuel Sanford Wertz, b.1856,son of Simon 209
Samuel Wert, chr.1828, son of Martin   249
Samuel Wert, m.1867 to Allice Witmer   237
Samuel Werts, b.a.1848, son of Charles   192
Samuel Werts, chr. 1847, son of Isaac   225
Samuel Wertz, 1753 emigrant   257
Samuel Wertz, 1829-1840, son of Jonathan 119
Samuel Wertz, 5 in 1850, son of John J.   179
Samuel Wertz, a. 1810   206
Samuel Wertz, b.1801, son of Adam   267
Samuel Wertz, b.a.1846, son of Michael   185
Samuel Wertz, b.a.1850, son of Jacob   181
Samuel Wertz, b.a.1854, son of Fable   193
Samuel Wertz, chr.1812, son of Johannes   205
Samuel Wertz, m.1802 to Susanna Kremer   259
Samuel Wertz, son of Andrew, 1813-1848   34
Samuel Wertz, son of William, b. 1836   35
Samuel Wirth, a. 1810   200
Sara Emerich Wert, m.1857 to Peter   237
Sara Oster Wertz, wife of Henry   178,179,180
Sara Werth, chr. 1822, dau. of John   200
Sara Wirtz, chr. 1795, dau. of Jacob   196
Sarah A. Schanook Wertz m.1858 to Jerome   76
Sarah A. Wertz, dau. of John 1829-1885   80
Sarah Agnes Wertz-Timmerman, b.1853   161,165
Sarah Amanda Werth, chr.1835,dau./Joh.Geo.228
Sarah Amelia Wert Mosser Garman, chr.1842,234
Sarah Ann Dicks Wert, wife of Robert F.   231
Sarah Ann Wertz-Rood, b.1838   69
Sarah B. Rood Wertz, wife of Jacob   69
Sarah B. Werts, b.a.1855, dau. of Josiah 185

About the Author

This Wertz Family History Book has been compiled by Mrs. Carolyn Cell Choppin, born 27 February 1938 in Evanston, Cook County, Illinois; daughter of Clark Wesley Cell and Erma C. Janssen Cell; and granddaughter of George Croft Cell and Cornelia Ellen Clark Cell (see page 53).

When I first married and moved to California in Sept. 1960, I suddenly discovered other families of our surname that I could not identify immediately. Establishing those ties that bind the generations together thus began for me in my early 20's, and has over the last 30 years become first a hobby and then a calling as a family history teacher and librarian, and now a profession as a family history writer.

It is my hope that this Wertz Family History Book will help many others to pick up the trail of their ancestors, explore it and learn to love their families and the heritage they have left to us. Those who are able to establish new ties or add additional information to that recorded here are encouraged to write to this author. As I write this, in March 1990, we are preparing to move — again — this summer, this time to Washington State. Check the LDS Family Registry, and I shall try to keep a current address there.

Carolyn Cell Choppin

www.ingramcontent.com/pod-product-compliance
Lightning Source LLC
Chambersburg PA
CBHW071828270326
41929CB00013B/1926